AF564635

Statistics

Statistics

Rama Nand Singh

RANDOM PUBLICATIONS
NEW DELHI (INDIA)

Statistics

ISBN 978-93-5111-451-2

Published in 2014 in India by

RANDOM PUBLICATIONS

4376-A/4B, Gali Murari Lal, Ansari Road
New Delhi-110 002
Phone : +91-11-43580356, +91-11-23289044
e-mail: randomexports@gmail.com, sales@randompublications.com,
info@randompublications.com

Reprinted 2022

Type Setting by: Friends Media, Delhi-110089
Digitally Printed at: Replika Press Pvt. Ltd.

Preface

Statistics is the study of the collection, organization, analysis, interpretation and presentation of data. It deals with all aspects of data, including the planning of data collection in terms of the design of surveys and experiments. The word statistics, when referring to the scientific discipline, is singular, as in "Statistics is an art." This should not be confused with the word statistic, referring to a quantity (such as mean or median) calculated from a set of data, whose plural is statistics. Statistics is alternately described as a mathematical body of science that pertains to the collection, analysis, interpretation or explanation, and presentation of data, or as a branch of mathematics concerned with collecting and interpreting data. Because of its empirical roots and its focus on applications, statistics is typically considered a distinct mathematical science rather than as a branch of mathematics. Some tasks a statistician may involve are less mathematical; for example, ensuring that data collection is undertaken in a way that produces valid conclusions, coding data, or reporting results in ways comprehensible to those who must use them.

Statisticians improve data quality by developing specific experiment designs and survey samples. Statistics itself also provides tools for prediction and forecasting the use of data and statistical models. Statistics is applicable to a wide variety of academic disciplines, including natural and social sciences, government, and business. Statistical consultants can help organizations and companies that don't have in-house expertise relevant to their particular questions. In applying statistics to a scientific, industrial, or societal problem, it is necessary to begin with a population or process to be studied. Populations can be diverse topics such as "all persons living in a country" or "every atom composing a crystal". A population can also be composed of observations of a process at various times, with the data from each observation serving as a different member of the overall group. Data collected about this kind of "population" constitutes what is called a time series. Statistics form a key basis tool in business and manufacturing as well. It is used to understand measurement systems variability, control processes (as in statistical process control or SPC), for summarizing data, and to make data-driven decisions. In these roles, it is a key tool, and perhaps the only reliable tool. The rapid and sustained increases in computing power starting from the second half of the 20th century have had a substantial impact on the practice of statistical science. Early statistical models were almost always from the class of linear models, but powerful computers, coupled with suitable numerical algorithms, caused an increased interest in nonlinear models (such as neural networks) as well as the creation of new types, such as generalized linear models and multilevel models.

This book is specially designed for students majoring in the life, health, and natural sciences. Through intensive exposure to the core concepts of statistics in the context of science, students acquire the skills and understanding they need to formulate valid research designs, implement statistical analysis, interpret data, and explain their results.

I thank all members of my team who have helped in the preparation of the book. My special thanks go to "Random Publications" who have published the book.

—Rama Nand Singh

Contents

1

Models of Statistics

Models for time series data can have many forms and represent different stochastic processes. When modelling variations in the level of a process, three broad classes of practical importance are the autoregressive (AR) models, the integrated (I) models, and the moving average (MA) models. These three classes depend linearly on previous data points. Combinations of these ideas produce autoregressive moving average (ARMA) and autoregressive integrated moving average (ARIMA) models.

The autoregressive fractionally integrated moving average (ARFIMA) model generalizes the former three. Extensions of these classes to deal with vector-valued data are available under the heading of multivariate time-series models and sometimes the preceding acronyms are extended by including an initial "V" for "vector". An additional set of extensions of these models is available for use where the observed time-series is driven by some "forcing" time-series (which may not have a causal effect on the observed series): the distinction from the multivariate case is that the forcing series may be deterministic or under the experimenter's control. For these models, the acronyms are extended with a final "X" for "exogenous".

Non-linear dependence of the level of a series on previous data points is of interest, partly because of the possibility of producing a chaotic time series. However, more importantly, empirical investigations can indicate the advantage of using predictions derived from non-linear models, over those from linear models, as for example in nonlinear autoregressive exogenous models.

Among other types of non-linear time series models, there are models to represent the changes of variance along time (heteroskedasticity). These models represent autoregressive conditional heteroskedasticity (ARCH) and the collection comprises a wide variety of representation (GARCH, TARCH, EGARCH, FIGARCH, CGARCH, etc.). Here changes in variability are related to, or predicted by, recent past values of the observed series.

This is in contrast to other possible representations of locally varying variability, where the variability might be modelled as being driven by a separate time-varying process, as in a doubly stochastic model. In recent work on model-free analyses, wavelet transform based methods (for example locally stationary wavelets and wavelet decomposed neural networks) have gained favour. Multiscale (often referred to as multiresolution) techniques decompose a given time series, attempting to illustrate time dependence at multiple scales.

Conditions

There are two sets of conditions under which much of the theory is built:

- Stationary process
- Ergodic process

However, ideas of stationarity must be expanded to consider two important ideas: strict stationarity and second-order stationarity. Both models and applications can be developed under each of these conditions, although the models in the latter case might be considered as only partly specified.

In addition, time-series analysis can be applied where the series are seasonally stationary or non-stationary. Situations where the amplitudes of frequency components change with time can be dealt with in time-frequency analysis which makes use of a time–frequency representation of a time-series or signal.

Models

The general representation of an autoregressive model, well known as AR(p), is

$$Y_t = \alpha_0 + \alpha_1 Y_{t-1} + \alpha_2 Y_{t-2} + \cdots + \alpha_p Y_{t-p} + \varepsilon_t$$

where the term ε*t* is the source of randomness and is called white noise. It is assumed to have the following characteristics:

- $E[\varepsilon_t] = 0,$
- $E[\varepsilon_t^2] = \sigma^2,$

- $E[\varepsilon_t \varepsilon_s] = 0$ for all $t \neq s$.

With these assumptions, the process is specified up to second-order moments and, subject to conditions on the coefficients, may be second-order stationary. If the noise also has a normal distribution, it is called normal or Gaussian white noise. In this case, the AR process may be strictly stationary, again subject to conditions on the coefficients.

Tools for investigating time-series data include:

- Consideration of the autocorrelation function and the spectral density function (also cross-correlation functions and cross-spectral density functions)
- Scaled cross- and auto-correlation functions
- Performing a Fourier transform to investigate the series in the frequency domain
- Use of a filter to remove unwanted noise
- Principal components analysis (or empirical orthogonal function analysis)
- Singular spectrum analysis
- "Structural" models:
  - o General State Space Models
  - o Unobserved Components Models
- Machine Learning
  - o Artificial neural networks
  - o Support Vector Machine
  - o Fuzzy Logic
- Hidden Markov model
- Control chart
  - o Shewhart individuals control chart
  - o CUSUM chart
  - o EWMA chart
  - o Real-time contrasts chart
- Detrended fluctuation analysis
- Dynamic time warping
- Dynamic Bayesian network
- Time-frequency analysis techniques:

  - Fast Fourier Transform
  - Continuous wavelet transform
  - Short-time Fourier transform
  - Chirplet transform
  - Fractional Fourier transform
- Chaotic analysis:
  - Correlation dimension
  - Recurrence plots
  - Recurrence quantification analysis
  - Lyapunov exponents
  - Entropy encoding

Measures

Time series metrics or features that can be used for time series classification or regression analysis:

- Univariate linear measures:
  - Moment (mathematics)
  - Spectral band power
  - Spectral edge frequency
  - Accumulated Energy (signal processing)
  - Characteristics of the autocorrelation function
  - Hjorth parameters
  - FFT parameters
  - Autoregressive model parameters
- Univariate non-linear measures:
  - Measures based on the correlation sum
  - Correlation dimension
  - Correlation integral
  - Correlation density
  - Correlation entropy
  - Approximate Entropy
  - Sample Entropy
  - Fourier entropy
  - Wavelet entropy
  - Rényi entropy

- Higher-order methods
- Marginal predictability
- Dynamical similarity index
- State space dissimilarity measures
- Lyapunov exponent
- Permutation methods
- Local flow

- Other univariate measures:
  - Algorithmic complexity
  - Kolmogorov complexity estimates
  - Hidden Markov Model states
  - Surrogate time series and surrogate correction
  - Loss of recurrence (degree of non-stationarity)
- Bivariate linear measures:
  - Maximum linear cross-correlation
  - Linear Coherence (signal processing)
- Bivariate non-linear measures:
  - Non-linear interdependence
  - Dynamical Entrainment (physics)
  - Measures for Phase synchronization
- Similarity measures:
  - Dynamic Time Warping
  - Hidden Markov Models
  - Edit distance
  - Total correlation
  - Newey–West estimator
  - Prais-Winsten transformation
  - Data as Vectors in a Metrizable Space
    - Minkowski distance
    - Mahalanobis distance
  - Data as Time Series with Envelopes
    - Global Standard Deviation
    - Local Standard Deviation
    - Windowed Standard Deviation

- o Data Interpreted as Stochastic Series
  - — Pearson product-moment correlation coefficient
  - — Spearman's rank correlation coefficient
- o Data Interpreted as a Probability Distribution Function
  - — Kolmogorov-Smirnov test
  - — Cramér-von Mises criterion

Misuse of Statistics

A misuse of statistics occurs when a statistical argument asserts a falsehood. In some cases, the misuse may be accidental. In others, it is purposeful and for the gain of the perpetrator. When the statistical reason involved is false or misapplied, this constitutes a statistical fallacy. The false statistics trap can be quite damaging to the quest for knowledge. For example, in medical science, correcting a falsehood may take decades and cost lives. Misuses can be easy to fall into. Professional scientists, even mathematicians and professional statisticians, can be fooled by even some simple methods, even if they are careful to check everything. Scientists have been known to fool themselves with statistics due to lack of knowledge of probability theory and lack of standardization of their tests.

Types of Misuse

Discarding Unfavourable Data

All a company has to do to promote a neutral (useless) product is to find or conduct, for example, 40 studies with a confidence level of 95%. If the product is really useless, this would on average produce one study showing the product was beneficial, one study showing it was harmful and thirty-eight inconclusive studies (38 is 95% of 40).

This tactic becomes more effective the more studies there are available.

Organizations that do not publish every study they carry out, such as tobacco companies denying a link between smoking and cancer, anti-smoking advocacy groups and media outlets trying to prove a link between smoking and various ailments, or miracle pill vendors, are likely to use this tactic.

Another common technique is to perform a study that tests a large number of dependent (response) variables at the same time. For example, a study testing the effect of a medical treatment might use as dependent variables the probability of survival, the average number of days spent in the hospital, the patient's self-reported level of pain, etc. This also increases the likelihood that at least one of the variables will by chance show a correlation with the independent (explanatory) variable.

Loaded Questions

The answers to surveys can often be manipulated by wording the question in such a way as to induce a prevalence towards a certain answer from the respondent. For example, in polling support for a war, the questions:

- Do you support the attempt by the USA to bring freedom and democracy to other places in the world?
- Do you support the unprovoked military action by the USA?
  will likely result in data skewed in different directions, although they are both polling about the support for the war. A better way of wording the question could be "Do you support the current US military action abroad?"

Another way to do this is to precede the question by information that supports the "desired" answer. For example, more people will likely answer "yes" to the question "Given the increasing burden of taxes on middle-class families, do you support cuts in income tax?" than to the question "Considering the rising federal budget deficit and the desperate need for more revenue, do you support cuts in income tax?"

Overgeneralization

Overgeneralization is a fallacy occurring when a statistic about a particular population is asserted to hold among members of a group for which the original population is not a representative sample.

For example, suppose 100% of apples are observed to be red in summer. The assertion "All apples are red" would be an instance of overgeneralization because the original statistic was true only of a specific subset of apples (those in summer), which is not expected to representative of the population of apples as a whole.

A real-world example of the overgeneralization fallacy can be observed as an artifact of modern polling techniques, which prohibit calling cell phones for over-the-phone political polls. As young people are more likely than other demographic groups to have only a cell phone, rather than also having a conventional "landline" phone, young people are more likely to be liberal, and young people who do not own a landline phone are even more likely to be liberal than their demographic as a whole, such polls effectively exclude many voters who are more likely to be liberal.

Thus, a poll examining the voting preferences of young people using this technique could not claim to be representative of young peoples' true voting preferences as a whole without overgeneralizing, because the sample used is not representative of the population as a whole. Overgeneralization often occurs when information is passed through nontechnical sources, in particular mass media.

Biased Samples

Misreporting or Misunderstanding of Estimated Error

If a research team wants to know how 300 million people feel about a certain topic, it would be impractical to ask all of them. However, if the team picks a random sample of about 1000 people, they can be fairly certain that the results given by this group are representative of what the larger group would have said if they had all been asked. This confidence can actually be quantified by the central limit theorem and other mathematical results. Confidence is expressed as a probability of the true result (for the larger group) being within a certain range of the estimate (the figure for the smaller group). This is the "plus or minus" figure often quoted for statistical surveys. The probability part of the confidence level is usually not mentioned; if so, it is assumed to be a standard number like 95%.

The two numbers are related. If a survey has an estimated error of ±5% at 95% confidence, it also has an estimated error of ±6.6% at 99% confidence. $\pm x$% at 95% confidence is always $\pm 1.32x$ % at 99% confidence.

The smaller the estimated error, the larger the required sample, at a given confidence level.

at 95.4% confidence:

±1% would require 10,000 people.

±2% would require 2,500 people.

±3% would require 1,111 people.

±4% would require 625 people.

±5% would require 400 people.

±10% would require 100 people.

±20% would require 25 people.

±25% would require 16 people.

±50% would require 4 people.

Most people assume, because the confidence figure is omitted, that there is a 100% certainty that the true result is within the estimated error. This is not mathematically correct.

Many people may not realize that the randomness of the sample is very important. In practice, many opinion polls are conducted by phone, which distorts the sample in several ways, including exclusion of people who do not have phones, favouring the inclusion of people who have more than one phone, favouring the inclusion of people who are willing to participate in a phone survey over those who refuse, etc. Non-random sampling makes the estimated error unreliable.

On the other hand, many people consider that statistics are inherently unreliable because not everybody is called, or because they themselves are never polled. Many people think that it is impossible to get data on the opinion of dozens of millions of people by just polling a few thousands. This is also inaccurate. A poll with perfect unbiased sampling and truthful answers has a mathematically determined margin of error, which only depends on the number of people polled. However, often only one margin of error is reported for a survey. When results are reported for population subgroups, a larger margin of error will apply, but this may not be made clear. For example, a survey of 1000 people may contain 100 people from a certain ethnic or economic group. The results focusing on that group will be much less reliable than results for the full population. If the margin of error for the full sample was 4%, say, then the margin of error for such a subgroup could be around 13%. There are also many other measurement problems in population surveys. The problems mentioned above apply to all statistical experiments, not just population surveys.

False Causality

When a statistical test shows a correlation between A and B, there are usually six possibilities:

1. A causes B.
2. B causes A.
3. A and B both partly cause each other.
4. A and B are both caused by a third factor, C.
5. B is caused by C which is correlated to A.
6. The observed correlation was due purely to chance.

The sixth possibility can be quantified by statistical tests that can calculate the probability that the correlation observed would be as large as it is just by chance if, in fact, there is no relationship between the variables. However, even if that possibility has a small probability, there are still the four others.

If the number of people buying ice cream at the beach is statistically related to the number of people who drown at the beach, then nobody would claim ice cream causes drowning because it's obvious that it isn't so. (In this case, both drowning and ice cream buying are clearly related by a third factor: the number of people at the beach).

This fallacy can be used, for example, to prove that exposure to a chemical causes cancer. Replace "number of people buying ice cream" with "number of people exposed to chemical X–, and "number of people who drown" with "number of people who get cancer", and many people will believe you. In such a situation, there may be a statistical correlation even if there is no real effect. For example, if there is a perception that a chemical site is "dangerous" (even if it really isn't) property values in the area will decrease, which will entice more low-income families to move to that area. If low-income families are more likely to get cancer than high-income families (this can happen for many reasons, such as a poorer diet or less access to medical care) then rates of cancer will go up, even though the chemical itself is not dangerous. It is believed that this is exactly what happened with some of the early studies showing a link between EMF (electromagnetic fields) from power lines and cancer.

In well-designed studies, the effect of false causality can be eliminated by assigning some people into a "treatment group" and some people into a "control group" at random, and giving the treatment group the treatment and not giving the control group the treatment. In the above example, a researcher might expose one group of people to chemical X and leave a second group unexposed. If the first group had higher cancer rates, the researcher knows that there is no third factor that affected whether a person was exposed because he controlled who was exposed or not, and he assigned people to the exposed and non-exposed groups at random.

However, in many applications, actually doing an experiment in this way is either prohibitively expensive, infeasible, unethical, illegal, or downright impossible. For example, it is highly unlikely that an IRB would accept an experiment that involved intentionally exposing people to a dangerous substance in order to test its toxicity. The obvious ethical implications of such types of experiments limit researchers' ability to empirically test causation.

Data Dredging

Data dredging is an abuse of data mining. In data dredging, large compilations of data are examined in order to find a correlation, without any pre-defined choice of a hypothesis to be tested. Since the required confidence interval to establish a relationship between two parameters is usually chosen to be 95% (meaning that there is a 95% chance that the relationship observed is not due to random chance), there is a thus a 5% chance of finding a correlation between any two sets of completely random variables. Given that data dredging efforts typically examine large datasets with many variables, and hence even larger numbers of pairs of variables, spurious but apparently statistically significant results are almost certain to be found by any such study.

Note that data dredging is a valid way of finding a possible hypothesis but that hypothesis must then be tested with data not used in the original dredging. The misuse comes in when that hypothesis is stated as fact without further validation.

Data Manipulation

Informally called "fudging the data," this practice includes selective reporting and even simply making up false data. Examples of selective reporting abound. The easiest and most common examples involve choosing a group of results that follow a pattern consistent with the preferred hypothesis while ignoring other results or "data runs" that contradict the hypothesis.

Psychic researchers have long disputed studies showing people with ESP ability. Critics accuse ESP proponents of only publishing experiments with positive results and shelving those that show negative results. A "positive result" is a test run (or data run) in which the subject guesses a hidden card, etc., at a much higher frequency than random chance. Scientists, in general, question the validity of study results that cannot be reproduced by other investigators. However, some scientists refuse to publish their data and methods.

Non-enduring Class Fallacies

This type of fallacy involves the claim or implication that members of a statistical class persist over time when this is in-fact not the case. The claims as applied to that statistical class may indeed be statistically correct, however the fallacy lies in the implication that the statistical class is composed of the same individuals from one point in time to the next.

For example, the claim by congressman Bernie Sanders in 2011 that "the top 1% of all income earners in the USA made 23.5% of all income", while being statistically correct, may still be fallacious due to the implication that this class composed of the top 1% is an enduring statistical class composed of the same individuals as in the previous year. While it may be true that many of the individuals in this class persist from the previous year, no indication of how many of these individuals do in fact persist was given in the original statement, and this led to the fallacious implication that all individuals in the class endured.

This fallacy can easily be avoided by specifying whether the statistics used refer to the same group of individuals over the period in question. When this precaution is not taken then suspicions of this fallacy may be raised, even if the fallacy has in fact not been committed.

Descriptive Statistics

Descriptive statistics is the discipline of quantitatively describing the main features of a collection of data. Descriptive statistics are distinguished from inferential statistics (or inductive statistics), in that descriptive statistics aim to summarize a sample, rather than use the data to learn about the population that the sample of data is thought to represent. This generally means that descriptive statistics, unlike inferential statistics, are not developed on the basis of probability theory. Even when a data analysis draws its main conclusions using inferential statistics, descriptive statistics are generally also presented.

For example in a paper reporting on a study involving human subjects, there typically appears a table giving the overall sample size, sample sizes in important subgroups (e.g., for each treatment or exposure group), and demographic or clinical characteristics such as the average age, the proportion of subjects of each sex, and the proportion of subjects with related comorbidities.

Descriptive statistics is also a set of brief descriptive coefficients that summarizes a given data set, which can either be a representation of the entire population or a sample. The measures used to describe the data set are measures of central tendency and measures of variability or dispersion. Measures of central tendency include the mean, median and mode, while measures of variability include the standard deviation (or variance), the minimum and maximum variables, kurtosis and skewness.

Use in Statistical Analysis

Descriptive statistics provides simple summaries about the sample and about the observations that have been made. Such summaries may be either quantitative, i.e. summary statistics, or visual, i.e. simple-to-understand graphs. These summaries may either form the basis of the initial description of the data as part of a more extensive statistical analysis, or they may be sufficient in and of themselves for a particular investigation.

For example, the shooting percentage in basketball is a descriptive statistic that summarizes the performance of a player or a team. This number is the number of shots made divided by the number of shots taken. For example, a player who shoots 33% is making approximately one shot in every three. The percentage summarizes or describes multiple discrete events. Consider also the grade point average. This single number describes the general performance of a student across the range of their course experiences.

The use of descriptive and summary statistics has an extensive history and, indeed, the simple tabulation of populations and of economic data was the first way in which the topic of statistics appeared. More recently, a collection of summarisation techniques has been formulated under the heading of exploratory data analysis: an example of such a technique is the box plot. In the business world, Descriptive statistics provide a useful summary of security returns when performing empirical and analytical analysis, as they provide a historical account of return behaviour. Although past information is useful in any analysis, one should always consider the expectations of future events.

Univariate Analysis

Univariate analysis involves describing the distribution of a single variable, including its central tendency (including the mean, median, and mode) and dispersion (including the range and quantiles of the data-set, and measures of spread such as the variance and standard deviation). The shape of the distribution may also be described via indices such as skewness and kurtosis. Characteristics of a variable's distribution may also be depicted in graphical or tabular format, including histograms and stem-and-leaf plots.

Bivariate Analysis

When a sample consists of more than one variable, descriptive statistics may be used to describe the relationship between pairs of variables. In this case, descriptive statistics include:

- Cross-tabulations and contingency tables
- Graphical representation via scatterplots
- Quantitative measures of dependence
- Descriptions of conditional distributions

Quantitative measures of dependence include correlation (such as Pearson's r when both variables are continuous, or Spearman's rho if one or both are not) and covariance (which reflects the scale upon which variables are measured). The slope, in regression analysis, also reflects the relationship between variables. The unstandardised slope indicates the unit change in the criterion variable for a one unit change in the predictor. The standardised slope indicates this change in standardised (z-score) units.

Average

In mathematics, an average is a measure of the "middle" or "typical" value of a data set. It is thus a measure of central tendency. In the most common case, the data set is a list of numbers. The average of a list of numbers is a single number intended to typify the numbers in the list. If all the numbers in the list are the same, then this number should be used. If the numbers are not the same, the average is calculated by combining the numbers from the list in a specific way and computing a single number as being the average of the list.

Many different descriptive statistics can be chosen as a measure of the central tendency of the data items. These include the arithmetic mean, the median, and the mode. Other statistics, such as the standard deviation and the range, are called measures of spread and describe how spread out the data is.

The most common statistic is the arithmetic mean, but depending on the nature of the data other types of central tendency may be more appropriate. For example, the median is used most often when the distribution of the values is skewed with a small number of very high or low values, as seen with house prices or incomes. It is also used when extreme values are likely to be anomalous or less reliable than the other values (e.g. as a result of measurement error), because the median takes less account of extreme values than the mean does.

Arithmetic Mean

In mathematics and statistics, the arithmetic mean, or simply the mean or average when the context is clear, is the central tendency of a collection of numbers taken as the sum of the numbers divided by the size of the collection. The collection is often the sample space of an experiment. The term "arithmetic mean" is preferred in mathematics and statistics because it helps distinguish it from other means such as the geometric and harmonic mean.

In addition to mathematics and statistics, the arithmetic mean is used frequently in fields such as economics, sociology, and history, though it is used in almost every academic field to some extent. For example, per capita GDP gives an approxi-mation of the arithmetic average income of a nation's population.

While the arithmetic mean is often used to report central tendencies, it is not a robust statistic, meaning that it is greatly influenced by outliers. Notably, for skewed distributions, the arithmetic mean may not accord with one's notion of "middle", and robust statistics such as the median may be a better description of central tendency.

Definition

Suppose we have sample space $\{a_1,\ldots,a_n\}$. Then the arithmetic mean $A$is defined via the equation

$$A := \frac{1}{n}\sum_{i=1}^{n} a_i \,.$$

If the list is a statistical population, then the mean of that population is called a population mean. If the list is a statistical sample, we call the resulting statistic a sample mean.

The arithmetic mean of a variable is often denoted by a bar, for example $\bar{x}$ (read "x bar") would be the mean of some sample space X.

Motivating Properties

The arithmetic mean has several properties that make it useful, especially as a measure of central tendency. These include:

- If numbers $x_1,\ldots..,x_n$ have mean X, then $(x_1 - X) + \ldots + (x_n - X) = 0$. Since $x_i - X$ is the distance from a given number to the mean, one way to interpret this property is as saying that the numbers to the left of the mean are balanced by the numbers to the right of the mean. The mean is the only single number for which the residuals defined this way sum to zero.
- If it is required to use a single number X as an estimate for the value of numbers $x_1,\ldots..,x_n$, then the arithmetic mean does this best, in the sense of minimizing the sum of squares (xi –

$X)^2$ of the residuals. (It follows that the mean is also the best single predictor in the sense of having the lowest root mean squared error.)

- For a normal distribution, the arithmetic mean is equal to both the median and the mode, other measures of central tendency.

Problems

The arithmetic mean may be misinterpreted as the median to imply that most values are higher or lower than is actually the case. If elements in the sample space increase arithmetically, when placed in some order, then the median and arithmetic average are equal. For example, consider the sample space {1,2,3,4}. The average is 2.5, as is the median.

However, when we consider a sample space that cannot be arranged into an arithmetic progression, such as {1,2,4,8,16}, the median and arithmetic average can differ significantly. In this case the arithmetic average is 6.2 and the median is 4. When one looks at the arithmetic average of a sample space, one must note that the average value can vary significantly from most values in the sample space.

There are applications of this phenomenon in many fields. For example, since the 1980s in the United States median income has increased more slowly than the arithmetic average of income. Researchers dealing with frequency data must also be careful when reporting summary statistics such as means or median. Where a phenomenon is rare in general (for example, emergency room visits among the general population), but occurs frequently in some people (for example, daredevils), then the mean value may be much lower than the median.

Angles

Particular care must be taken when using cyclic data such as phases or angles. Naïvely taking the arithmetic mean of 1° and 359° yields a result of 180°. This is incorrect for two reasons:

- Firstly, angle measurements are only defined up to a factor of 360° (or 2π, if measuring in radians). Thus one could as easily call these 1° and −1°, or 1° and 719° – each of which gives a different average.
- Secondly, in this situation, 0° (equivalently, 360°) is geometrically a better average value: there is lower dispersion about it (the points are both 1° from it, and 179° from 180°, the putative average).

In general application such an oversight will lead to the average value artificially moving towards the middle of the numerical range. A solution to this problem is to use the optimization formulation (viz, define the mean as the central point: the point about which one has the lowest dispersion), and redefine the difference as a modular distance (i.e., the distance on the circle: so the modular distance between 1° and 359° is 2°, not 358°).

Geometric Mean

In mathematics, the geometric mean is a type of mean or average, which indicates the central tendency or typical value of a set of numbers. A geometric mean is often used when comparing different items – finding a single "figure of merit" for these items – when each item has multiple properties that have different numeric ranges. For example, the geometric mean can give a meaningful "average" to compare two companies which are each rated at 0 to 5 for their environmental sustainability, and are rated at 0 to 100 for their financial viability.

If an arithmetic mean was used instead of a geometric mean, the financial viability is given more weight because its numeric range is larger- so a small percentage change in the financial rating (e.g. going from 80 to 90) makes a much larger difference in the arithmetic mean than a large percentage change in environmental sustainability (e.g. going from 2 to 5).

The use of a geometric mean "normalizes" the ranges being averaged, so that no range dominates the weighting, and a given percentage change in any of the properties has the same effect on the geometric mean. So, a 20% change in environmental sustainability from 4 to 4.8 has the same effect on the geometric mean as a 20% change in financial viability from 60 to 72.

The geometric mean is similar to the arithmetic mean, except that the numbers are multiplied and then the nth root (where n is the count of numbers in the set) of the resulting product is taken.

For instance, the geometric mean of two numbers, say 2 and 8, is just the square root of their product; that is $^{2}–2 \times 8 = 4$. As another example, the geometric mean of the three numbers 4, 1, and 1/32 is the cube root of their product (1/8), which is 1/2; that is $^{3}–4 \times 1 \times 1/32 = ½$.

More generally, if the numbers are $x_1,\ldots,x_n$, the geometric mean G satisfies

$$G = \sqrt[n]{x_1 x_2 \cdots x_n},$$

and hence

$$\log G = \frac{1}{n}\sum_{i=1}^{n} \log x_i.$$

The latter expression states that the log of the geometric mean is the arithmetic mean of the logs of the numbers.

The geometric mean can also be understood in terms of geometry. The geometric mean of two numbers, a and b, is the length of one side of a square whose area is equal to the area of a rectangle with sides of lengths a and b.

Similarly, the geometric mean of three numbers, a, b, and c, is the length of one side of a cube whose volume is the same as that of a cuboid with sides whose lengths are equal to the three given numbers.

The geometric mean applies only to positive numbers. It is also often used for a set of numbers whose values are meant to be multiplied together or are exponential in nature, such as data on the growth of the human population or interest rates of a financial investment. The geometric mean is also one of the three classical Pythagorean means, together with the aforementioned arithmetic mean and the harmonic mean. For all positive data sets containing at least one pair of unequal values, the harmonic mean is always the least of the three means, while the arithmetic mean is always the greatest of the three and the geometric mean is always in between.

Calculation

The geometric mean of a data set $\{a_1, a_2, \ldots, a_n\}$ is given by:

$$\Big(\prod_{i=1}^{n} a_i\Big)^{1/n} = \sqrt[n]{a_1 a_2 \cdots a_n}.$$

The geometric mean of a data set is less than the data set's arithmetic mean unless all members of the data set are equal, in which case the geometric and arithmetic means are equal. This allows the definition of the arithmetic-geometric mean, a mixture of the two which always lies in between.

The geometric mean is also the arithmetic-harmonic mean in the sense that if two sequences (an) and (hn) are defined:

$$a_{n+1} = \frac{a_n + h_n}{2}, \quad a_0 = x$$

and

$$h_{n+1} = \frac{2}{\frac{1}{a_n} + \frac{1}{h_n}}, \quad h_0 = y$$

then a*n* and h*n* will converge to the geometric mean of x and y.

This can be seen easily from the fact that the sequences do converge to a common limit (which can be shown by Bolzano–Weierstrass theorem) and the fact that geometric mean is preserved:

$$\sqrt{a_i h_i} = \sqrt{\frac{a_i + h_i}{\frac{a_i + h_i}{h_i a_i}}} = \sqrt{\frac{a_i + h_i}{\frac{1}{a_i} + \frac{1}{h_i}}} = \sqrt{a_{i+1} h_{i+1}}$$

Replacing the arithmetic and harmonic mean by a pair of generalized means of opposite, finite exponents yields the same result.

Relationship with Arithmetic Mean of Logarithms

By using logarithmic identities to transform the formula, the multiplications can be expressed as a sum and the power as a multiplication.

$$\left(\prod_{i=1}^{n} a_i\right)^{1/n} = \exp\left[\frac{1}{n}\sum_{i=1}^{n} \ln a_i\right]$$

This is sometimes called the log-average. It is simply computing the arithmetic mean of the logarithm-transformed values of a_i (i.e., the arithmetic mean on the log scale) and then using the exponentiation to return the computation to the original scale, i.e., it is the generalised f-mean with $f(x) = \log x$. For example, the geometric mean of 2 and 8 can be calculated as:

$$b^{(\log_b(2)+\log_b(8))/2} = 4,$$

where b is any base of a logarithm (commonly 2, e or 10).

Relationship with Arithmetic Mean and Mean-preserving Spread

If a set of non-identical numbers is subjected to a mean-preserving spread — that is, two or more elements of the set are “spread apart” from each other while leaving the arithmetic mean unchanged — then the geometric mean always decreases.

Computation in Constant Time

In cases where the geometric mean is being used to determine the average growth rate of some quantity, and the initial and final values a_0 and a_n of that quantity are known, the product of the measured growth rate at every step need not be taken. Instead, the geometric mean is simply

$$\left(\frac{a_n}{a_0}\right)^{\frac{1}{n}},$$

where $n$is the number of steps from the initial to final state.

If the values are $a_0,\ldots,a_n$, then the growth rate between measurement a_k and a_k+1 is a_k+1/a_k. The geometric mean of these growth rates is just

$$\left(\frac{a_1}{a_0}\frac{a_2}{a_1}\cdots\frac{a_n}{a_{n-1}}\right)^{\frac{1}{n}}=\left(\frac{a_n}{a_0}\right)^{\frac{1}{n}}$$

Properties

The fundamental property of the geometric mean, which can be proven to be false for any other mean, is

$$GM\left(\frac{X_i}{Y_i}\right)=\frac{GM(X_i)}{GM(Y_i)}$$

This makes the geometric mean the only correct mean when averaging normalized results, that is results that are presented as ratios to reference values. This is the case when presenting computer performance with respect to a reference computer, or when computing a single average index from several heterogeneous sources (for example life expectancy, education years and infant mortality). In this scenario, using the arithmetic or harmonic mean would change the ranking of the results depending on what is used as a reference. For example, take the following comparison of execution time of computer programmes:

	Computer A	***Computer B***	***Computer C***
Programme 1	1	10	20
Programme 2	1000	100	20
Arithmetic mean	500.5	55	20
Geometric mean	31.622 . . .	31.622 . . .	20

The arithmetic and geometric means “agree” that computer C is the fastest. However, by presenting appropriately normalized values and using the arithmetic mean, we can show either of the other two computers to be the fastest. Normalizing by A's result gives A as the fastest computer according to the arithmetic mean:

	Computer A	*Computer B*	*Computer C*
Programme 1	1	10	20
Programme 2	1	0.1	0.02
Arithmetic mean	1	5.05	10.01
Geometric mean	1	1	0.632 . . .

while normalizing by B's result gives B as the fastest computer according to the arithmetic mean:

	Computer A	*Computer B*	*Computer C*
Programme 1	0.1	1	2
Programme 2	10	1	0.2
Arithmetic mean	5.05	1	1.1
Geometric mean	1	1	0.632

In all cases, the ranking given by the geometric mean stays the same as the one obtained with unnormalized values.

Applications

Proportional Growth

The geometric mean is more appropriate than the arithmetic mean for describing proportional growth, both exponential growth (constant proportional growth) and varying growth; in business the geometric mean of growth rates is known as the compound annual growth rate (CAGR). The geometric mean of growth over periods yields the equivalent constant growth rate that would yield the same final amount.

Suppose an orange tree yields 100 oranges one year and then 180, 210 and 300 the following years, so the growth is 80%, 16.6666% and 42.8571% for each year respectively. Using the arithmetic mean calculates a (linear) average growth of 46.5079% (80% + 16.6666% + 42.8571% divided by 3). However, if we start with 100 oranges and let it grow 46.5079% each year, the result is 314 oranges, not 300, so the linear average over-states the year-on-year growth. Instead, we can use the geometric mean. Growing with 80% corresponds to multiplying with 1.80, so we take the geometric mean of 1.80, 1.166666 and 1.428571, i.e. $\sqrt[3]{1.80 \times 1.166666 \times 1.428571} = 1.442249$; thus the "average" growth per year is 44.2249%. If we start with 100 oranges and let the number grow with 44.2249% each year, the result is 300 oranges.

Applications in the Social Sciences

Although the geometric mean has been relatively rare in computing social statistics, starting from 2010 the United Nations Human Development Index did switch to this mode of calculation, on the grounds that it better reflected the non-substitutable nature of the statistics being compiled and compared:

The geometric mean reduces the level of substitutability between dimensions [being compared] and at the same time ensures that a 1 percent decline in say life expectancy at birth has the same impact on the HDI as a 1 percent decline in education or income. Thus, as a basis for comparisons of achievements, this method is also more respectful of the intrinsic differences across the dimensions than a simple average.

Note that not all values used to compute the HDI are normalized; some of them instead have the form $(X - X_{min})/(X_{norm} - X_{min})$. This makes the choice of the geometric mean less obvious than one would expect from the "Properties" section above.

Aspect Ratios

The geometric mean has been used in choosing a compromise aspect ratio in film and video: given two aspect ratios, the geometric mean of them provides a compromise between them, distorting or cropping both in some sense equally. Concretely, two equal area rectangles (with the same center and parallel sides) of different aspect ratios intersect in a rectangle whose aspect ratio is the geometric mean, and their hull (smallest rectangle which contains both of them) likewise has aspect ratio their geometric mean.

In the choice of 16:9 aspect ratio by the SMPTE, balancing 2.35 and 4:3, the geometric mean is $\sqrt{2.35 \times \frac{4}{3}} \approx 1.7701$, and thus 16:9 = 1.777... was chosen. This was discovered empirically by Kerns Powers, who cut out rectangles with equal areas and shaped them to match each of the popular aspect ratios. When overlapped with their center points aligned, he found that all of those aspect ratio rectangles fit within an outer rectangle with an aspect ratio of 1.77:1 and all of them also covered a smaller common inner rectangle with the same aspect ratio 1.77:1. The value found by Powers is exactly the geometric mean of the extreme aspect ratios, 4:3 (1.33:1) and CinemaScope (2.35:1), which is coincidentally close to 16:9 (1.777:1). Note that the intermediate ratios have no effect on the result, only the two extreme ratios.

Applying the same geometric mean technique to 16:9 and 4:3 approximately yields the 14:9 (1.555...) aspect ratio, which is likewise used as a compromise between these ratios. In this case 14:9 is exactly the arithmetic mean of 16:9 and 4:3 = 12:9, since 14 is the average of 16 and 12, while the precise geometric mean is $\sqrt{\frac{16}{9} \times \frac{4}{3}} \approx 1.5396 \approx 13.8:9$, but the two different means, arithmetic and geometric, are approximately equal because both numbers are sufficiently close to each other (a difference of less than 2%).

Spectral Flatness

In signal processing, spectral flatness, a measure of how flat or spiky a spectrum is, is defined as the ratio of the geometric mean of the power spectrum to its arithmetic mean.

Geometry

The length of the altitude of a right triangle from the hypotenuse to the right angle, where the altitude is perpendicular to the hypotenuse, is the geometric mean of the two segments into which the hypotenuse is divided.

In an ellipse, the semi-minor axis is the geometric mean of the maximum and minimum distances of the ellipse from a focus; and the semi-major axis of the ellipse is the geometric mean of the distance from the center to either focus and the distance from the center to either directrix.

Frequency Distribution

In statistics, a frequency distribution is an arrangement of the values that one or more variables take in a sample. Each entry in the table contains the frequency or count of the occurrences of values within a particular group or interval, and in this way, the table summarizes the distribution of values in the sample.

Applications

Managing and operating on frequency tabulated data is much simpler than operation on raw data. There are simple algorithms to calculate median, mean, standard deviation etc. from these tables.

Statistical hypothesis testing is founded on the assessment of differences and similarities between frequency distributions. This assessment involves measures of central tendency or averages, such as the mean and median, and measures of variability or statistical dispersion, such as the standard deviation or variance.

A frequency distribution is said to be skewed when its mean and median are different. The kurtosis of a frequency distribution is the concentration of scores at the mean, or how peaked the distribution appears if depicted graphically—for example, in a histogram.

If the distribution is more peaked than the normal distribution it is said to be leptokurtic; if less peaked it is said to be platykurtic. Letter frequency distributions are also used in frequency analysis to crack codes and are referred to the relative frequency of letters in different languages.

Failure Rate

Failure rate is the frequency with which an engineered system or component fails, expressed, for example, in failures per hour. It is often denoted by the Greek letter λ (lambda) and is important in reliability engineering.

The failure rate of a system usually depends on time, with the rate varying over the life cycle of the system. For example, an automobile's failure rate in its fifth year of service may be many times greater than its failure rate during its first year of service. One does not expect to replace an exhaust pipe, overhaul the brakes, or have major transmission problems in a new vehicle. In practice, the mean time between failures (MTBF, 1/λ) is often reported instead of the failure rate. This is valid and useful if the failure rate may be assumed constant - often used for complex units / systems, electronics - and is a general agreement in some reliability standards (Military and Aerospace).

It does in this case *only* relate to the flat region of the bathtub curve, also called the "useful life period". Because of this, it is incorrect to extrapolate MTBF to give an estimate of the service life time of a component, which will typically be much less than suggested by the MTBF due to the much higher failure rates in the "end-of-life wearout" part of the "bathtub curve". The reason for the preferred use for MTBF numbers is that the use of large positive numbers (like 150.000 hours) is more intuitive and easier to remember than very small numbers (like 1.3e-4 per hour). The MTBF is an important system parameter in systems where failure rate needs to be managed, in particular for safety systems. The MTBF appears frequently in the engineering design requirements, and governs frequency of required system maintenance and inspections. In special processes called renewal processes, where the time to recover from failure can be neglected and the likelihood of failure remains constant with respect to time, the failure rate is simply the multiplicative inverse of the MTBF ($1/\lambda$). A similar ratio used in the transport industries, especially in railways and trucking is 'mean distance between failures', a variation which attempts to correlate actual loaded distances to similar reliability needs and practices.

Failure rates are important factors in the insurance, finance, commerce and regulatory industries and fundamental to the design of safe systems in a wide variety of applications.

Estimation

The Nelson–Aalen estimator can be used to estimate the cumulative hazard rate function.

Statistical Inference

In statistics, statistical inference is the process of drawing conclusions from data that is subject to random variation, for example, observational errors or sampling variation. More substantially, the terms statistical inference, statistical induction and inferential statistics are used to describe systems of procedures that can be used to draw conclusions from datasets arising from systems affected by random variation, such as observational errors, random sampling, or random experi-mentation.

Initial requirements of such a system of procedures for inference and induction are that the system should produce reasonable answers when applied to well-defined situations and that it should be general enough to be applied across a range of situations. The outcome of statistical inference may be an answer to the question "what should be done next?", where this might be a decision about making further experiments or surveys, or about drawing a conclusion before implementing some organizational or governmental policy.

Introduction

Scope

For the most part, statistical inference makes propositions about populations, using data drawn from the population of interest via some form of random sampling. More generally, data about a random process is obtained from its observed behaviour during a finite period of time. Given a parameter or hypothesis about which one wishes to make inference, statistical inference most often uses:

- A statistical model of the random process that is supposed to generate the data, which is known when randomization has been used, and
- A particular realization of the random process; i.e., a set of data.

The conclusion of a statistical inference is a statistical proposition. Some common forms of statistical proposition are:

- An estimate; i.e., a particular value that best approximates some parameter of interest,
- A confidence interval (or set estimate); i.e., an interval constructed using a dataset drawn from a population so that, under repeated sampling of such datasets, such intervals would contain the true parameter value with the probability at the stated confidence level,
- A credible interval; i.e., a set of values containing, for example, 95% of posterior belief,
- Rejection of a hypothesis
- Clustering or classification of data points into groups

Comparison to Descriptive Statistics

Statistical inference is generally distinguished from descriptive statistics. In simple terms, descriptive statistics can be thought of as being just a straightforward presentation of facts, in which modelling decisions made by a data analyst have had minimal influence.

Models/Assumptions

Any statistical inference requires some assumptions. A statistical model is a set of assumptions concerning the generation of the observed data and similar data. Descriptions of statistical models usually emphasize the role of population quantities of interest, about which we wish to draw inference. Descriptive statistics are typically used as a preliminary step before more formal inferences are drawn.

Degree of Models/assumptions

Statisticians distinguish between three levels of modelling assumptions;

- *Fully parametric:* The probability distributions describing the data-generation process are assumed to be fully described by a family of probability distributions involving only a finite number of unknown parameters. For example, one may assume that the distribution of population values is truly Normal, with unknown mean and variance, and that datasets are generated by 'simple' random sampling. The family of generalized linear models is a widely used and flexible class of parametric models.
- *Non-parametric:* The assumptions made about the process generating the data are much less than in parametric statistics and may be minimal. For example, every continuous probability distribution has a median, which may be estimated using the sample median or the Hodges-Lehmann-Sen estimator, which has good properties when the data arise from simple random sampling.
- *Semi-parametric:* This term typically implies assump-tions 'between' fully and non-parametric approaches. For example, one may assume that a population distribution have a finite mean. Furthermore, one may assume that the mean response level in the population depends in a truly linear manner on some covariate (a parametric assumption) but not make any parametric assumption describing the variance around that mean (i.e., about the presence or possible form of any heteroscedasticity). More generally, semi-parametric models can often be separated into 'structural' and 'random variation' components. One component is treated para-metrically and the other non-parametrically. The well-known Cox model is a set of semi-parametric assumptions.

Importance of Valid Models/assumptions

Whatever level of assumption is made, correctly calibrated inference in general requires these assumptions to be correct; i.e., that the data-generating mechanisms really has been correctly specified.

Incorrect assumptions of 'simple' random sampling can invalidate statistical inference. More complex semi- and fully parametric assumptions are also cause for concern. For example, incorrectly assuming the Cox model can in some cases lead to faulty conclusions. Incorrect assumptions of Normality in the population also invalidates some forms of regression-based inference. The use of any parametric model is viewed skeptically by most experts in sampling human populations: "most sampling statisticians, when they deal with confidence intervals at all, limit themselves to statements about [estimators] based on very large samples, where the central limit theorem ensures that these [estimators] will have distributions that are nearly normal." In particular, a normal distribution "would be a totally unrealistic and catastrophically unwise assumption to make if we were dealing with any kind of economic population." Here, the central limit theorem states that the distribution of the sample mean "for very large samples" is approximately normally distributed, if the distribution is not heavy tailed.

Approximate Distributions

Given the difficulty in specifying exact distributions of sample statistics, many methods have been developed for approximating these.

With finite samples, approximation results measure how close a limiting distribution approaches the statistic's sample distribution: For example, with 10,000 independent samples the normal distribution approximates (to two digits of accuracy) the distribution of the sample mean for many population distributions, by the Berry–Esseen theorem. Yet for many practical purposes, the normal approximation provides a good approximation to the sample-mean's distribution when there are 10 (or more) independent samples, according to simulation studies and statisticians' experience. Following Kolmogorov's work in the 1950s, advanced statistics uses approximation theory and functional analysis to quantify the error of approximation. In this approach, the metric geometry of probability distributions is studied; this approach quantifies approximation error with, for example, the Kullback–Leibler distance, Bregman divergence, and the Hellinger distance.

With indefinitely large samples, limiting results like the central limit theorem describe the sample statistic's limiting distribution, if one exists. Limiting results are not statements about finite samples, and indeed are irrelevant to finite samples. However, the asymptotic theory of limiting distributions is often invoked for work with finite samples. For example, limiting results are often invoked to justify the generalized method of moments and the use of generalized estimating equations, which are popular in econometrics and biostatistics. The magnitude of the difference between the limiting distribution and the true distribution (formally, the 'error' of the approximation) can be assessed using simulation. The heuristic application of limiting results to finite samples is common practice in many applications, especially with low-dimensional models with log-concave likelihoods (such as with one-parameter exponential families).

Randomization-based Models

For a given dataset that was produced by a randomization design, the randomization distribution of a statistic (under the null-hypothesis) is defined by evaluating the test statistic for all of the plans that could have been generated by the randomization design. In frequentist inference, randomization allows inferences to be based on the randomization distribution rather than a subjective model, and this is important especially in survey sampling and design of experiments. Statistical inference from randomized studies is also more straightforward than many other situations. In Bayesian inference, randomization is also of importance: in survey sampling, use of sampling without replacement ensures the exchangeability of the sample with the population; in randomized experiments, randomization warrants a missing at random assumption for covariate information.

Objective randomization allows properly inductive procedures. Many statisticians prefer randomization-based analysis of data that was generated by well-defined randomi-zation procedures. (However, it is true that in fields of science with developed theoretical knowledge and experimental control, randomized experiments may increase the costs of experi-mentation without improving the quality of inferences.) Similarly, results from randomized experiments are recom-mended by leading statistical authorities as allowing inferences with greater reliability than do observational studies of the same phenomena. However, a good observational study may be better than a bad randomized experiment.

The statistical analysis of a randomized experiment may be based on the randomization scheme stated in the experimental protocol and does not need a subjective model.

However, at any time, some hypotheses cannot be tested using objective statistical models, which accurately describe randomized experiments or random samples. In some cases, such randomized studies are uneconomical or unethical.

Model-based Analysis of Randomized Experiments

It is standard practice to refer to a statistical model, often a linear model, when analysing data from randomized experiments. However, the randomization scheme guides the choice of a statistical model. It is not possible to choose an appropriate model without knowing the randomization scheme. Seriously misleading results can be obtained analysing data from randomized experiments while ignoring the experimental protocol; common mistakes include forgetting the blocking used in an experiment and confusing repeated measurements on the same experimental unit with independent replicates of the treatment applied to different experimental units.

Modes of Inference

Different schools of statistical inference have become established. These schools (or 'paradigms') are not mutually exclusive, and methods which work well under one paradigm often have attractive interpretations under other paradigms. The two main paradigms in use are frequentist and Bayesian inference, which are both summarized below.

Frequentist inference

This paradigm calibrates the production of propositions by considering (notional) repeated sampling of datasets similar to the one at hand. By considering its characteristics under repeated sample, the frequentist properties of any statistical inference procedure can be described — although in practice this quantification may be challenging.

Frequentist Inference, Objectivity, and Decision Theory

One interpretation of frequentist inference (or classical inference) is that it is applicable only in terms of frequency probability; that is, in terms of repeated sampling from a population. However, the approach of Neyan develops these procedures in terms of pre-experiment probabilities. That is, before undertaking an experiment, one decides on a rule for coming to a conclusion such that the probability of being correct is controlled in a suitable way: such a probability need not have a frequentist or repeated sampling interpretation. In contrast, Bayesian inference works in terms of conditional probabilities (i.e. probabilities conditional on the observed data), compared to the marginal (but conditioned on unknown parameters) probabilities used in the frequentist approach.

The frequentist procedures of significance testing and confidence intervals can be constructed without regard to utility functions. However, some elements of frequentist statistics, such as statistical decision theory, do incorporate utility functions. In particular, frequentist developments of optimal inference (such as minimum-variance unbiased estimators, or uniformly most powerful testing) make use of loss functions, which play the role of (negative) utility functions.

Loss functions need not be explicitly stated for statistical theorists to prove that a statistical procedure has an optimality property. However, loss-functions are often useful for stating optimality properties: for example, median-unbiased estimators are optimal under absolute value loss functions, in that they minimize expected loss, and least squares estimators are optimal under squared error loss functions, in that they minimize expected loss.

While statisticians using frequentist inference must choose for themselves the parameters of interest, and the estimators/test statistic to be used, the absence of obviously explicit utilities and prior distributions has helped frequentist procedures to become widely viewed as 'objective'.

Bayesian Inference

The Bayesian calculus describes degrees of belief using the 'language' of probability; beliefs are positive, integrate to one, and obey probability axioms. Bayesian inference uses the available posterior beliefs as the basis for making statistical propositions. There are several different justifications for using the Bayesian approach.

Examples of Bayesian Inference

- Credible intervals for interval estimation
- Bayes factors for model comparison

Bayesian Inference, Subjectivity and Decision Theory

Many informal Bayesian inferences are based on "intuitively reasonable" summaries of the posterior. For example, the posterior mean, median and mode, highest posterior density intervals, and Bayes Factors can all be motivated in this way. While a user's utility function need not be stated for this sort of inference, these summaries do all depend (to some extent) on stated prior beliefs, and are generally viewed as subjective conclusions. (Methods of prior construction which do not require external input have been proposed but not yet fully developed.)

Formally, Bayesian inference is calibrated with reference to an explicitly stated utility, or loss function; the 'Bayes rule' is the one which maximizes expected utility, averaged over the posterior uncertainty. Formal Bayesian inference therefore automatically provides optimal decisions in a decision theoretic sense. Given assumptions, data and utility, Bayesian inference can be made for essentially any problem, although not every statistical inference need have a Bayesian interpretation. Analyses which are not formally Bayesian can be (logically) incoherent; a feature of Bayesian procedures which use proper priors (i.e., those integrable to one) is that they are guaranteed to be coherent.

Some advocates of Bayesian inference assert that inference *must* take place in this decision-theoretic framework, and that Bayesian inference should not conclude with the evaluation and summarization of posterior beliefs.

Other Modes of Inference (besides frequentist and Bayesian)

Information and Computational Complexity

Other forms of statistical inference have been developed from ideas in information theory and the theory of Kolmogorov complexity. For example, the minimum description length (MDL) principle selects statistical models that maximally compress the data; inference proceeds without assuming counterfactual or non-falsifiable 'data-generating mechanisms' or probability models for the data, as might be done in frequentist or Bayesian approaches.

However, if a 'data generating mechanism' does exist in reality, then according to Shannon's source coding theorem it provides the MDL description of the data, on average and asymptotically. In minimizing description length (or descriptive complexity), MDL estimation is similar to maximum likelihood estimation and maximum a posteriori estimation (using maximum-entropy Bayesian priors). However, MDL avoids assuming that the underlying probability model is known; the MDL principle can also be applied without assumptions that e.g. the data arose from independent sampling. The MDL principle has been applied in communication-coding theory in information theory, in linear regression, and in time-series analysis (particularly for choosing the degrees of the polynomials in Autoregressive moving average (ARMA) models).

Information-theoretic statistical inference has been popular in data mining, which has become a common approach for very large observational and heterogeneous datasets made possible by the computer revolution and internet. The evaluation of statistical inferential procedures often uses techniques or criteria from computational complexity theory or numerical analysis.

Fiducial Inference

Fiducial inference was an approach to statistical inference based on fiducial probability, also known as a "fiducial distribution". In subsequent work, this approach has been called ill-defined, extremely limited in applicability, and even fallacious. However this argument is the same as that which shows that a so-called confidence distribution is not a valid probability distribution and, since this has not invalidated the application of confidence intervals, it does not necessarily invalidate conclusions drawn from fiducial arguments.

Structural Inference

Developing ideas of Fisher and of Pitman from 1938 to 1939, George A. Barnard developed "structural inference" or "pivotal inference", an approach using invariant probabilities on group families. Barnard reformulated the arguments behind fiducial inference on a restricted class of models on which "fiducial" procedures would be well-defined and useful.

Estimation Theory

Estimation theory is a branch of statistics and signal processing that deals with estimating the values of parameters based on measured/ empirical data that has a random component. The parameters describe an underlying physical setting in such a way that their value affects the distribution of the measured data. An estimator attempts to approximate the unknown parameters using the measurements.

For example, it is desired to estimate the proportion of a population of voters who will vote for a particular candidate. That proportion is the parameter sought; the estimate is based on a small random sample of voters.

Or, for example, in radar the goal is to estimate the range of objects (airplanes, boats, etc.) by analysing the two-way transit timing of received echoes of transmitted pulses. Since the reflected pulses are unavoidably embedded in electrical noise, their measured values are randomly distributed, so that the transit time must be estimated.

In estimation theory, it is assumed the measured data is random with probability distribution dependent on the parameters of interest. For example, in electrical communication theory, the measurements which contain information regarding the parameters of interest are often associated with a noisy signal. Without randomness, or noise, the problem would be deterministic and estimation would not be needed.

Recursive Bayesian Estimation

Recursive Bayesian estimation, also known as a Bayes filter, is a general probabilistic approach for estimating an unknown probability density function recursively over time using incoming measurements and a mathematical process model.

In Robotics

A Bayes filter is an algorithm used in computer science for calculating the probabilities of multiple beliefs to allow a robot to infer its position and orientation. Essentially, Bayes filters allow robots to continuously update their most likely position within a coordinate system, based on the most recently acquired sensor data.

This is a recursive algorithm. It consists of two parts: prediction and innovation. If the variables are linear and normally distributed the Bayes filter becomes equal to the Kalman filter. In a simple example, a robot moving throughout a grid may have several different sensors that provide it with information about its surroundings. The robot may start out with certainty that it is at position (0,0). However, as it moves farther and farther from its original position, the robot has continuously less certainty about its position; using a Bayes filter, a probability can be assigned to the robot's belief about its current position, and that probability can be continuously updated from additional sensor information.

Model

The true state x is assumed to be an unobserved Markov process, and the measurements z are the observed states of a Hidden Markov Model (HMM). The following picture presents a Bayesian Network of a HMM.

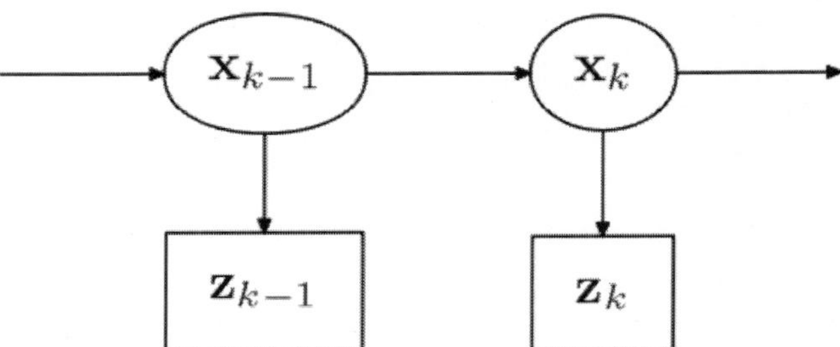

Figure: *Because of the Markov assumption, the probability of the current true state given the immediately previous one is conditionally independent of the other earlier states.*

$$p(\mathrm{x}_k \mid \mathrm{x}_{k-1}, \mathrm{x}_{k-2}, \ldots, \mathrm{x}_0) = p(\mathrm{x}_k \mid \mathrm{x}_{k-1})$$

Similarly, the measurement at the k-th timestep is dependent only upon the current state, so is conditionally independent of all other states given the current state.

$$p(z_k \mid x_k, x_{k-1}, \ldots, x_0) = p(z_k \mid x_k)$$

Using these assumptions the probability distribution over all states of the HMM can be written simply as:

$$p(x_0, \ldots, x_k, z_1, \ldots, z_k) = p(x_0)\prod_{i=1}^{k} p(z_i \mid x_i)p(x_i \mid x_{i-1}).$$

However, when using the Kalman filter to estimate the state x, the probability distribution of interest is associated with the current states conditioned on the measurements up to the current timestep. (This is achieved by marginalising out the previous states and dividing by the probability of the measurement set.) This leads to the *predict* and *update* steps of the Kalman filter written probabilistically. The probability distribution associated with the predicted state is the sum (integral) of the products of the probability distribution associated with the transition from the (k - 1)-th timestep to the k-th and the probability distribution associated with the previous state, over all possible x_{k_1}.

$$p(x_k \mid Z_{k-1}) = \int p(x_k \mid x_{k-1})p(x_{k-1} \mid Z_{k-1})dx_{k-1}$$

The probability distribution of update is proportional to the product of the measurement likelihood and the predicted state.

$$p(x_k \mid Z_k) = \frac{p(z_k \mid x_k)p(x_k \mid Z_{k-1})}{p(z_k \mid Z_{k-1})} = \alpha\, p(z_k \mid x_k)p(x_k \mid Z_{k-1})$$

The denominator

$$p(z_k \mid Z_{k-1}) = \int p(z_k \mid x_k)p(x_k \mid Z_{k-1})dx_k$$

is constant relative to x, so we can always substitute it for a coefficient α, which can usually be ignored in practice. The numerator can be calculated and then simply normalized, since its integral must be unitary.

2

Exploratory Factor Analysis

In multivariate statistics, exploratory factor analysis (EFA) is a statistical method used to uncover the underlying structure of a relatively large set of variables. EFA is a technique within factor analysis whose overarching goal is to identify the underlying relationships between measured variables. It is commonly used by researchers when developing a scale (a scale is a collection of questions used to measure a particular research topic) and serves to identify a set of latent constructs underlying a battery of measured variables.

It should be used when the researcher has no a priori hypothesis about factors or patterns of measured variables. Measured variables are any one of several attributes of people that may be observed and measured. An example of a measured variable would be one item on a scale. Researchers must carefully consider the number of measured variables to include in the analysis. EFA procedures are more accurate when each factor is represented by multiple measured variables in the analysis. There should be at least 3 to 5 measured variables per factor.

EFA is based on the common factor model. Within the common factor model, measured variables are expressed as a function of common factors, unique factors, and errors of measurement. Common factors inûuence two or more measured variables, while each unique factor inûuences only one measured variable and does not explain correlations among measured variables.

An assumption of EFA is that any indicator/measured variable may be associated with any factor. When developing a scale, researchers should use EFA first before moving on to confirmatory factor analysis (CFA). EFA requires the researcher to make a number of important decisions about how to conduct the analysis because there is no one set method.

Fitting Procedures

Fitting procedures are used to estimate the factor loadings and unique variances of the model (Factor loadings are the regression coefûcients between items and factors and measure the inûuence of a common factor on a measured variable). There are several factor analysis fitting methods to choose from, however there is little information on all of their strengths and weaknesses and many don't even have an exact name that is used consistently. Principal axis factoring (PAF) and maximum likelihood (ML) are two extraction methods that are generally recommended. In general, ML or PAF give the best results, depending on whether data are normally-distributed or if the assumption of normality has been violated.

Maximum Likelihood (ML)

The maximum likelihood method has many advantages in that it allows researchers to compute of a wide range of indexes of the goodness of fit of the model, it allows researchers to test the statistical significance of factor loadings, calculate correlations among factors and compute confidence intervals for these parameters. ML is the best choice when data are normally distributed because "it allows for the computation of a wide range of indexes of the goodness of fit of the model [and] permits statistical significance testing of factor loadings and correlations among factors and the computation of confidence intervals". ML should not be used if the data are not normally distributed.

Principal Axis Factoring (PAF)

Called "principal" axis factoring because the first factor accounts for as much common variance as possible, then the second factor next most variance, and so on. PAF is a descriptive procedure so it is best to use when the focus is just on your sample and you do not plan to generalize the results beyond your sample. An advantage of PAF is that it can be used when the assumption of normality has been violated. Another advantage of PAF is that it is less likely than ML to produce improper solutions. A downside of PAF is that it provides a limited range of goodness-of-fit indexes compared to ML and does not allow for the computation of confidence intervals and significance tests.

Selecting the Appropriate Number of Factors

When selecting how many factors to include in a model, researchers must try to balance parsimony (a model with relatively few factors) and plausibility (that there are enough factors to adequately account for correlations among measured variables). It is better to include too many factors (overfactoring) than too few factors (underfactoring).

Overfactoring occurs when too many factors are included in a model. It is not as bad as underfactoring because major factors will usually be accurately represented and extra factors will have no measured variables load onto them. Still, it should be avoided because overfactoring may lead researchers to put forward constructs with little theoretical value.

Underfactoring occurs when too few factors are included in a model. This is considered to be a greater error than overfactoring. If not enough factors are included in a model, there is likely to be substantial error. Measured variables that load onto a factor not included in the model can falsely loaded on factors that are included, altering true factor loadings . This can result in rotated solutions in which two factors are combined into a single factor, obscuring the true factor structure.

There are a number of procedures in order to determine the best number of factors, including scree plot, parallel analysis, kaiser criterion, and model comparison. The first three measures rely on eigenvalues. The eigenvalue of a factor represents the amount of variance of the variables accounted for by that factor. The lower the eigenvalue, the less that factor contributes to the explanation of variances in the variables.

Scree Plot

Compute the eigenvalues for the correlation matrix and plot the values from largest to smallest. Examine the graph to determine the last substantial drop in the magnitude of eigenvalues. The number of plotted points before the last drop is the number of factors to include in the model. This method has been criticized because of its subjective nature (i.e., there is no clear objective definition of what constitutes a substantial drop).

Parallel Analysis

Compute the eigenvalues for the correlation matrix and plot the values from largest to smallest and then plot a set of random eigenvalues. The number of eigenvalues before the intersection points indicates how many factors to include in your model. This procedure can be somewhat artbitrary (i.e. a factor just meeting the cutoff will be included and one just below will not).

Kaiser Criterion

Compute the eigenvalues for the correlation matrix and determine how many of these eigenvalues are greater than 1. This number is the number of factors to include in the model. A disadvantage of this procedure is that it is quite arbitrary (e.g., an eigenvalue of 1.01 is included whereas an eigenvalue of .99 is not). This procedure often leads to overfactoring and sometimes underfactoring. Therefore, this procedure should not be used.

Model Comparison

Choose the best model from a series of models that differ in complexity. Researchers use goodness-of-fit measures to fit models beginning with a model with zero factors and gradually increase the number of factors. The goal is to ultimately choose a model that explains the data significantly better than simpler models (with fewer factors) and explains the data as well as more complex models (with more factors).

There are different methods that can be used to assess model fit:

Likelihood Ratio Statistic

Used to test the null hypothesis that a model has perfect model fit. It should be applied to models with an increasing number of factors until the result is nonsignificant, indicating that the model is not rejected as good model fit of the population. This statistic should be used with a large sample size and normally distributed data. There are some drawbacks to the likelihood ratio test. First, when there is a large sample size, even small discrepancies between the model and the data result in model rejection. When there is a small sample size, even large discrepancies between the model and data may not be significant, which leads to underfactoring. Another disadvantage of the likelihood ratio test is that the null hypothesis of perfect fit is an unrealistic standard.

Root mean square error of approximation (RMSEA) fit index: RMSEA is an estimate of the discrepancy between the model and the data per degree of freedom for the model. Values less that .05 constitute good fit, values between 0.05 and 0.08 constitute acceptable fit, a values between 0.08 and 0.10 constitute marginal fit and values greater than 0.10 indicate poor fit . An advantage of the RMSEA fit index is that it provides confidence intervals which allow researchers to compare a series of models with varying numbers of factors.

Factor Rotation

Factor rotation is the process for interpreting factor matrixes. For any solution with two or more factors there are an infinite number of orientations of the factors that will explain the data equally well. Because there is no unique solution, a researcher must select a single solution from the infinite possibilities. The goal of factor rotation is to rotate factors in multidimensional space to arrive at a solution with best simple structure. There are two types of factor rotation: orthogonal and oblique rotation.

Orthogonal Rotation

Orthogonal rotations constrain factors to be uncorrelated. Varimax is considered the best orthogonal rotation and consequently is used the most often in psychology research. An advantage of orthogonal rotation is its simplicity and conceptual clarity, although there are several disadvantages. In the social sciences, there is often a theoretical basis for expecting constructs to be correlated, therefore orthogonal rotations may not be very realistic because it ignores this possibility. Also, because orthogonal rotations require factors to be uncorrelated, they are less likely to produce solutions with simple structure.

Factor Interpretation

Factor loadings are numerical values that indicate the strength and direction of a factor on a measured variable. Factor loadings indicate how strongly the factor influences the measured variable. In order to label the factors in the model, researchers should examine the factor pattern to see which items load highly on which factors and then determine what those items have in common. Whatever the items have in common will indicate the meaning of the factor.

Confirmatory Factor Analysis

In statistics, confirmatory factor analysis (CFA) is a special form of factor analysis, most commonly used in social research. It is used to test whether measures of a construct are consistent with a researcher's understanding of the nature of that construct (or factor). As such, the objective of confirmatory factor analysis is to test whether the data fit a hypothesized measurement model. This hypothesized model is based on theory and/or previous analytic research. CFA was first developed by Jöreskog and has built upon and replaced older methods of analysing construct validity such as the MTMM Matrix as described in Campbell & Fiske (1959).

In confirmatory factor analysis, the researcher first develops a hypothesis about what factors s/he believes are underlying the measures s/he has used (e.g., "Depression" being the factor underlying the Beck Depression Inventory and the Hamilton Rating Scale for Depression) and may impose constraints on the model based on these a priori hypotheses. By imposing these constraints, the researcher is forcing the model to be consistent with his/her theory.

For example, if it is posited that there are two factors accounting for the covariance in the measures, and that these factors are unrelated to one another, the researcher can create a model where the correlation between factor A and factor B is constrained to zero. Model fit measures could then be obtained to assess how well the proposed model captured the covariance between all the items or measures in the model.

If the constraints the researcher has imposed on the model are inconsistent with the sample data, then the results of statistical tests of model fit will indicate a poor fit, and the model will be rejected. If the fit is poor, it may be due to some items measuring multiple factors. It might also be that some items within a factor are more related to each other than others.

For some applications, the requirement of "zero loadings" (for indicators not supposed to load on a certain factor) has been regarded as too strict. A newly developed analysis method, "exploratory structural equation modelling", specifies hypotheses about the relation between observed indicators and their supposed primary latent factors while allowing for estimation of loadings with other latent factors as well.

Confirmatory Factor Analysis and Exploratory Factor Analysis

Both exploratory factor analysis (EFA) and confirmatory factor analysis are employed to understand shared variance of measured variables that is believed to be attributable to a factor or latent construct. Despite this similarity, however, EFA and CFA are conceptually and statistically distinct analyses.

The goal of EFA is to identify factors based on data and to maximize the amount of variance explained. The researcher is not required to have any specific hypotheses about how many factors will emerge, and what items or variables these factors will comprise.

If these hypotheses exist, they are not incorporated into and do not affect the results of the statistical analyses. By contrast, CFA evaluates a priori hypotheses and is largely driven by theory. CFA analyses require the researcher to hypothesize, in advance, the number of factors, whether or not these factors are correlated, and which items/measures load onto and reflect which factors. As such, in contrast to exploratory factor analysis, where all loadings are free to vary, CFA allows for the explicit constraint of certain loadings to be zero.

EFA is sometimes reported in research when CFA would be a better statistical approach. It has been argued that CFA can be restrictive and inappropriate when used in an exploratory fashion.

However, the idea that CFA is solely a "confirmatory" analysis may sometimes be misleading, as modification indices used in CFA are somewhat exploratory in nature. Modification indices show the improvement in model fit if a particular coefficient were to become unconstrained. Likewise, EFA and CFA do not have to be mutually exclusive analyses; EFA has been argued to be a reasonable follow up to a poor-fitting CFA model.

Confirmatory Factor Analysis and Structural Equation Modelling

Structural equation modelling software is typically used for performing confirmatory factor analysis. LISREL, EQS, AMOS, and Mplus are popular software programmes. CFA is also frequently used as a first step to assess the proposed measurement model in a structural equation model. Many of the rules of interpretation regarding assessment of model fit and model modification in structural equation modelling apply equally to CFA. CFA is distinguished from structural equation modelling by the fact that in CFA, there are no directed arrows between latent factors.

In other words, while in CFA factors are not presumed to directly cause one another, SEM often does specify particular factors and variables to be causal in nature. In the context of SEM, the CFA is often called 'the measurement model', while the relations between the latent variables (with directed arrows) are called 'the structural model'.

Evaluating Model Fit

Most statistical methods only require one statistical test to determine the significance of the analyses. However, in CFA, several statistical tests are used to determine how well the model fits to the data. Note that a good fit between the model and the data does not mean that the model is "correct", or even that it explains a large proportion of the covariance. A "good model fit" only indicates that the model is plausible. When reporting the results of a confirmatory factor analysis, one is urged to report: (*a*) the proposed models, (*b*) any modifications made, (*c*) which measures identify each latent variable, (*d*) correlations between latent variables, d) any other pertinent information, such as whether constraints are used. With regard to selecting model fit statistics to report, one should not simply report the statistics that estimate the best fit, though this may be tempting. Though several varying opinions exist, Kline (2010) recommends reporting the Chi-squared test, the RMSEA, the CFI, and the SRMR.

Absolute Fit Indices

Absolute fit indices determine how well the a priori model fits, or reproduces the data. Absolute fit indices include, but are not limited to, the Chi-Squared test, RMSEA, GFI, AGFI, RMR, and SRMR.

Chi-squared Test

The chi-squared test indicates the difference between observed and expected covariance matrices. Values closer to zero indicate a better fit; smaller difference between expected and observed covariance matrices. Chi-squared statistics can also be used to directly compare the fit of nested models to the data. One difficulty with the chi-squared test of model fit, however, is that researchers may fail to reject the hypothesis (or "accept" the model) due to a lack of statistical power due to small sample sizes (Type I error). Likewise, when a large sample size is used, one may fail to find a model that fits (Type II error). As a result, other measures of fit have been developed.

Root Mean Square Error of Approximation

The root mean square error of approximation (RMSEA) avoids issues of sample size by analysing the discrepancy between the hypothesized model, with optimally chosen parameter estimates, and the population covariance matrix. The RMSEA ranges from 0 to 1, with smaller values indicating better model fit. A value of .06 or less is indicative of acceptable model fit.

Root Mean Square Residual and Standardized Root Mean Square Residual

The root mean square residual (RMR) and standardized root mean square residual (SRMR) are the square root of the discrepancy between the sample covariance matrix and the model covariance matrix.

The RMR may be somewhat difficult to interpret, however, as its range is based on the scales of the indicators in the model (this becomes tricky when you have multiple indicators with varying scales; e.g., two questionnaires, one on a 0-10 scale, the other on a 1-3 scale). The standardized root mean square residual removes this difficulty in interpretation, and ranges from 0 to 1, with a value of .08 or less being indicative of an acceptable model.

Goodness of Fit Index and Adjusted Goodness of Fit Index

The goodness of fit index (GFI) is a measure of fit between the hypothesized model and the observed covariance matrix. The adjusted goodness of fit index (AGFI) corrects the GFI, which is affected by the number of indicators of each latent variable. The GFI and AGFI range between 0 and 1, with a cutoff value of .9 generally indicating acceptable model fit.

Relative Fit Indices

Relative fit indices (also called "incremental fit indices" and "comparative fit indices") compare the chi-square for the hypothesized model to one from a "null", or "baseline" model. This null model almost always contains a model in which all of the variables are uncorrelated, and as a result, has a very large chi-square (indicating poor fit). Relative fit indices include the normed fit index and comparative fit index.

Normed fit Index and non-normed Fit Index

The normed fit index (NFI) analyzes the discrepancy between the chi-squared value of the hypothesized model and the chi-squared value of the null model. However, this NFI was found to be very susceptible to sample size. The non-normed fit index (NNFI; also known as the Tucker-Lewis index, as it was built on an index formed by Tucker and Lewis, in 1973) resolves some of the issues of sample size, though NNFI values may sometimes erroneously fall beyond the 0 to 1 range. Values for both the NFI and NNFI should range between 0 and 1, with a cutoff of .95 or greater indicating a good model fit.

Comparative Fit Index

The comparative fit index (CFI) analyzes the model fit by examining the discrepancy between the data and the hypothesized model, while adjusting for the issues of sample size inherent in the chi-squared test of model fit, and the normed fit index. CFI values range from 0 to 1, with larger values indicating better fit; a CFI value of 0.90 or larger is generally considered to indicate acceptable model fit.

Identification and Underidentification

To estimate the parameters of a model, the model must be properly identified. That is, the number of estimated (unknown) parameters (q) must be less than or equal to the number of unique variances and covariances among the measured variables; $p(p + 1)/2$. This equation is known as the "t rule". If there is too little information available on which to base the parameter estimates, then the model is said to be underidentified, and model parameters cannot be estimated appropriately.

Principal Component Analysis

Principal component analysis (PCA) is a mathematical procedure that uses an orthogonal transformation to convert a set of observations of possibly correlated variables into a set of values of linearly uncorrelated variables called principal components. The number of principal components is less than or equal to the number of original variables. This transformation is defined in such a way that the first principal component has the largest possible variance (that is, accounts for as much of the variability in the data as possible), and each succeeding component in turn has the highest variance possible under the constraint that it be orthogonal to (i.e., uncorrelated with) the preceding components. Principal components are guaranteed to be independent only if the data set is jointly normally distributed. PCA is sensitive to the relative scaling of the original variables. Depending on the field of application, it is also named the discrete Karhunen–Loève transform (KLT), the Hotelling transform or proper orthogonal decomposition (POD).

PCA was invented in 1901 by Karl Pearson. Now it is mostly used as a tool in exploratory data analysis and for making predictive models. PCA can be done by eigenvalue decomposition of a data covariance (or correlation) matrix or singular value decomposition of a data matrix, usually after mean centering (and normalizing or using Z-scores) the data matrix for each attribute. The results of a PCA are usually discussed in terms of component scores, sometimes called factor scores (the transformed variable values corresponding to a particular data point), and loadings (the weight by which each standardized original variable should be multiplied to get the component score).

PCA is the simplest of the true eigenvector-based multivariate analyses. Often, its operation can be thought of as revealing the internal structure of the data in a way that best explains the variance in the data. If a multivariate dataset is visualised as a set of coordinates in a high-dimensional data space (1 axis per variable), PCA can supply the user with a lower-dimensional picture, a "shadow" of this object when viewed from its (in some sense) most informative viewpoint. This is done by using only the first few principal components so that the dimensionality of the transformed data is reduced.

PCA is closely related to factor analysis. Factor analysis typically incorporates more domain specific assumptions about the underlying structure and solves eigenvectors of a slightly different matrix.

Details

PCA is mathematically defined as an orthogonal linear transformation that transforms the data to a new coordinate system such that the greatest variance by any projection of the data comes to lie on the first coordinate (called the first principal component), the second greatest variance on the second coordinate, and so on.

Define a data matrix, X^T, with zero empirical mean (the empirical (sample) mean of the distribution has been subtracted from the data set), where each of the n rows represents a different repetition of the experiment, and each of the m columns gives a particular kind of datum (say, the results from a particular probe). (Note that X^T is defined here and not X itself, and what we are calling X^T is often alternatively denoted as X itself.) The singular value decomposition of X is $X = W\Sigma V^T$, where the $m \times m$ matrix W is the matrix of eigenvectors of the covariance matrix XX^T, the matrix Σ is an $m \times n$ rectangular diagonal matrix with nonnegative real numbers on the diagonal, and the $n \times n$ matrix V is the matrix of eigenvectors of X^TX. The PCA transformation that preserves dimensionality (that is, gives the same number of principal components as original variables) is then given by:

$$\begin{aligned} Y^T &= X^TW \\ &= V\Sigma^TW^TW \\ &= V\Sigma^T \end{aligned}$$

V is not uniquely defined in the usual case when $m < n - 1$, but Y will usually still be uniquely defined. Since W (by definition of the SVD of a real matrix) is an orthogonal matrix, each row of Y^T is simply a linear transformation of the corresponding row of X^T. The first column of Y^T is made up of the "scores" of the cases with respect to the "principal" component, the next column has the scores with respect to the "second principal" component, and so on.

If we want a reduced-dimensionality representation, we can project X down into the reduced space defined by only the first L singular vectors, WL:

$$Y = W_L^T X = \Sigma_L V^T \text{ where } \Sigma_L = I_{L\times m}\Sigma \text{ with}$$

$I_{L\times m}$ the $L \times m$ rectangular identity matrix.

The matrix W of singular vectors of X is equivalently the matrix W of eigenvectors of the matrix of observed covariances $C = X X^T$,

$$XX^T = W\Sigma\Sigma^T W^T$$

Given a set of points in Euclidean space, the first principal component corresponds to a line that passes through the multidimensional mean and minimizes the sum of squares of the distances of the points from the line. The second principal component corresponds to the same concept after all correlation with the first principal component has been subtracted from the points. The singular values (in Σ) are the square roots of the eigenvalues of the matrix XX^T. Each eigenvalue is proportional to the portion of the "variance" (more correctly of the sum of the squared distances of the points from their multidimensional mean) that is correlated with each eigenvector. The sum of all the eigenvalues is equal to the sum of the squared distances of the points from their multidimensional mean. PCA essentially rotates the set of points around their mean in order to align with the principal components. This moves as much of the variance as possible (using an orthogonal transformation) into the first few dimensions. The values in the remaining dimensions, therefore, tend to be small and may be dropped with minimal loss of information. PCA is often used in this manner for dimensionality reduction. PCA has the distinction of being the optimal orthogonal transformation for keeping the subspace that has largest "variance" (as defined above). This advantage, however, comes at the price of greater computational requirements if compared, for example and when applicable, to the discrete cosine transform, and in particular to the DCT-II which is simply known as the "DCT"; introduced by N. Ahmed, T.Natarajan and K.R.Rao in 1974.

PCA is sensitive to the scaling of the variables. If we have just two variables and they have the same sample variance and are positively correlated, then the PCA will entail a rotation by 45° and the "loadings" for the two variables with respect to the principal component will be equal. But if we multiply all values of the first variable by 100, then the principal component will be almost the same as that variable, with a small contribution from the other variable, whereas the second component will be almost aligned with the second original variable.

This means that whenever the different variables have different units (like temperature and mass), PCA is a somewhat arbitrary method of analysis. (Different results would be obtained if one used Fahrenheit rather than Celsius for example.) Note that Pearson's original paper was entitled "On Lines and Planes of Closest Fit to Systems of Points in Space" – "in space" implies physical Euclidean space where such concerns do not arise. One way of making the PCA less arbitrary is to use variables scaled so as to have unit variance.

Discussion

Mean subtraction (a.k.a. "mean centering") is necessary for performing PCA to ensure that the first principal component describes the direction of maximum variance. If mean subtraction is not performed, the first principal component might instead correspond more or less to the mean of the data. A mean of zero is needed for finding a basis that minimizes the mean square error of the approximation of the data. Assuming zero empirical mean (the empirical mean of the distribution has been subtracted from the data set), the principal component w*1* of a data set *X* can be defined as:

$$\mathrm{w}_1 = \underset{\|\mathrm{w}\|=1}{\arg\max}\, \mathrm{Var}\{\mathrm{w}^{\mathrm{T}}\mathrm{X}\} = \underset{\|\mathrm{w}\|=1}{\arg\max}\, E\left\{\left(\mathrm{w}^{\mathrm{T}}\mathrm{X}\right)^2\right\}$$

With the first $k - 1$ components, the kth component can be found by subtracting the first $k-1$ principal components from *X*:

$$\hat{\mathrm{X}}_{k-1} = \mathrm{X} - \sum_{i=1}^{k-1} \mathrm{w}_i \mathrm{w}_i^{\mathrm{T}} \mathrm{X}$$

and by substituting this as the new data set to find a principal component in

$$\hat{\mathrm{X}}_{k-1} = \mathrm{X} - \sum_{i=1}^{k-1} \mathrm{w}_i \mathrm{w}_i^{\mathrm{T}} \mathrm{X}$$

PCA is equivalent to empirical orthogonal functions (EOF), a name which is used in meteorology. An autoencoder neural network with a linear hidden layer is similar to PCA. Upon convergence, the weight vectors of the K neurons in the hidden layer will form a basis for the space spanned by the first K principal components. Unlike PCA, this technique will not necessarily produce orthogonal vectors.

PCA is a popular primary technique in pattern recognition. It is not, however, optimized for class separability. An alternative is the linear discriminant analysis, which does take this into account.

Properties and Limitations of PCA

As noted above, the results of PCA depend on the scaling of the variables. The applicability of PCA is limited by certain assumptions made in its derivation.

Computing PCA Using the Covariance Method

The following is a detailed description of PCA using the covariance method. But note that it is better to use the singular value decomposition (using standard software). The goal is to transform a given data set X of dimension M to an alternative data set Y of smaller dimension L. Equivalently, we are seeking to find the matrix Y, where Y is the Karhunen–Loève transform (KLT) of matrix X:

$$Y = \mathbb{KLT}\{X\}$$

Organize the Data Set

Suppose you have data comprising a set of observations of M variables, and you want to reduce the data so that each observation can be described with only L variables, $L < M$. Suppose further, that the data are arranged as a set of N data vectors $x_1 \ldots x_N$ ith each x_n representing a single grouped observation of the M variables.

- Write as column vectors, each of which has M rows.
- Place the column vectors into a single matrix X of dimensions $M \times N$.

Calculate the Empirical Mean

- Find the empirical mean along each dimension m = 1, ..., M.
- Place the calculated mean values into an empirical mean vector u of dimensions $M \times 1$.

$$u[m] = \frac{1}{N} \sum_{n=1}^{N} X[m,n]$$

Calculate the Deviations From the Mean

Mean subtraction is an integral part of the solution towards finding a principal component basis that minimizes the mean square error of approximating the data. Hence we proceed by centering the data as follows:

- Subtract the empirical mean vector u from each column of the data matrix X.
- Store mean-subtracted data in the $M \times N$ matrix B. $\mathrm{B} = \mathrm{X} - \mathrm{uh}$

where h is a $1 \times N$ row vector of all 1s: $h[n] = 1$ for $n = 1, \ldots, N$

Find the Covariance Matrix

Find the $M \times M$ empirical covariance matrix C from the outer product of matrix B with itself:

$$\mathrm{C} = \mathbb{E}\left[\mathrm{B} \otimes \mathrm{B}\right] = \mathbb{E}\left[\mathrm{B} \cdot \mathrm{B}^{*}\right] = \frac{1}{N-1} \mathrm{B} \cdot \mathrm{B}^{*}$$

where

$\mathbb{E}$ is the expected value operator,

$\otimes$ is the outer product operator, and

* is the conjugate transpose operator. Note that if B consists entirely of real numbers, which is the case in many applications, the "conjugate transpose" is the same as the regular transpose.

Please note that the information in this section is indeed a bit fuzzy. Outer products apply to vectors. For tensor cases we should apply tensor products, but the covariance matrix in PCA is a sum of outer products between its sample vectors; indeed, it could be represented as $B.B^*$.

Find the Eigenvectors and Eigenvalues of the Covariance Matrix

Compute the matrix V of eigenvectors which diagonalizes the covariance matrix C:

$$\mathrm{V}^{-1}\mathrm{C}\mathrm{V} = \mathrm{D}$$

where D is the diagonal matrix of eigenvalues of C. This step will typically involve the use of a computer-based algorithm for computing eigenvectors and eigenvalues. These algorithms are readily available as sub-components of most matrix algebra systems, such as R, MATLAB, Mathematica, SciPy, IDL (Interactive Data Language), or GNU Octave as well as OpenCV.

Matrix D will take the form of an $\mathrm{M} \times \mathrm{M}$ diagonal matrix, where

$$D[p, q] = \lambda_m \qquad \text{for } p = q = m$$

is the mth eigenvalue of the covariance matrix C, and

$$D[p,q]=0 \qquad \text{for } p \neq q.$$

Matrix V, also of dimension M × M, contains M column vectors, each of length M, which represent the M eigenvectors of the covariance matrix C.

The eigenvalues and eigenvectors are ordered and paired. The mth eigenvalue corresponds to the mth eigenvector.

Rearrange the Eigenvectors and Eigenvalues

Sort the columns of the eigenvector matrix V and eigenvalue matrix D in order of decreasing eigenvalue magnitude (i.e. in absolute value).

Make sure to maintain the correct pairings between the columns in each matrix.

Compute the Cumulative Energy Content for Each Eigenvector

The eigenvalues represent the distribution of the source data's energy among each of the eigenvectors, where the eigenvectors form a basis for the data. The cumulative energy content g for the mth eigenvector is the sum of the energy content across all of the eigenvalues from 1 through m:

$$g[m]=\sum_{q=1}^{m}\left|D[q,q]\right| \qquad \text{for} \qquad m=1,\ldots,M$$

Select a Subset of the Eigenvectors as Basis Vectors

Save the first L columns of V as the M × L matrix W:

$$W[p,q]=V[p,q] \qquad \text{for} \qquad p=1,\ldots,M \qquad q=1,\ldots,L$$

where $\quad 1 \leq L \leq M.$

Use the vector g as a guide in choosing an appropriate value for L. The goal is to choose a value of L as small as possible while achieving a reasonably high value of g on a percentage basis. For example, you may want to choose L so that the cumulative energy g is above a certain threshold, like 90 percent. In this case, choose the smallest value of L such that

$$\frac{g[L]}{g[M]} \geq 0.9$$

Convert the Source Data to z-scores (optional)

Create an M × 1 empirical standard deviation vector s from the square root of each element along the main diagonal of the diagonalized covariance matrix C. (Note, that scaling operations do not commute with the KLT thus we must scale by the variances of the already-decorrelated vector, which is the diagonal of C) :

$$s = \{s[m]\} = \{\sqrt{C[m,m]}\} \qquad \text{for } m = 1,\ldots,M$$

Calculate the M × N z-score matrix: $Z = \frac{B}{s \cdot h}$ (divide element-by-element)

Note: While this step is useful for various applications as it normalizes the data set with respect to its variance, it is not integral part of PCA/KLT

Project the z-scores of the Data Onto the New Basis

The projected vectors are the columns of the matrix

$$Y = W^{*} \cdot Z = \mathbb{KLT}\{X\}.$$

W* is the conjugate transpose of the eigenvector basis.

The columns of matrix Y represent the Karhunen–Loeve transforms (KLT) of the data vectors in the columns of matrix X.

Derivation of PCA Using the Covariance Method

Let X be a d-dimensional random vector expressed as column vector. Without loss of generality, assume X has zero mean.

We want to find (*)a$d \times d$ orthonormal transformation matrix P so that PX has a diagonal covariant matrix (i.e. PX is a random vector with all its distinct components pairwise uncorrelated).

A quick computation assuming P were unitary yields:

$$\begin{aligned} t]rcl\,\mathrm{var}(PX) &= \mathbb{E}[PX\;(PX)^{\dagger}] \\ &= \mathbb{E}[PX\,X^{\dagger}P^{\dagger}] \\ &= P\,\mathbb{E}[XX^{\dagger}]P^{\dagger} \\ &= P\,\mathrm{cov}(X)P^{-1} \end{aligned}$$

Hence (*) holds if and only if $\mathrm{cov}(X)$ were diagonalisable by P.

This is very constructive, as var(X) is guaranteed to be a non-negative definite matrix and thus is guaranteed to be diagonalisable by some unitary matrix.

The NIPALS Method

For very high-dimensional datasets, such as those generated in the *omics sciences (e.g., genomics, metabolomics) it is usually only necessary to compute the first few PCs. The non-linear iterative partial least squares (NIPALS) algorithm calculates t*1* and p*1*' from *X*. The outer product, t*1*p*1*' can then be subtracted from X leaving the residual matrix E*1*. This can be then used to calculate subsequent PCs. This results in a dramatic reduction in computational time since calculation of the covariance matrix is avoided.

However, for large data matrices, or matrices that have a high degree of column collinearity, NIPALS suffers from loss of orthogonality due to machine precision limitations accumulated in each iteration step. A Gram-Schmidt (GS) re-orthogonalization algorithm is applied to both the scores and the loadings at each iteration step to eliminate this loss of orthogonality.

Online/sequential Estimation

In an "online" or "streaming" situation with data arriving piece by piece rather than being stored in a single batch, it is useful to make an estimate of the PCA projection that can be updated sequentially. This can be done efficiently, but requires different algorithms.

Relation Between PCA and K-means Clustering

It has been shown recently (2001,2004) that the relaxed solution of K-means clustering, specified by the cluster indicators, is given by the PCA principal components, and the PCA subspace spanned by the principal directions is identical to the cluster centroid subspace specified by the between-class scatter matrix. Thus PCA automatically projects to the subspace where the global solution of K-means clustering lies, and thus facilitates K-means clustering to find near-optimal solutions.

Correspondence Analysis

Correspondence analysis (CA) was developed by Jean-Paul Benzécri and is conceptually similar to PCA, but scales the data (which should be non-negative) so that rows and columns are treated equivalently. It is traditionally applied to contingency tables. CA decomposes the chi-squared statistic associated to this table into orthogonal factors. Because CA is a descriptive technique, it can be applied to tables for which the chi-squared statistic is appropriate or not. Several variants of CA are available including detrended correspondence analysis and canonical correspondence analysis. One special extension is multiple correspondence analysis, which may be seen as the counterpart of principal component analysis for categorical data.

Criteria for Determining the Mumber of Factors

Using one or more of the methods below, the researcher determines an appropriate range of solutions to investigate. Methods may not agree. For instance, the Kaiser criterion may suggest five factors and the scree test may suggest two, so the researcher may request 3-, 4-, and 5-factor solutions discuss each in terms of their relation to external data and theory.

Comprehensibility: A purely subjective criterion would be to retain those factors whose meaning is comprehensible to the researcher. This is not recommended.

Kaiser criterion: The Kaiser rule is to drop all components with eigenvalues under 1.0 – this being the eigenvalue equal to the information accounted for by an average single item. The Kaiser criterion is the default in SPSS and most statistical software but is not recommended when used as the sole cut-off criterion for estimating the number of factors as it tends to overextract factors.

Variance explained criteria: Some researchers simply use the rule of keeping enough factors to account for 90% (sometimes 80%) of the variation. Where the researcher's goal emphasizes parsimony (explaining variance with as few factors as possible), the criterion could be as low as 50%

Scree plot: The Cattell scree test plots the components as the X axis and the corresponding eigenvalues as the Y-axis. As one moves to the right, towards later components, the eigenvalues drop. When the drop ceases and the curve makes an elbow towards less steep decline, Cattell's scree test says to drop all further components after the one starting the elbow. This rule is sometimes criticised for being amenable to researcher-controlled "fudging". That is, as picking the "elbow" can be subjective because the curve has multiple elbows or is a smooth curve, the researcher may be tempted to set the cut-off at the number of factors desired by his or her research agenda.

Horn's Parallel Analysis (PA): A Monte-Carlo based simulation method that compares the observed eigenvalues with those obtained from uncorrelated normal variables. A factor or component is retained if the associated eigenvalue is bigger than the 95th of the distribution of eigenvalues derived from the random data. PA is one of the most recommendable rules for determining the number of components to retain, but only few programmes include this option. Before dropping a factor below one's cut-off, however, the researcher should check its correlation with the dependent variable. A very small factor can have a large correlation with the dependent variable, in which case it should not be dropped.

Rotation Methods

The unrotated output maximises the variance accounted for by the first and subsequent factors, and forcing the factors to be orthogonal. This data-compression comes at the cost of having most items load on the early factors, and usually, of having many items load substantially on more than one factor. Rotation serves to make the output more understandable, by seeking so-called "Simple Structure": A pattern of loadings where items load most strongly on one factor, and much more weakly on the other factors. Rotations can be orthogonal or oblique (allowing the factors to correlate).

Varimax rotation is an orthogonal rotation of the factor axes to maximize the variance of the squared loadings of a factor (column) on all the variables (rows) in a factor matrix, which has the effect of differentiating the original variables by extracted factor. Each factor will tend to have either large or small loadings of any particular variable. A varimax solution yields results which make it as easy as possible to identify each variable with a single factor.

This is the most common rotation option. However, the orthogonality (i.e., independence) of factors is often an unrealistic assumption. Oblique rotations are inclusive of orthogonal rotation, and for that reason, oblique rotations are a preferred method.

Quartimax rotation is an orthogonal alternative which minimizes the number of factors needed to explain each variable. This type of rotation often generates a general factor on which most variables are loaded to a high or medium degree. Such a factor structure is usually not helpful to the research purpose.

Equimax rotation is a compromise between Varimax and Quartimax criteria. Direct oblimin rotation is the standard method when one wishes a non-orthogonal (oblique) solution – that is, one in which the factors are allowed to be correlated. This will result in higher eigenvalues but diminished interpretability of the factors.

Promax rotation is an alternative non-orthogonal (oblique) rotation method which is computationally faster than the direct oblimin method and therefore is sometimes used for very large datasets.

History

Charles Spearman pioneered the use of factor analysis in the field of psychology and is sometimes credited with the invention of factor analysis. He discovered that school children's scores on a wide variety of seemingly unrelated subjects were positively correlated, which led him to postulate that a general mental ability, or g, underlies and shapes human cognitive performance. His postulate now enjoys broad support in the field of intelligence research, where it is known as the g theory.

Raymond Cattell expanded on Spearman's idea of a two-factor theory of intelligence after performing his own tests and factor analysis. He used a multi-factor theory to explain intelligence. Cattell's theory addressed alternate factors in intellectual development, including motivation and psychology. Cattell also developed several mathematical methods for adjusting psychometric graphs, such as his "scree" test and similarity coefficients. His research led to the development of his theory of fluid and crystallized intelligence, as well as his 16 Personality Factors theory of personality. Cattell was a strong advocate of factor analysis and psychometrics. He believed that all theory should be derived from research, which supports the continued use of empirical observation and objective testing to study human intelligence.

Applications in Psychology

Factor analysis is used to identify "factors" that explain a variety of results on different tests. For example, intelligence research found that people who get a high score on a test of verbal ability are also good on other tests that require verbal abilities. Researchers explained this by using factor analysis to isolate one factor, often called crystallized intelligence or verbal intelligence, which represents the degree to which someone is able to solve problems involving verbal skills.

Factor analysis in psychology is most often associated with intelligence research. However, it also has been used to find factors in a broad range of domains such as personality, attitudes, beliefs, etc. It is linked to psychometrics, as it can assess the validity of an instrument by finding if the instrument indeed measures the postulated factors.

Advantages

Reduction of number of variables, by combining two or more variables into a single factor. For example, performance at running, ball throwing, batting, jumping and weight lifting could be combined into a single factor such as general athletic ability. Usually, in an item by people matrix, factors are selected by grouping related items. In the Q factor analysis technique, the matrix is transposed and factors are created by grouping related people: For example, liberals, libertarians, conservatives and socialists, could form separate groups.

Identification of groups of inter-related variables, to see how they are related to each other. For example, Carroll used factor analysis to build his Three Stratum Theory. He found that a factor called "broad visual perception" relates to how good an individual is at visual tasks. He also found a "broad auditory perception" factor, relating to auditory task capability. Furthermore, he found a global factor, called "g" or general intelligence, that relates to both "broad visual perception" and "broad auditory perception".

This means someone with a high "g" is likely to have both a high "visual perception" capability and a high "auditory perception" capability, and that "g" therefore explains a good part of why someone is good or bad in both of those domains.

Disadvantages

"...each orientation is equally acceptable mathematically. But different factorial theories proved to differ as much in terms of the orientations of factorial axes for a given solution as in terms of anything else, so that model fitting did not prove to be useful in distinguishing among theories." (Sternberg, 1977).

This means all rotations represent different underlying processes, but all rotations are equally valid outcomes of standard factor analysis optimization. Therefore, it is impossible to pick the proper rotation using factor analysis alone.

Factor analysis can be only as good as the data allows. In psychology, where researchers often have to rely on less valid and reliable measures such as self-reports, this can be problematic.

Interpreting factor analysis is based on using a "heuristic", which is a solution that is "convenient even if not absolutely true". More than one interpretation can be made of the same data factored the same way, and factor analysis cannot identify causality.

Exploratory Factor Analysis Versus Principal Components Analysis

While exploratory factor analysis and principal component analysis are treated as synonymous techniques in some fields of statistics, this has been criticised (e.g. Fabrigar et al., 1999; Suhr, 2009). In factor analysis, the researcher makes the assumption that an underlying causal model exists, whereas PCA is simply a variable reduction technique. Researchers have argued that the distinctions between the two techniques may mean that there are objective benefits for preferring one over the other based on the analytic goal.

Arguments Contrasting PCA and EFA

Fabrigar et al. (1999) address a number of reasons used to suggest that principal components analysis is equivalent to factor analysis:

1. It is sometimes suggested that principal components analysis is computationally quicker and requires fewer resources than factor analysis. Fabrigar et al. suggest that the ready availability of computer resources have rendered this practical concern irrelevant.
2. PCA and factor analysis can produce similar results. This point is also addressed by Fabrigar et al.; in certain cases, whereby the communalities are low (e.g., .40), the two techniques produce divergent results. In fact, Fabrigar et al. argue that in cases where the data correspond to assumptions of the common factor model, the results of PCA are inaccurate results.
3. There are certain cases where factor analysis leads to 'Heywood cases'. These encompass situations whereby 100% or more of the variance in a measured variable is estimated to be accounted for by the model. Fabrigar et al. suggest that these cases are actually informative to the researcher, indicating a misspecified model or a violation of the common factor model. The lack of Heywood cases in the PCA approach may mean that such issues pass unnoticed.
4. Researchers gain extra information from a PCA approach, such as an individual's score on a certain component – such information is not yielded from factor analysis. However, as Fabrigar et al. contend, the typical aim of factor analysis – i.e. to determine the factors accounting for the structure of the correlations between measured variables – does not require knowledge of factor scores and thus this advantage is negated. It is also possible to compute factor scores from a factor analysis.

Variance Versus Covariance

Factor analysis takes into account the random error that is inherent in measurement, whereas PCA fails to do so. This point is exemplified by Brown (2009), who indicated that, in respect to the correlation matrices involved in the calculations:

> *"In PCA, 1.00s are put in the diagonal meaning that all of the variance in the matrix is to be accounted for (including variance unique to each variable, variance common among variables, and error variance). That would, therefore, by definition, include all of the variance in the variables. In contrast, in EFA, the communalities are put in the diagonal meaning that only the variance shared with other variables is to be accounted for (excluding variance unique to each variable and error variance). That would, therefore, by definition, include only variance that is common among the variables."*
>
> *— Brown (2009), Principal components analysis and exploratory factor analysis – Definitions, differences and choices*

For this reason, Brown (2009) recommends using factor analysis when theoretical ideas about relationships between variables exist, whereas PCA should be used if the goal of the researcher is to explore patterns in their data.

Differences in Procedure and Results

The differences between principal components analysis and factor analysis are further illustrated by Suhr (2009):

- PCA results in principal components that account for a maximal amount of variance for observed variables; FA account for common variance in the data.
- PCA inserts ones on the diagonals of the correlation matrix; FA adjusts the diagonals of the correlation matrix with the unique factors.
- PCA minimizes the sum of squared perpendicular distance to the component axis; FA estimates factors which influence responses on observed variables.
- The component scores in PCA represent a linear combination of the observed variables weighted by eigenvectors; the observed variables in FA are linear combinations of the underlying and unique factors.
- In PCA, the components yielded are uninterpretable, i.e. they do not represent underlying 'constructs'; in FA, the underlying constructs can be labeled and readily interpreted, given an accurate model specification.

Factor Analysis in Marketing

The basic steps are:

- Identify the salient attributes consumers use to evaluate products in this category.
- Use quantitative marketing research techniques (such as surveys) to collect data from a sample of potential customers concerning their ratings of all the product attributes.
- Input the data into a statistical programme and run the factor analysis procedure. The computer will yield a set of underlying attributes (or factors).
- Use these factors to construct perceptual maps and other product positioning devices.

Information Collection

The data collection stage is usually done by marketing research professionals. Survey questions ask the respondent to rate a product sample or descriptions of product concepts on a range of attributes. Anywhere from five to twenty attributes are chosen. They could include things like: ease of use, weight, accuracy, durability, colourfulness, price, or size. The attributes chosen will vary depending on the product being studied. The same question is asked about all the products in the study. The data for multiple products is coded and input into a statistical programme such as R, SPSS, SAS, Stata, STATISTICA, JMP and SYSTAT.

Analysis

The analysis will isolate the underlying factors that explain the data using a matrix of associations. Factor analysis is an interdependence technique. The complete set of interdependent relationships is examined. There is no specification of dependent variables, independent variables, or causality. Factor analysis assumes that all the rating data on different attributes can be reduced down to a few important dimensions. This reduction is possible because the attributes relate. The rating given to any one attribute is partially the result of the influence of other attributes. The statistical algorithm deconstructs the rating (called a raw score) into its various components, and reconstructs the partial scores into underlying factor scores. The degree of correlation between the initial raw score and the final factor score is called a factor loading.

Advantages

- Both objective and subjective attributes can be used provided the subjective attributes can be converted into scores.
- Factor analysis can identify latent dimensions or constructs that direct analysis may not.
- It is easy and inexpensive.

Disadvantages

- Usefulness depends on the researchers' ability to collect a sufficient set of product attributes. If important attributes are excluded or neglected, the value of the procedure is reduced.
- If sets of observed variables are highly similar to each other and distinct from other items, factor analysis will assign a single factor to them. This may obscure factors that represent more interesting relationships.
- Naming factors may require knowledge of theory because seemingly dissimilar attributes can correlate strongly for unknown reasons.

Factor Analysis in Physical Sciences

Factor analysis has also been widely used in physical sciences such as geochemistry, ecology, and hydrochemistry. In groundwater quality management, it is important to relate the spatial distribution of different chemical parameters to different possible sources, which have different chemical signatures. For example, a sulfide mine is likely to be associated with high levels of acidity, dissolved sulphates and transition metals. These signatures can be identified as factors through R-mode factor analysis, and the location of possible sources can be suggested by contouring the factor scores.

In geochemistry, different factors can correspond to different mineral associations, and thus to mineralisation.

Factor Analysis in Microarray Analysis

Factor analysis can be used for summarizing high-density oligonucleotide DNA microarrays data at probe level for Affymetrix GeneChips. In this case, the latent variable corresponds to the RNA concentration in a sample.

Implementation

Factor analysis has been implemented in several statistical analysis programmes since the 1980s: SAS, BMDP and SPSS. It is also implemented in the R programming language (with the factanal function) and in OpenOpt. Rotations are implemented in the GPArotation R package.

Mann–Whitney U

In statistics, the Mann–Whitney U test (also called the Mann–Whitney–Wilcoxon (MWW) , Wilcoxon rank-sum test or Wilcoxon-Mann-Whitney test) is a non-parametric statistical hypothesis test for assessing whether one of two samples of independent observations tends to have larger values than the other. It is one of the most well-known non-parametric significance tests.

It was proposed initially by the German Gustav Deuchler in 1914 (with a missing term in the variance) and later independently by Frank Wilcoxon in 1945, for equal sample sizes, and extended to arbitrary sample sizes and in other ways by Henry Mann and his student Donald Ransom Whitney in 1947.

Assumptions and Formal Statement of Hypotheses

Although Mann and Whitney developed the MWW test under the assumption of continuous responses with the alternative hypothesis being that one distribution is stochastically greater than the other, there are many other ways to formulate the null and alternative hypotheses such that the MWW test will give a valid test.

A very general formulation is to assume that:

1. All the observations from both groups are independent of each other,
2. The responses are ordinal (i.e. one can at least say, of any two observations, which is the greater),
3. Under the null hypothesis the distributions of both groups are equal, so that the probability of an observation from one population (X) exceeding an observation from the second population (Y) equals the probability of an observation from Y exceeding an observation from X, that is, there is a symmetry between populations with respect to probability of random drawing of a larger observation.
4. Under the alternative hypothesis the probability of an observation from one population (X) exceeding an observation from the second population (Y) (after exclusion of ties) is not equal to 0.5. The alternative may also be stated in terms of a one-sided test, for example: $P(X > Y) + 0.5\ P(X = Y) > 0.5$.

Under more strict assumptions than those above, e.g., if the responses are assumed to be continuous and the alternative is restricted to a shift in location (i.e. $F1(x) = F2(x + \delta)$), we can interpret a significant MWW test as showing a difference in medians. Under this location shift assumption, we can also interpret the MWW as assessing whether the Hodges–Lehmann estimate of the difference in central tendency between the two populations differs from zero. The Hodges–Lehmann estimate for this two-sample problem is the median of all possible differences between an observation in the first sample and an observation in the second sample.

Calculations

The test involves the calculation of a statistic, usually called U, whose distribution under the null hypothesis is known. In the case of small samples, the distribution is tabulated, but for sample sizes above ~20 approximation using the normal distribution is fairly good. Some books tabulate statistics equivalent to U, such as the sum of ranks in one of the samples, rather than U itself.

The U test is included in most modern statistical packages. It is also easily calculated by hand, especially for small samples. There are two ways of doing this.

First, arrange all the observations into a single ranked series. That is, rank all the observations without regard to which sample they are in.

Method one: For small samples a direct method is recommended. It is very quick, and gives an insight into the meaning of the U statistic.

1. Choose the sample for which the ranks seem to be smaller (The only reason to do this is to make computation easier). Call this “sample 1,– and call the other sample “sample 2.–
2. For each observation in sample 1, count the number of observations in sample 2 that have a smaller rank (count a half for any that are equal to it). The sum of these counts is *U*.

Method two: For larger samples, a formula can be used:

Add up the ranks for the observations which came from sample 1. The sum of ranks in sample 2 is now determinate, since the sum of all the ranks equals $N(N + 1)/2$ where N is the total number of observations.

U is then given by:

$$U_1 = R_1 - \frac{n_1(n_1+1)}{2}$$

where n*1* is the sample size for sample 1, and R*1* is the sum of the ranks in sample 1.

Note that it doesn't matter which of the two samples is considered sample 1. An equally valid formula for *U* is

$$U_2 = R_2 - \frac{n_2(n_2+1)}{2}.$$

The smaller value of U*1* and U*2* is the one used when consulting significance tables. The sum of the two values is given by

$$U_1 + U_2 = R_1 - \frac{n_1(n_1+1)}{2} + R_2 - \frac{n_2(n_2+1)}{2}.$$

Knowing that R*1* + R*2* = *N*(*N* + 1)/2 and *N* = n*1* + n*2* , and doing some algebra, we find that the sum is

$$U_1 + U_2 = n_1 n_2.$$

Properties

The maximum value of *U* is the product of the sample sizes for the two samples. In such a case, the "other" *U* would be 0.

Examples

Illustration of Calculation Methods: Suppose that Aesop is dissatisfied with his classic experiment in which one tortoise was found to beat one hare in a race, and decides to carry out a significance test to discover whether the results could be extended to tortoises and hares in general. He collects a sample of 6 tortoises and 6 hares, and makes them all run his race at once. The order in which they reach the finishing post (their rank order, from first to last crossing the finish line) is as follows, writing T for a tortoise and H for a hare:

T H H H H H T T T T T H

What is the value of *U*?

Using the direct method, we take each tortoise in turn, and count the number of hares it is beaten by, getting 0, 5, 5, 5, 5, 5, which means *U* = 25. Alternatively, we could take each hare in turn, and count the number of tortoises it is beaten by. In this case, we get 1, 1, 1, 1, 1, 6. So *U* = 6 + 1 + 1 + 1 + 1 + 1 = 11. Note that the sum of these two values for *U* is 36, which is 6 × 6.

Using the indirect method: the sum of the ranks achieved by the tortoises is 1 + 7 + 8 + 9 + 10 + 11 = 46.

Therefore $U = 46 - (6\times7)/2 = 46 - 21 = 25$. the sum of the ranks achieved by the hares is 2 + 3 + 4 + 5 + 6 + 12 = 32, leading to $U = 32 - 21 = 11$.

Illustration of Object of Test: A second example race, with 19 participants of each species, in which the outcomes are as follows:

H H H H H H H H H T T T T T T T T T T H H H H H H H H H H T T T T T T T T T

The median tortoise here comes in at position 19, and thus actually beats the median hare, which comes in at position 20.

However, the value of *U* (for hares) is 100

(9 Hares beaten by (x) 0 tortoises) + (10 hares beaten by (x) 10 tortoises) = 0 + 100 = 100

Value of U(for tortoises) is 261

(10 tortoises beaten by 9 hares) + (9 tortoises beaten by 19 hares) = 90 + 171 = 261

Consulting tables, or using the approximation below, shows that this *U* value gives significant evidence that hares tend to do better than tortoises ($p < 0.05$, two-tailed). Obviously this is an extreme distribution that would be spotted easily, but in a larger sample something similar could happen without it being so apparent. Notice that the problem here is not that the two distributions of ranks have different variances; they are mirror images of each other, so their variances are the same, but they have very different mean.

Normal Approximation

For large samples, *U* is approximately normally distributed. In that case, the standardized value

$$z = \frac{U - m_U}{\sigma_U},$$

where m*U* and σ*U* are the mean and standard deviation of *U*, is approximately a standard normal deviate whose significance can be checked in tables of the normal distribution. m*U* and σ*U* are given by

$$m_U = \frac{n_1 n_2}{2}.$$

$$\sigma_U = \sqrt{\frac{n_1 n_2 (n_1 + n_2 + 1)}{12}}.$$

The formula for the standard deviation is more complicated in the presence of tied ranks; the full formula is given in the text books referenced below.

However, if the number of ties is small (and especially if there are no large tie bands) ties can be ignored when doing calculations by hand. The computer statistical packages will use the correctly adjusted formula as a matter of routine.

Note that since $U1 + U2 = n1\ n2$, the mean $n1\ n2/2$ used in the normal approximation is the mean of the two values of U. Therefore, the absolute value of the z statistic calculated will be same whichever value of U is used.

Relation to Other Tests

Comparison to Student's t-test

The U test is useful in the same situations as the independent samples Student's t-test, and the question arises of which should be preferred.

Ordinal data: U remains the logical choice when the data are ordinal but not interval scaled, so that the spacing between adjacent values cannot be assumed to be constant.

Robustness: As it compares the sums of ranks, the Mann–Whitney test is less likely than the t-test to spuriously indicate significance because of the presence of outliers – i.e. Mann–Whitney is more robust.

Efficiency: When normality holds, MWW has an (asymptotic) efficiency of $3/\pi$ or about 0.95 when compared to the t test. For distributions sufficiently far from normal and for sufficiently large sample sizes, the MWW can be considerably more efficient than the t.

Overall, the robustness makes the MWW more widely applicable than the t test, and for large samples from the normal distribution, the efficiency loss compared to the t test is only 5%, so one can recommend MWW as the default test for comparing interval or ordinal measurements with similar distributions.

The relation between efficiency and power in concrete situations isn't trivial though. For small sample sizes one should investigate the power of the MWW vs t.

MWW will give very similar results to performing an ordinary parametric two-sample *t* test on the rankings of the data.

Different Distributions

If one is only interested in stochastic ordering of the two populations (i.e., the concordance probability $P(Y > X)$), the *U* test can be used even if the shapes of the distributions are different. The concordance probability is exactly equal to the area under the receiver operating characteristic curve (ROC) that is often used in the context.

Alternatives

If one desires a simple shift interpretation, the U test should not be used when the distributions of the two samples are very different, as it can give erroneously significant results. In that situation, the unequal variances version of the t test is likely to give more reliable results, but only if normality holds.

Alternatively, some authors (e.g. Conover) suggest transforming the data to ranks (if they are not already ranks) and then performing the *t* test on the transformed data, the version of the *t* test used depending on whether or not the population variances are suspected to be different. Rank transformations do not preserve variances, but variances are recomputed from samples after rank transformations.

The Brown–Forsythe test has been suggested as an appropriate non-parametric equivalent to the *F* test for equal variances.

Related Test Statistics

Kendall's τ: The *U* test is related to a number of other non-parametric statistical procedures. For example, it is equivalent to Kendall's τ correlation coefficient if one of the variables is binary (that is, it can only take two values).

ρ *statistic:* A statistic called ρ that is linearly related to *U* and widely used in studies of categorization (discrimination learning involving concepts), and elsewhere, is calculated by dividing *U* by its maximum value for the given sample sizes, which is simply $n_1 \times n_2$. ρ is thus a non-parametric measure of the overlap between two distributions; it can take values between 0 and 1, and it is an estimate of $P(Y > X) + 0.5\ P(Y = X)$, where *X* and *Y* are randomly chosen observations from the two distributions. Both extreme values represent complete separation of the distributions, while a ρ of 0.5 represents complete overlap. The usefulness of the ρ statistic can be seen in the case of the odd example used above, where two distributions that were significantly different on a U-test nonetheless had nearly identical medians: the ρ value in this case is approximately 0.723 in favour of the hares, correctly reflecting the fact that even though the median tortoise beat the median hare, the hares collectively did better than the tortoises collectively.

Example Statement of Results

In reporting the results of a Mann–Whitney test, it is important to state:

- A measure of the central tendencies of the two groups (means or medians; since the Mann–Whitney is an ordinal test, medians are usually recommended)
- The value of U
- The sample sizes
- The significance level.

In practice some of this information may already have been supplied and common sense should be used in deciding whether to repeat it. A typical report might run,

"Median latencies in groups E and C were 153 and 247 ms; the distributions in the two groups differed significantly (Mann–Whitney $U = 10.5$, $n1 = n2 = 8$, $P < 0.05$ two-tailed)."

A statement that does full justice to the statistical status of the test might run,

"Outcomes of the two treatments were compared using the Wilcoxon–Mann–Whitney two-sample rank-sum test. The treatment effect (difference between treatments) was quantified using the Hodges–Lehmann (HL) estimator, which is consistent with the Wilcoxon test. This estimator (HLΔ) is the median of all possible differences in outcomes between a subject in group B and a subject in group A. A non-parametric 0.95 confidence interval for HLΔ accompanies these estimates as does ρ, an estimate of the probability that a randomly chosen subject from population B has a higher weight than a randomly chosen subject from population A.

The median [quartiles] weight for subjects on treatment A and B respectively are 147 [121, 177] and 151 [130, 180] kg. Treatment A decreased weight by HLΔ = 5 kg (0.95 CL [2, 9] kg, 2P = 0.02, ρ = 0.58)."

However it would be rare to find so extended a report in a document whose major topic was not statistical inference.

Implementations

- Online implementation using javascript
- ALGLIB includes implementation of the Mann–Whitney U test in C++, C#, Delphi, Visual Basic, etc.
- R includes an implementation of the test (there referred to as the Wilcoxon two-sample test) as wilcox.test.
- SAS implements the test in the PROC NPAR1WAY procedure
- Stata includes implementation of Wilcoxon-Mann-Whitney rank-sum test with ranksum command.
- SciPy has the mannwhitneyu function in the stats module.
- MATLAB implements the test with function ranksum in the statistics toolbox.
- Mathematica implements the function as MannWhitneyTest.

Mean Square Weighted Deviation

Mean square weighted deviation is used extensively in geochronology, the science of obtaining information about the time of formation of, for example, rocks, minerals, bones, corals, or charcoal, or the time at which particular processes took place in a rock mass, for example recrystallization and grain growth, or alteration associated with the emplacement of metalliferous ore deposits..

Often the geochronologist will determine a series of age measurements on a single sample, with the measured value x_i having a weighting w_i and an associated error σ_{x_i} for each age determination. As regards weighting, one can either weight all of the measured ages equally, or weight them by the proportion of the sample that they represent.

For example, if two thirds of the sample was used for the first measurement and one third for the second and final measurement then one might weight the first measurement twice that of the second.

The arithmetic mean of the age determinations is:

$$\overline{x} = \frac{\sum_{i=1}^{N} x_i}{N}$$

but this value can be misleading unless each determination of the age is of equal significance.

When each measured value can be assumed to have the same weighting, or significance, the biased and unbiased (or “population” and "sample", respectively) estimators of the variance are computed as follows:

$$\sigma^2 = \frac{\sum_{i=1}^{N}(x_i - \bar{x})^2}{N} \quad \text{and} \quad s^2 = \frac{N}{N-1}\cdot\sigma^2 = \frac{N}{N^2 - N}\cdot\sum_{i=1}^{N}(x_i - \bar{x})^2.$$

The standard deviation is the square root of the variance.

When individual determinations of an age are not of equal significance it is better to use a weighted mean to obtain an 'average' age, as follows:

$$\bar{x}^* = \frac{\sum_{i=1}^{N} w_i x_i}{\sum_{i=1}^{N} w_i}$$

The biased weighted estimator of variance can be shown to be:

$$\sigma^2 = \frac{\sum_{i=1}^{N} w_i (x_i - \bar{x}^*)^2}{\sum_{i=1}^{N} w_i}$$

which can be computed on the fly as

$$\sigma^2 = \frac{\sum_{i=1}^{N} w_i x_i^2 \cdot \sum_{i=1}^{N} w_i - (\sum_{i=1}^{N} w_i x_i)^2}{(\sum_{i=1}^{N} w_i)^2}$$

The unbiased weighted estimator of the sample variance can be computed as follows:

$$s^2 = \frac{\sum_{i=1}^{N} w_i}{(\sum_{i=1}^{N} w_i)^2 - \sum_{i=1}^{N} w_i^2} \cdot \sum_{i=1}^{N} w_i (x_i - \bar{x}^*)^2$$

Again the corresponding standard deviation is the square root of the variance. The unbiased weighted estimator of the sample variance can also be computed on the fly as follows:

$$s^2 = \frac{\sum_{i=1}^{N} w_i x_i^2 \cdot \sum_{i=1}^{N} w_i - (\sum_{i=1}^{N} w_i x_i)^2}{(\sum_{i=1}^{N} w_i)^2 - \sum_{i=1}^{N} w_i^2}$$

The unweighted mean square of the weighted deviations (unweighted MSWD) can then be computed, as follows:

$$\text{MSWD}_u = \frac{1}{N-1} \cdot \sum_{i=1}^{N} \frac{(x_i - \overline{x})^2}{\sigma_{x_i}^2}$$

By analogy the weighted mean square of the weighted deviations (weighted MSWD) can be computed, as follows:

$$\text{MSWD}_w = \frac{\sum_{i=1}^{N} w_i}{(\sum_{i=1}^{N} w_i)^2 - \sum_{i=1}^{N} w_i^2} \cdot \sum_{i=1}^{N} \frac{w_i.(x_i - \overline{x}^*)^2}{(\sigma_{x_i})^2}$$

Regression Analysis

In statistics, regression analysis is a statistical technique for estimating the relationships among variables. It includes many techniques for modelling and analysing several variables, when the focus is on the relationship between a dependent variable and one or more independent variables. More specifically, regression analysis helps one understand how the typical value of the dependent variable changes when any one of the independent variables is varied, while the other independent variables are held fixed.

Most commonly, regression analysis estimates the conditional expectation of the dependent variable given the independent variables — that is, the average value of the dependent variable when the independent variables are fixed. Less commonly, the focus is on a quantile, or other location parameter of the conditional distribution of the dependent variable given the independent variables. In all cases, the estimation target is a function of the independent variables called the regression function. In regression analysis, it is also of interest to characterize the variation of the dependent variable around the regression function, which can be described by a probability distribution.

Regression analysis is widely used for prediction and forecasting, where its use has substantial overlap with the field of machine learning. Regression analysis is also used to understand which among the independent variables are related to the dependent variable, and to explore the forms of these relationships.

In restricted circumstances, regression analysis can be used to infer causal relationships between the independent and dependent variables. However this can lead to illusions or false relationships, so caution is advisable. A large body of techniques for carrying out regression analysis has been developed. Familiar methods such as linear regression and ordinary least squares regression are parametric, in that the regression function is defined in terms of a finite number of unknown parameters that are estimated from the data. Nonparametric regression refers to techniques that allow the regression function to lie in a specified set of functions, which may be infinite-dimensional.

The performance of regression analysis methods in practice depends on the form of the data generating process, and how it relates to the regression approach being used. Since the true form of the data-generating process is generally not known, regression analysis often depends to some extent on making assumptions about this process. These assumptions are sometimes testable if a large amount of data is available. Regression models for prediction are often useful even when the assumptions are moderately violated, although they may not perform optimally. However, in many applications, especially with small effects or questions of causality based on observational data, regression methods give misleading results.

History

The earliest form of regression was the method of least squares, which was published by Legendre in 1805, and by Gauss in 1809. Legendre and Gauss both applied the method to the problem of determining, from astronomical observations, the orbits of bodies about the Sun (mostly comets, but also later the then newly discovered minor planets). Gauss published a further development of the theory of least squares in 1821, including a version of the Gauss–Markov theorem.

The term "regression" was coined by Francis Galton in the nineteenth century to describe a biological phenomenon. The phenomenon was that the heights of descendants of tall ancestors tend to regress down towards a normal average (a phenomenon also known as regression towards the mean). For Galton, regression had only this biological meaning, but his work was later extended by Udny Yule and Karl Pearson to a more general statistical context. In the work of Yule and Pearson, the joint distribution of the response and explanatory variables is assumed to be Gaussian. This assumption was weakened by R.A. Fisher in his works of 1922 and 1925. Fisher assumed that the conditional distribution of the response variable is Gaussian, but the joint distribution need not be. In this respect, Fisher's assumption is closer to Gauss's formulation of 1821.

In the 1950s and 1960s, economists used electromechanical desk calculators to calculate regressions. Before 1970, it sometimes took up to 24 hours to receive the result from one regression.

Regression methods continue to be an area of active research. In recent decades, new methods have been developed for robust regression, regression involving correlated responses such as time series and growth curves, regression in which the predictor or response variables are curves, images, graphs, or other complex data objects, regression methods accommodating various types of missing data, nonparametric regression, Bayesian methods for regression, regression in which the predictor variables are measured with error, regression with more predictor variables than observations, and causal inference with regression.

Regression Models

Regression models involve the following variables:

- The unknown parameters, denoted as β, which may represent a scalar or a vector.
- The independent variables, X.
- The dependent variable, Y.

In various fields of application, different terminologies are used in place of dependent and independent variables.

A regression model relates Y to a function of X and β.

$$Y \approx f(X, \beta)$$

The approximation is usually formalized as $E(Y \mid X) = f(X, \beta)$. To carry out regression analysis, the form of the function f must be specified. Sometimes the form of this function is based on knowledge about the relationship between Y and X that does not rely on the data. If no such knowledge is available, a flexible or convenient form for f is chosen.

Assume now that the vector of unknown parameters β is of length k. In order to perform a regression analysis the user must provide information about the dependent variable Y:

- If N data points of the form (Y,X) are observed, where $N < k$, most classical approaches to regression analysis cannot be performed: since the system of equations defining the regression model is underdetermined, there is not enough data to recover β.
- If exactly $N = k$ data points are observed, and the function f is linear, the equations $Y = f(X, \beta)$ can be solved exactly rather

than approximately. This reduces to solving a set of N equations with N unknowns (the elements of β), which has a unique solution as long as the X are linearly independent. If f is nonlinear, a solution may not exist, or many solutions may exist.

- The most common situation is where $N > k$ data points are observed. In this case, there is enough information in the data to estimate a unique value for β that best fits the data in some sense, and the regression model when applied to the data can be viewed as an overdetermined system in β.

In the last case, the regression analysis provides the tools for:

1. Finding a solution for unknown parameters β that will, for example, minimize the distance between the measured and predicted values of the dependent variable Y (also known as method of least squares).
2. Under certain statistical assumptions, the regression analysis uses the surplus of information to provide statistical information about the unknown parameters β and predicted values of the dependent variable Y.

Necessary Number of Independent Measurements

Consider a regression model which has three unknown parameters, β0, β1, and β2. Suppose an experimenter performs 10 measurements all at exactly the same value of independent variable vector X (which contains the independent variables $X1$, X2, and $X3$). In this case, regression analysis fails to give a unique set of estimated values for the three unknown parameters; the experimenter did not provide enough information. The best one can do is to estimate the average value and the standard deviation of the dependent variable Y. Similarly, measuring at two different values of X would give enough data for a regression with two unknowns, but not for three or more unknowns.

If the experimenter had performed measurements at three different values of the independent variable vector X, then regression analysis would provide a unique set of estimates for the three unknown parameters in β.

In the case of general linear regression, the above statement is equivalent to the requirement that matrix X^TX is invertible.

Statistical Assumptions

When the number of measurements, N, is larger than the number of unknown parameters, k, and the measurement errors εi are normally distributed then the excess of information contained in $(N - k)$ measurements is used to make statistical predictions about the unknown parameters. This excess of information is referred to as the degrees of freedom of the regression.

Underlying Assumptions

Classical assumptions for regression analysis include:

- The sample is representative of the population for the inference prediction.
- The error is a random variable with a mean of zero conditional on the explanatory variables.
- The independent variables are measured with no error. (Note: If this is not so, modelling may be done instead using errors-in-variables model techniques).
- The predictors are linearly independent, i.e. it is not possible to express any predictor as a linear combination of the others.
- The errors are uncorrelated, that is, the variance–covariance matrix of the errors is diagonal and each non-zero element is the variance of the error.
- The variance of the error is constant across observations (homoscedasticity). (Note: If not, weighted least squares or other methods might instead be used).

These are sufficient conditions for the least-squares estimator to possess desirable properties; in particular, these assumptions imply that the parameter estimates will be unbiased, consistent, and efficient in the class of linear unbiased estimators. It is important to note that actual data rarely satisfies the assumptions. That is, the method is used even though the assumptions are not true. Variation from the assumptions can sometimes be used as a measure of how far the model is from being useful. Many of these assumptions may be relaxed in more advanced treatments. Reports of statistical analyses usually include analyses of tests on the sample data and methodology for the fit and usefulness of the model.

Assumptions include the geometrical support of the variables (Cressie, 1996). Independent and dependent variables often refer to values measured at point locations. There may be spatial trends and spatial autocorrelation in the variables that violates statistical assumptions of regression. Geographic weighted regression is one technique to deal with such data (Fotheringham et al., 2002). Also, variables may include values aggregated by areas. With aggregated data the Modifiable Areal Unit Problem can cause extreme variation in regression parameters (Fotheringham and Wong, 1991). When analysing data aggregated by political boundaries, postal codes or census areas results may be very different with a different choice of units.

Linear Regression

In statistics, linear regression is an approach to modelling the relationship between a scalar dependent variable *y* and one or more explanatory variables denoted *X*. The case of one explanatory variable is called simple regression. More than one explanatory variable is multiple regression. (This in turn should be distinguished from multivariate linear regression, where multiple correlated dependent variables are predicted, rather than a single scalar variable.)

In linear regression, data is modelled using linear predictor functions, and unknown model parameters are estimated from the data. Such models are called linear models. Most commonly, linear regression refers to a model in which the conditional mean of y given the value of *X* is an affine function of *X*. Less commonly, linear regression could refer to a model in which the median, or some other quantile of the conditional distribution of *y given X* is expressed as a linear function of *X*. Like all forms of regression analysis, linear regression focuses on the conditional probability distribution of *y* given *X, r*ather than on the joint probability distribution of *y and X,* which is the domain of multivariate analysis.

Linear regression was the first type of regression analysis to be studied rigorously, and to be used extensively in practical applications. This is because models which depend linearly on their unknown parameters are easier to fit than models which are non-linearly related to their parameters and because the statistical properties of the resulting estimators are easier to determine.

Linear regression has many practical uses. Most applications of linear regression fall into one of the following two broad categories:

- If the goal is prediction, or forecasting, linear regression can be used to fit a predictive model to an observed data set of *y* and *X* values. After developing such a model, if an additional value of *X* is then given without its accompanying value of *y*, the fitted model can be used to make a prediction of the value of *y*.
- Given a variable *y* and a number of variables X1, ..., Xp that may be related to *y, l*inear regression analysis can be applied

to quantify the strength of the relationship between y and the *Xj*, to assess which *Xj* may have no relationship with y at all, and to identify which subsets of the *Xj* contain redundant information about *y*.

Linear regression models are often fitted using the least squares approach, but they may also be fitted in other ways, such as by minimizing the "lack of fit" in some other norm (as with least absolute deviations regression), or by minimizing a penalized version of the least squares loss function as in ridge regression. Conversely, the least squares approach can be used to fit models that are not linear models. Thus, while the terms "least squares" and "linear model" are closely linked, they are not synonymous.

Interpretation

A fitted linear regression model can be used to identify the relationship between a single predictor variable *xj* and the response variable *y* when all the other predictor variables in the model are "held fixed". Specifically, the interpretation of b*j* is the expected change in y for a one-unit change in *xj* when the other covariates are held fixed—that is, the expected value of the partial derivative of y with respect to *xj*.

This is sometimes called the unique effect of x*j* on y. In contrast, the marginal effect of *xj* on y can be assessed using a correlation coefficient or simple linear regression model relating x*j* to y; this effect is the total derivative of y with respect to *xj*.

Care must be taken when interpreting regression results, as some of the regressors may not allow for marginal changes (such as dummy variables, or the intercept term), while others cannot be held fixed (recall the example from the introduction: it would be impossible to "hold *ti* fixed" and at the same time change the value of ti^2).

It is possible that the unique effect can be nearly zero even when the marginal effect is large. This may imply that some other covariate captures all the information in *xj*, so that once that variable is in the model, there is no contribution of *xj* to the variation in *y*. Conversely, the unique effect of *xj* can be large while its marginal effect is nearly zero. This would happen if the other covariates explained a great deal of the variation of *y*, but they mainly explain variation in a way that is complementary to what is captured by *xj*. In this case, including the other variables in the model reduces the part of the variability of y that is unrelated to xj, thereby strengthening the apparent relationship with xj.

The meaning of the expression "held fixed" may depend on how the values of the predictor variables arise. If the experimenter directly sets the values of the predictor variables according to a study design, the comparisons of interest may literally correspond to comparisons among units whose predictor variables have been "held fixed" by the experimenter. Alternatively, the expression "held fixed" can refer to a selection that takes place in the context of data analysis. In this case, we "hold a variable fixed" by restricting our attention to the subsets of the data that happen to have a common value for the given predictor variable. This is the only interpretation of "held fixed" that can be used in an observational study.

The notion of a "unique effect" is appealing when studying a complex system where multiple interrelated components influence the response variable. In some cases, it can literally be interpreted as the causal effect of an intervention that is linked to the value of a predictor variable.

However, it has been argued that in many cases multiple regression analysis fails to clarify the relationships between the predictor variables and the response variable when the predictors are correlated with each other and are not assigned following a study design.

Extensions

Numerous extensions of linear regression have been developed, which allow some or all of the assumptions underlying the basic model to be relaxed.

Simple and Multiple Regression

The very simplest case of a single scalar predictor variable x and a single scalar response variable y is known as simple linear regression. The extension to multiple and/or vector-valued predictor variables (denoted with a capital X) is known as multiple linear regression. Nearly all real-world regression models involve multiple predictors, and basic descriptions of linear regression are often phrased in terms of the multiple regression model. Note, however, that in these cases the response variable y is still a scalar.

General Linear Models

The general linear model considers the situation when the response variable Y is not a scalar but a vector. Conditional linearity of $E(y \mid x) = Bx$ is still assumed, with a matrix B replacing the vector β

of the classical linear regression model. Multivariate analogues of OLS and GLS have been developed.

Heteroskedastic Models

Various models have been created that allow for heteroskedasticity, i.e. the errors for different response variables may have different variances. For example, weighted least squares is a method for estimating linear regression models when the response variables may have different error variances, possibly with correlated errors. Weighted linear least squares, and generalized least squares.) Heteroscedasticity-consistent standard errors is an improved method for use with uncorrelated but potentially heteroskedastic errors.

Generalized Linear Models

Generalized linear models (GLM's) are a framework for modelling a response variable y that is bounded or discrete. This is used, for example:

- when modelling positive quantities (e.g. prices or populations) that vary over a large scale — which are better described using a skewed distribution such as the log-normal distribution or Poisson distribution (although GLM's are not used for log-normal data, instead the response variable is simply transformed using the logarithm function);
- when modelling categorical data, such as the choice of a given candidate in an election (which is better described using a Bernoulli distribution/binomial distribution for binary choices, or a categorical distribution/multinomial distribution for multi-way choices), where there are a fixed number of choices that cannot be meaningfully ordered;
- when modelling ordinal data, e.g. ratings on a scale from 0 to 5, where the different outcomes can be ordered but where the quantity itself may not have any absolute meaning (e.g. a rating of 4 may not be "twice as good" in any objective sense as a rating of 2, but simply indicates that it is better than 2 or 3 but not as good as 5).

Generalized linear models allow for an arbitrary link function g that relates the mean of the response variable to the predictors, i.e. $E(y) = g(\beta 2\ x)$. The link function is often related to the distribution of the response, and in particular it typically has the effect of transforming between the $(-\infty, \infty)$ range of the linear predictor and the range of the response variable.

Some common examples of GLM's are:

- Poisson regression for count data.
- Logistic regression and probit regression for binary data.
- Multinomial logistic regression and multinomial probit regression for categorical data.
- Ordered probit regression for ordinal data.

Single index models allow some degree of nonlinearity in the relationship between x and y, *w*hile preserving the central role of the linear predictor β2 x as in the classical linear regression model. Under certain conditions, simply applying OLS to data from a single-index model will consistently estimate β up to a proportionality constant.

Hierarchical Linear Models

Hierarchical linear models (or multilevel regression) organizes the data into a hierarchy of regressions, for example where A is regressed on *B*, and *B is* regressed on *C*. It is often used where the data have a natural hierarchical structure such as in educational statistics, where students are nested in classrooms, classrooms are nested in schools, and schools are nested in some administrative grouping such as a school district. The response variable might be a measure of student achievement such as a test score, and different covariates would be collected at the classroom, school, and school district levels.

Errors-in-variables

Errors-in-variables models (or "measurement error models") extend the traditional linear regression model to allow the predictor variables *X* to be observed with error. This error causes standard estimators of β to become biased. Generally, the form of bias is an attenuation, meaning that the effects are biased towards zero.

Others

In Dempster–Shafer theory, or a linear belief function in particular, a linear regression model may be represented as a partially swept matrix, which can be combined with similar matrices representing observations and other assumed normal distributions and state equations. The combination of swept or unswept matrices provides an alternative method for estimating linear regression models.

Estimation Methods

A large number of procedures have been developed for parameter estimation and inference in linear regression. These methods differ in computational simplicity of algorithms, presence of a closed-form solution, robustness with respect to heavy-tailed distributions, and theoretical assumptions needed to validate desirable statistical properties such as consistency and asymptotic efficiency. Some of the more common estimation techniques for linear regression are summarized below.

Least-squares Estimation and Related Techniques

Ordinary least squares (OLS) is the simplest and thus most common estimator. It is conceptually simple and computationally straightforward. OLS estimates are commonly used to analyse both experimental and observational data.

The OLS method minimizes the sum of squared residuals, and leads to a closed-form expression for the estimated value of the unknown parameter β:

$$\hat{\beta} = (X^T X)^{-1} X^T y = \left(\tfrac{1}{n}\sum x_i x_i^T\right)^{-1}\left(\tfrac{1}{n}\sum x_i y_i\right).$$

The estimator is unbiased and consistent if the errors have finite variance and are uncorrelated with the regressors

$$E[x_i \varepsilon_i] = 0.$$

It is also efficient under the assumption that the errors have finite variance and are homoscedastic, meaning that $E[\varepsilon i^2 \mid xi]$ does not depend on i. The condition that the errors are uncorrelated with the regressors will generally be satisfied in an experiment, but in the case of observational data, it is difficult to exclude the possibility of an omitted covariate z that is related to both the observed covariates and the response variable.

The existence of such a covariate will generally lead to a correlation between the regressors and the response variable, and hence to an inconsistent estimator of β. The condition of homoscedasticity can fail with either experimental or observational data. If the goal is either inference or predictive modelling, the performance of OLS estimates can be poor if multicollinearity is present, unless the sample size is large.

In simple linear regression, where there is only one regressor (with a constant), the OLS coefficient estimates have a simple form that is closely related to the correlation coefficient between the covariate and the response.

Generalized least squares (GLS) is an extension of the OLS method, that allows efficient estimation of β when either heteroscedasticity, or correlations, or both are present among the error terms of the model, as long as the form of heteroscedasticity and correlation is known independently of the data. To handle heteroscedasticity when the error terms are uncorrelated with each other, GLS minimizes a weighted analogue to the sum of squared residuals from OLS regression, where the weight for the ith case is inversely proportional to var(εi). This special case of GLS is called "weighted least squares". The GLS solution to estimation problem is

$$\hat{\beta} = (X^T\Omega^{-1}X)^{-1}X^T\Omega^{-1}y,$$

where Ω is the covariance matrix of the errors. GLS can be viewed as applying a linear transformation to the data so that the assumptions of OLS are met for the transformed data. For GLS to be applied, the covariance structure of the errors must be known up to a multiplicative constant.

Percentage least squares focuses on reducing percentage errors, which is useful in the field of forecasting or time series analysis. It is also useful in situations where the dependent variable has a wide range without constant variance, as here the larger residuals at the upper end of the range would dominate if OLS were used. When the percentage or relative error is normally distributed, least squares percentage regression provides maximum likelihood estimates. Percentage regression is linked to a multiplicative error model, whereas OLS is linked to models containing an additive error term.

Iteratively reweighted least squares (IRLS) is used when heteroscedasticity, or correlations, or both are present among the error terms of the model, but where little is known about the covariance structure of the errors independently of the data. In the first iteration, OLS, or GLS with a provisional covariance structure is carried out, and the residuals are obtained from the fit. Based on the residuals, an improved estimate of the covariance structure of the errors can usually be obtained. A subsequent GLS iteration is then performed using this estimate of the error structure to define the weights. The process can be iterated to convergence, but in many cases, only one iteration is sufficient to achieve an efficient estimate of β.

Instrumental variables regression (IV) can be performed when the regressors are correlated with the errors. In this case, we need the existence of some auxiliary instrumental variables zi such that $E[zi\varepsilon i] = 0$. If Z is the matrix of instruments, then the estimator can be given in closed form as

$$\hat{\beta} = (X^T Z(Z^T Z)^{-1} Z^T X)^{-1} X^T Z(Z^T Z)^{-1} Z^T y.$$

Optimal instruments regression is an extension of classical IV regression to the situation where $E[\varepsilon i \mid zi] = 0$.

Total least squares (TLS) is an approach to least squares estimation of the linear regression model that treats the covariates and response variable in a more geometrically symmetric manner than OLS. It is one approach to handling the "errors in variables" problem, and is sometimes used when the covariates are assumed to be error-free.

Maximum-likelihood Estimation and Related Techniques

Maximum likelihood estimation can be performed when the distribution of the error terms is known to belong to a certain parametric family $f\theta$ of probability distributions. When $f\theta$ is a normal distribution with mean zero and variance θ, the resulting estimate is identical to the OLS estimate. GLS estimates are maximum likelihood estimates when ε follows a multivariate normal distribution with a known covariance matrix.

Ridge regression, and other forms of penalized estimation such as Lasso regression, deliberately introduce bias into the estimation of β in order to reduce the variability of the estimate. The resulting estimators generally have lower mean squared error than the OLS estimates, particularly when multicollinearity is present. They are generally used when the goal is to predict the value of the response variable y for values of the predictors x that have not yet been observed. These methods are not as commonly used when the goal is inference, since it is difficult to account for the bias.

Least absolute deviation (LAD) regression is a robust estimation technique in that it is less sensitive to the presence of outliers than OLS (but is less efficient than OLS when no outliers are present). It is equivalent to maximum likelihood estimation under a Laplace distribution model for ε.

Adaptive estimation. If we assume that error terms are independent from the regressors $\varepsilon_i \perp x_i$, the optimal estimator is the 2-step MLE, where the first step is used to non-parametrically estimate the distribution of the error term.

Other Estimation Techniques

Bayesian linear regression applies the framework of Bayesian statistics to linear regression. In particular, the regression coefficients β are assumed to be random variables with a specified prior distribution.

The prior distribution can bias the solutions for the regression coefficients, in a way similar to (but more general than) ridge regression or lasso regression. In addition, the Bayesian estimation process produces not a single point estimate for the "best" values of the regression coefficients but an entire posterior distribution, completely describing the uncertainty surrounding the quantity. This can be used to estimate the "best" coefficients using the mean, mode, median, any quantile, or any other function of the posterior distribution.

Quantile regression focuses on the conditional quantiles of y given X rather than the conditional mean of y given X. Linear quantile regression models a particular conditional quantile, often the conditional median, as a linear function $\beta^T x$ of the predictors.

Mixed models are widely used to analyse linear regression relationships involving dependent data when the dependencies have a known structure. Common applications of mixed models include analysis of data involving repeated measurements, such as longitudinal data, or data obtained from cluster sampling. They are generally fit as parametric models, using maximum likelihood or Bayesian estimation. In the case where the errors are meddled as normal random variables, there is a close connection between mixed models and generalized least squares. Fixed effects estimation is an alternative approach to analysing this type of data.

Principal component regression (PCR) is used when the number of predictor variables is large, or when strong correlations exist among the predictor variables. This two-stage procedure first reduces the predictor variables using principal component analysis then uses the reduced variables in an OLS regression fit. While it often works well in practice, there is no general theoretical reason that the most informative linear function of the predictor variables should lie among the dominant principal components of the multivariate distribution of the predictor variables. The partial least squares regression is the extension of the PCR method which does not suffer from the mentioned deficiency.

Least-angle regression is an estimation procedure for linear regression models that was developed to handle high-dimensional covariate vectors, potentially with more covariates than observations.

The Theil–Sen estimator is a simple robust estimation technique that chooses the slope of the fit line to be the median of the slopes of the lines through pairs of sample points. It has similar statistical efficiency properties to simple linear regression but is much less sensitive to outliers.

Other robust estimation techniques, including the α-trimmed mean approach, and L-, M-, S-, and R-estimators have been introduced.

Further Discussion

In statistics, the problem of numerical methods for linear least squares is an important one because linear regression models are one of the most important types of model, both as formal statistical models and for exploration of data sets.

The majority of statistical computer packages contain facilities for regression analysis that make use of linear least squares computations. Hence it is appropriate that considerable effort has been devoted to the task of ensuring that these computations are undertaken efficiently and with due regard to numerical precision.

Individual statistical analyses are seldom undertaken in isolation, but rather are part of a sequence of investigatory steps. Some of the topics involved in considering numerical methods for linear least squares relate to this point. Thus important topics can be

Computations where a number of similar, and often nested, models are considered for the same data set. That is, where models with the same dependent variable but different sets of independent variables are to be considered, for essentially the same set of data points.

Computations for analyses that occur in a sequence, as the number of data points increases.

Special considerations for very extensive data sets. Fitting of linear models by least squares often, but not always, arises in the context of statistical analysis.

It can therefore be important that considerations of computational efficiency for such problems extend to all of the auxiliary quantities required for such analyses, and are not restricted to the formal solution of the linear least squares problem.

Matrix calculations, like any others, are affected by rounding errors. An early summary of these effects, regarding the choice of computational methods for matrix inversion, was provided by Wilkinson.

Applications of Linear Regression

Linear regression is widely used in biological, behavioural and social sciences to describe possible relationships between variables. It ranks as one of the most important tools used in these disciplines.

Trend Line

A trend line represents a trend, the long-term movement in time series data after other components have been accounted for. It tells whether a particular data set (say GDP, oil prices or stock prices) have increased or decreased over the period of time. A trend line could simply be drawn by eye through a set of data points, but more properly their position and slope is calculated using statistical techniques like linear regression. Trend lines typically are straight lines, although some variations use higher degree polynomials depending on the degree of curvature desired in the line.

Trend lines are sometimes used in business analytics to show changes in data over time. This has the advantage of being simple. Trend lines are often used to argue that a particular action or event (such as training, or an advertising campaign) caused observed changes at a point in time. This is a simple technique, and does not require a control group, experimental design, or a sophisticated analysis technique. However, it suffers from a lack of scientific validity in cases where other potential changes can affect the data.

Epidemiology

Early evidence relating tobacco smoking to mortality and morbidity came from observational studies employing regression analysis. In order to reduce spurious correlations when analysing observational data, researchers usually include several variables in their regression models in addition to the variable of primary interest. For example, suppose we have a regression model in which cigarette smoking is the independent variable of interest, and the dependent variable is lifespan measured in years. Researchers might include socio-economic status as an additional independent variable, to ensure that any observed effect of smoking on lifespan is not due to some effect of education or income.

However, it is never possible to include all possible confounding variables in an empirical analysis. For example, a hypothetical gene might increase mortality and also cause people to smoke more. For this reason, randomized controlled trials are often able to generate more compelling evidence of causal relationships than can be obtained using regression analyses of observational data. When controlled experiments are not feasible, variants of regression analysis such as instrumental variables regression may be used to attempt to estimate causal relationships from observational data.

Finance

The capital asset pricing model uses linear regression as well as the concept of Beta for analysing and quantifying the systematic risk of an investment. This comes directly from the Beta coefficient of the linear regression model that relates the return on the investment to the return on all risky assets.

Economics

Linear regression is the predominant empirical tool in economics. For example, it is used to predict consumption spending, fixed investment spending, inventory investment, purchases of a country's exports, spending on imports, the demand to hold liquid assets, labour demand, and labour supply.

Environmental Science

Linear regression finds application in a wide range of environmental science applications. In Canada, the Environmental Effects Monitoring Programme uses statistical analyses on fish and benthic surveys to measure the effects of pulp mill or metal mine effluent on the aquatic ecosystem.

Regression Diagnostics

Once a regression model has been constructed, it may be important to confirm the goodness of fit of the model and the statistical significance of the estimated parameters. Commonly used checks of goodness of fit include the R-squared, analyses of the pattern of residuals and hypothesis testing. Statistical significance can be checked by an F-test of the overall fit, followed by t-tests of individual parameters.

Interpretations of these diagnostic tests rest heavily on the model assumptions. Although examination of the residuals can be used to invalidate a model, the results of a t-test or F-test are sometimes more difficult to interpret if the model's assumptions are violated. For example, if the error term does not have a normal distribution, in small samples the estimated parameters will not follow normal distributions and complicate inference. With relatively large samples, however, a central limit theorem can be invoked such that hypothesis testing may proceed using asymptotic approximations.

Regression with "limited dependent" Variables

The phrase "limited dependent" is used in econometric statistics for categorical and constrained variables.

The response variable may be non-continuous ("limited" to lie on some subset of the real line). For binary (zero or one) variables, if analysis proceeds with least-squares linear regression, the model is called the linear probability model. Nonlinear models for binary dependent variables include the probit and logit model.

The multivariate probit model is a standard method of estimating a joint relationship between several binary dependent variables and some independent variables. For categorical variables with more than two values there is the multinomial logit. For ordinal variables with more than two values, there are the ordered logit and ordered probit models. Censored regression models may be used when the dependent variable is only sometimes observed, and Heckman correction type models may be used when the sample is not randomly selected from the population of interest. An alternative to such procedures is linear regression based on polychoric correlation (or polyserial correlations) between the categorical variables.

Such procedures differ in the assumptions made about the distribution of the variables in the population. If the variable is positive with low values and represents the repetition of the occurrence of an event, then count models like the Poisson regression or the negative binomial model may be used instead.

Interpolation and Extrapolation

Regression models predict a value of the *Y* variable given known values of the *X* variables. Prediction within the range of values in the dataset used for model-fitting is known informally as interpolation. Prediction outside this range of the data is known as extrapolation. Performing extrapolation relies strongly on the regression assumptions. The further the extrapolation goes outside the data, the more room there is for the model to fail due to differences between the assumptions and the sample data or the true values.

It is generally advised that when performing extrapolation, one should accompany the estimated value of the dependent variable with a prediction interval that represents the uncertainty. Such intervals tend to expand rapidly as the values of the independent variable(s) moved outside the range covered by the observed data.

For such reasons and others, some tend to say that it might be unwise to undertake extrapolation. However, this does not cover the full set of modelling errors that may be being made: in particular, the assumption of a particular form for the relation between *Y* and *X*. A properly conducted regression analysis will include an assessment of how well the assumed form is matched by the observed data, but it can only do so within the range of values of the independent variables actually available. This means that any extrapolation is particularly reliant on the assumptions being made about the structural form of the regression relationship. Best-practice advice here is that a linear-in-variables and linear-in-parameters relationship should not be chosen simply for computational convenience, but that all available knowledge should be deployed in constructing a regression model.

If this knowledge includes the fact that the dependent variable cannot go outside a certain range of values, this can be made use of in selecting the model — even if the observed dataset has no values particularly near such bounds. The implications of this step of choosing an appropriate functional form for the regression can be great when extrapolation is considered. At a minimum, it can ensure that any extrapolation arising from a fitted model is "realistic" (or in accord with what is known).

Nonlinear Regression

In statistics, nonlinear regression is a form of regression analysis in which observational data are meddled by a function which is a nonlinear combination of the model parameters and depends on one or more independent variables. The data are fitted by a method of successive approximations.

General

The data consist of error-free independent variables (explanatory variables), *x*, and their associated observed dependent variables (response variables), *y*. Each y is meddled as a random variable with a mean given by a nonlinear function $f(x,\beta)$. Systematic error may be present but its treatment is outside the scope of regression analysis. If the independent variables are not error-free, this is an errors-in-variables model, also outside this scope.

For example, the Michaelis–Menten model for enzyme kinetics

$$v = \frac{V_{\max}[\mathrm{S}]}{K_m + [\mathrm{S}]}$$

can be written as

$$f(x,\beta) = \frac{\beta_1 x}{\beta_2 + x}$$

where β_1 is the parameter V_{max}, β_2 is the parameter K_m and [S] is the independent variable, x. This function is nonlinear because it cannot be expressed as a linear combination of the βs.

Other examples of nonlinear functions include exponential functions, logarithmic functions, trigonometric functions, power functions, Gaussian function, and Lorenz curves. Some functions, such as the exponential or logarithmic functions, can be transformed so that they are linear. When so transformed, standard linear regression can be performed but must be applied with caution.

In general, there is no closed-form expression for the best-fitting parameters, as there is in linear regression. Usually numerical optimization algorithms are applied to determine the best-fitting parameters. Again in contrast to linear regression, there may be many local minima of the function to be optimized and even the global minimum may produce a biased estimate.

In practice, estimated values of the parameters are used, in conjunction with the optimization algorithm, to attempt to find the global minimum of a sum of squares.

Regression Statistics

The assumption underlying this procedure is that the model can be approximated by a linear function.

$$f(x_i, \beta) \approx f^0 + \sum_j J_{ij}\beta_j$$

where $J_{ij} = \dfrac{\partial f(x_i, \beta)}{\partial \beta_j}$.

It follows from this that the least squares estimators are given by

$$\hat{\beta} \approx (J^T J)^{-1} J^T y.$$

The nonlinear regression statistics are computed and used as in linear regression statistics, but using J in place of X in the formulas. The linear approximation introduces bias into the statistics. Therefore more caution than usual is required in interpreting statistics derived from a nonlinear model.

Ordinary and Weighted Least Squares

The best-fit curve is often assumed to be that which minimizes the sum of squared residuals. This is the (ordinary) least squares

(OLS) approach. However, in cases where the dependent variable does not have constant variance a sum of weighted squared residuals may be minimized. Each weight should ideally be equal to the reciprocal of the variance of the observation, but weights may be recomputed on each iteration, in an iteratively weighted least squares algorithm.

Linearization

Transformation

Some nonlinear regression problems can be moved to a linear domain by a suitable transformation of the model formulation.

For example, consider the nonlinear regression problem

$$y = ae^{bx}U$$

with parameters a and b and with multiplicative error term U. If we take the logarithm of both sides, this becomes

$$\ln(y) = \ln(a) + bx + u,$$

where u = log(U), suggesting estimation of the unknown parameters by a linear regression of ln(y) on x, a computation that does not require iterative optimization. However, use of a nonlinear transformation requires caution. The influences of the data values will change, as will the error structure of the model and the interpretation of any inferential results. These may not be desired effects. On the other hand, depending on what the largest source of error is, a nonlinear transformation may distribute your errors in a normal fashion, so the choice to perform a nonlinear transformation must be informed by modelling considerations.

For Michaelis–Menten kinetics, the linear Lineweaver–Burk plot

$$\frac{1}{v} = \frac{1}{V_{\max}} + \frac{K_m}{V_{\max}[S]}$$

of 1/v against 1/[S] has been much used. However, since it is very sensitive to data error and is strongly biased towards fitting the data in a particular range of the independent variable, [S], its use is strongly discouraged. For error distributions that belong to the Exponential family, a link function may be used to transform the parameters under the Generalised Linear Model framework.

Segmentation

The independent or explanatory variable (say *X*) can be split up into classes or segments and linear regression can be performed per segment. Segmented regression with confidence analysis may yield the result that the dependent or response variable (say *Y*) behaves differently in the various segments.

The figure shows that the soil salinity (*X*) initially exerts no influence on the crop yield *(Y)* of mustard (colza), until a critical or threshold value (breakpoint), after which the yield is affected negatively.

Nonlinear Regression Algorithms

- Gauss–Newton algorithm
- Gradient descent
- Levenberg–Marquardt algorithm: a hybrid of Gauss-Newton and gradient descent

Power and Sample Size Calculations

There are no generally agreed methods for relating the number of observations versus the number of independent variables in the model. One rule of thumb suggested by Good and Hardin is $N = m^n$, where *N* is the sample size, *n* is the number of independent variables and *m* is the number of observations needed to reach the desired precision if the model had only one independent variable. For example, a researcher is building a linear regression model using a dataset that contains 1000 patients ( ). If he decides that five observations are needed to precisely define a straight line ( ), then the maximum number of independent variables his model can support is 4, because

$$\frac{\log 1000}{\log 5} = 4.29 .$$

Other Methods

Although the parameters of a regression model are usually estimated using the method of least squares, other methods which have been used include:

- Bayesian methods, e.g. Bayesian linear regression
- Percentage regression, for situations where reducing percentage errors is deemed more appropriate.
- Least absolute deviations, which is more robust in the presence of outliers, leading to quantile regression
- Nonparametric regression, requires a large number of observations and is computationally intensive

- Distance metric learning, which is learned by the search of a meaningful distance metric in a given input space.

Software

All major statistical software packages perform least squares regression analysis and inference. Simple linear regression and multiple regression using least squares can be done in some spreadsheet applications and on some calculators. While many statistical software packages can perform various types of nonparametric and robust regression, these methods are less standardized; different software packages implement different methods, and a method with a given name may be implemented differently in different packages. Specialized regression software has been developed for use in fields such as survey analysis and neuroimaging.

Student's t-test

A t-test is any statistical hypothesis test in which the test statistic follows a Student's t distribution if the null hypothesis is supported. It is most commonly applied when the test statistic would follow a normal distribution if the value of a scaling term in the test statistic were known. When the scaling term is unknown and is replaced by an estimate based on the data, the test statistic (under certain conditions) follows a Student's t distribution.

History

The t-statistic was introduced in 1908 by William Sealy Gosset, a chemist working for the Guinness brewery in Dublin, Ireland ("Student" was his pen name). Gosset had been hired due to Claude Guinness's policy of recruiting the best graduates from Oxford and Cambridge to apply biochemistry and statistics to Guinness's industrial processes. Gosset devised the t-test as a cheap way to monitor the quality of stout.

He published the test in Biometrika in 1908, but was forced to use a pen name by his employer, who regarded the fact that they were using statistics as a trade secret. In fact, Gosset's identity was known to fellow statisticians.

Uses

Among the most frequently used t-tests are:

- A one-sample location test of whether the mean of a normally distributed population has a value specified in a null hypothesis.

- A two sample location test of the null hypothesis that the means of two normally distributed populations are equal. All such tests are usually called Student's t-tests, though strictly speaking that name should only be used if the variances of the two populations are also assumed to be equal; the form of the test used when this assumption is dropped is sometimes called Welch's t-test. These tests are often referred to as "unpaired" or "independent samples" t-tests, as they are typically applied when the statistical units underlying the two samples being compared are non-overlapping.
- A test of the null hypothesis that the difference between two responses measured on the same statistical unit has a mean value of zero. For example, suppose we measure the size of a cancer patient's tumor before and after a treatment. If the treatment is effective, we expect the tumor size for many of the patients to be smaller following the treatment. This is often referred to as the "paired" or "repeated measures" t-test.
- A test of whether the slope of a regression line differs significantly from 0.

Assumptions

Most t-test statistics have the form $T = Z / s$, where Z and s are functions of the data. Typically, Z is designed to be sensitive to the alternative hypothesis (i.e. its magnitude tends to be larger when the alternative hypothesis is true), whereas s is a scaling parameter that allows the distribution of T to be determined.

As an example, in the one-sample t-test $Z = \overline{X} / \sigma / \sqrt{n}$ where $\overline{X}$ is the sample mean of the data, n is the sample size, and σ is the population standard deviation of the data; s in the one-sample t-test is $\hat{\sigma} / \sqrt{n}$, where $\hat{\sigma}$ is the sample standard deviation.

The assumptions underlying a t-test are that

- Z follows a standard normal distribution under the null hypothesis
- s^2 follows a χ^2 distribution with p degrees of freedom under the null hypothesis, where p is a positive constant
- Z and s are independent.

In a specific type of t-test, these conditions are consequences of the population being studied, and of the way in which the data are sampled. For example, in the t-test comparing the means of two independent samples, the following assumptions should be met:

- Each of the two populations being compared should follow a normal distribution. This can be tested using a normality test, such as the Shapiro-Wilk or Kolmogorov–Smirnov test, or it can be assessed graphically using a normal quantile plot.
- If using Student's original definition of the t-test, the two populations being compared should have the same variance (testable using *F* test, Levene's test, Bartlett's test, or the Brown–Forsythe test; or assessable graphically using a *Q-Q* plot). If the sample sizes in the two groups being compared are equal, Student's original t-test is highly robust to the presence of unequal variances. Welch's t-test is insensitive to equality of the variances regardless of whether the sample sizes are similar.
- The data used to carry out the test should be sampled independently from the two populations being compared. This is in general not testable from the data, but if the data are known to be dependently sampled (i.e. if they were sampled in clusters), then the classical t-tests discussed here may give misleading results.

Alternatives to the t-test for Location Problems

The t-test provides an exact test for the equality of the means of two normal populations with unknown, but equal, variances. (The Welch's t-test is a nearly exact test for the case where the data are normal but the variances may differ.) For moderately large samples and a one tailed test, the t is relatively robust to moderate violations of the normality assumption.

For exactness, the t-test and Z-test require normality of the sample means, and the t-test additionally requires that the sample variance follows a scaled χ^2 distribution, and that the sample mean and sample variance be statistically independent. Normality of the individual data values is not required if these conditions are met. By the central limit theorem, sample means of moderately large samples are often well-approximated by a normal distribution even if the data are not normally distributed. For non-normal data, the distribution of the sample variance may deviate substantially from a χ^2 distribution. However, if the sample size is large, Slutsky's theorem implies that the distribution of the sample variance has little effect on the distribution of the test statistic.

If the data are substantially non-normal and the sample size is small, the t-test can give misleading results.

When the normality assumption does not hold, a non-parametric alternative to the t-test can often have better statistical power. For example, for two independent samples when the data distributions are asymmetric (that is, the distributions are skewed) or the distributions have large tails, then the Wilcoxon Rank Sum test (also known as the Mann-Whitney U test) can have three to four times higher power than the t-test. The nonparametric counterpart to the paired samples t test is the Wilcoxon signed-rank test for paired samples. For a discussion on choosing between the t and nonparametric alternatives.

One-way analysis of variance generalizes the two-sample t-test when the data belong to more than two groups.

Hotelling's T-squared Distribution

In statistics Hotelling's T-squared distribution is important because it arises as the distribution of a set of statistics which are natural generalisations of the statistics underlying Student's t distribution. In particular, the distribution arises in multivariate statistics in undertaking tests of the differences between the (multivariate) means of different populations, where tests for univariate problems would make use of a t-test. It is proportional to the F distribution.

The distribution is named for Harold Hotelling, who developed it as a generalization of Student's *t* distribution.

The Distribution

If the notation $T^2_{p,m}$ is used to denote a random variable having Hotelling's T-squared distribution with parameters *p*and *m*then, if a random variable *X*has Hotelling's T-squared distribution,

$$X \sim T^2_{p,m}$$

then

$$\frac{m-p+1}{pm} X \sim F_{p,m-p+1}$$

where $F_{p,m-p+1}$ is the F-distribution with parameters and .

Software Implementations

Most spreadsheet programmes and statistics packages, such as QtiPlot, OpenOffice.org Calc, LibreOffice Calc, Microsoft Excel, SAS,

SPSS, Stata, DAP, gretl, R, Python ([1]), PSPP, and Minitab, include implementations of Student's t-test.

Time Series

In statistics, signal processing, pattern recognition, econometrics, mathematical finance, Weather forecasting, Earthquake prediction, Electroencephalography, Control engineering and Communications engineering a time series is a sequence of data points, measured typically at successive time instants spaced at uniform time intervals.

Examples of time series are the daily closing value of the Dow Jones index or the annual flow volume of the Nile River at Aswan. Time series analysis comprises methods for analysing time series data in order to extract meaningful statistics and other characteristics of the data. Time series forecasting is the use of a model to predict future values based on previously observed values. Time series are very frequently plotted via line charts.

Time series data have a natural temporal ordering. This makes time series analysis distinct from other common data analysis problems, in which there is no natural ordering of the observations (e.g. explaining people's wages by reference to their respective education levels, where the individuals' data could be entered in any order). Time series analysis is also distinct from spatial data analysis where the observations typically relate to geographical locations (e.g. accounting for house prices by the location as well as the intrinsic characteristics of the houses).

A stochastic model for a time series will generally reflect the fact that observations close together in time will be more closely related than observations further apart. In addition, time series models will often make use of the natural one-way ordering of time so that values for a given period will be expressed as deriving in some way from past values, rather than from future values.

Methods for time series analyses may be divided into two classes: frequency-domain methods and time-domain methods. The former include spectral analysis and recently wavelet analysis; the latter include auto-correlation and cross-correlation analysis.

Additionally time series analysis techniques may be divided into parametric and non-parametric methods. The parametric approaches assume that the underlying stationary Stochastic process has a certain structure which can be described using a small number of parameters (for example, using an autoregressive or moving average model).

In these approaches, the task is to estimate the parameters of the model that describes the stochastic process. By contrast, non-parametric approaches explicitly estimate the covariance or the spectrum of the process without assuming that the process has any particular structure.

Additionally methods of time series analysis may be divided into linear and non-linear, univariate and multivariate.

Time series analysis can be applied to:

- real-valued, continuous data
- discrete numeric data
- discrete symbolic data (i.e. sequences of characters, such as letters and words in English language).

Analysis

There are several types of data analysis available for time series which are appropriate for different purposes.

In the context of statistics, econometrics, quantitative finance, seismology, meteorology, geophysics the primary goal of time series analysis is forecasting, in the context of signal processing, control engineering and communication engineering it is used for signal detection and estimation while in the context of data mining, pattern recognition and machine learning time series analysis can be used for clustering, classification, query by content, anomaly detection as well as forecasting.

Exploratory Analysis

The clearest way to examine a regular time series manually is with a line chart such as the one shown for tuberculosis in the United States, made with a spreadsheet programme. The number of cases was standardized to a rate per 100,000 and the percent change per year in this rate was calculated. The nearly steadily dropping line shows that the TB incidence was decreasing in most years, but the percent change in this rate varied by as much as +/- 10%, with 'surges' in 1975 and around the early 1990s. The use of both vertical axes allows the comparison of two time series in one graphic. Other techniques include:

- Autocorrelation analysis to examine serial dependence
- Spectral analysis to examine cyclic behaviour which need not be related to seasonality. For example, sun spot activity varies over 11 year cycles. Other common examples include celestial

phenomena, weather patterns, neural activity, commodity prices, and economic activity.

- Separation into components representing trend, seasonality, slow and fast variation, cyclical irregular.
- Simple properties of marginal distributions

Prediction and Forecasting

- Fully formed statistical models for stochastic simulation purposes, so as to generate alternative versions of the time series, representing what might happen over non-specific time-periods in the future
- Simple or fully formed statistical models to describe the likely outcome of the time series in the immediate future, given knowledge of the most recent outcomes (forecasting).
- Forecasting on time series is usually done using automated statistical software packages and programming languages, such as R (programming language), S (programming language), SAS (software), SPSS, Minitab and many others.

Classification

Assigning time series pattern to a specific category, for example identify a word based on series of hand movements in Sign language

Regression Analysis

Estimating future value of a signal based on its previous behaviour, e.g. predict the price of AAPL stock based on its previous price movements for that hour, day or month, or predict position of Apollo 11 spacecraft at a certain future moment based on its current trajectory (i.e. time series of its previous locations).

Regression analysis is usually based on statistical interpretation of time series properties in time domain, pioneered by statisticians George Box and Gwilym Jenkins in the 50s.

Signal Estimation

This approach is based on Harmonic analysis and filtering of signals in Frequency domain using Fourier transform, and Spectral density estimation, the development of which was significantly accelerated during World War II by mathematician Norbert Weiner, electrical engineers Rudolf E. Kálmán, Dennis Gabor and others for filtering signal from noise and predicting signal value at a certain point in time.

3

History of Statistics

The history of statistics can be said to start around 1749 although, over time, there have been changes to the interpretation of the word statistics. In early times, the meaning was restricted to information about states.

This was later extended to include all collections of information of all types, and later still it was extended to include the analysis anturies, particularly in the analysis of games of chance (gambling). By 1800, astronomy used probability models and statistical theories, particularly the method of least squares, which was invented by Legendre and Gauss. Early probability theory and statistics was systematized and extended by Laplace; following Laplace, probability and statistics have been in continual development. In the 19th century, statistical reasoning and probability models were used by social scientists to advance the new sciences of experimental psychology and sociology, and by physical scientists in thermodynamics and statistical mechanics. The development of statistical reasoning was closely associated with the development of inductive logic and the scientific method.

Statistics can be regarded as not a field of mathematics but an autonomous mathematical science, like computer science and operations research. Unlike mathematics, statistics had its origins in public administration. It is used in demography and economics. With its emphasis on learning from data and making best predictions, statistics has a considerable overlap with decision science and microeconomics. With its concerns with data, statistics has overlap with information science and computer science.

Etymology

The term statistics is ultimately derived from the New Latin statisticum collegium ("council of state") and the Italian word statista ("statesman" or "politician"). The German Statistik, first introduced by Gottfried Achenwall (1749), originally designated the analysis of data about the state, signifying the "science of state" (then called political arithmetic in English).

It acquired the meaning of the collection and classification of data generally in the early 19th century. It was introduced into English in 1791 by Sir John Sinclair when he published the first of 21 volumes titled Statistical Account of Scotland.

Thus, the original principal purpose of Statistik was data to be used by governmental and (often centralized) administrative bodies. The collection of data about states and localities continues, largely through national and international statistical services. In particular, censuses provide frequently updated information about the population. The first book to have 'statistics' in its title was "Contributions to Vital Statistics" by Francis GP Neison, actuary to the Medical Invalid and General Life Office (1st ed., 1845; 2nd ed., 1846; 3rd ed., 1857).

Origins in Probability

The use of statistical methods dates back to least to the 5th century BCE. The historian Thucydides in his History of the Peloponnesian War describes how the Athenians calculated the height of the wall of Platea by counting the number of bricks in an unplastered section of the wall sufficiently near them to be able to count them. The count was repeated several times by a number of soldiers.

The most frequent value (in modern terminology - the mode) so determined was taken to be the most likely value of the number of bricks. Multiplying this value by the height of the bricks used in the wall allowed the Athenians to determine the height of the ladders necessary to scale the walls.

In the Indian epic - the Mahabharata (Book 3: The Story of Nala) - King Rtuparna estimated the number of fruit and leaves (2095 fruit and 50,000,000 - five crores - leaves) on two great branches of a Vibhitaka tree by counting them on a single twig. This number was then multiplied by the number of twigs on the branches. This estimate was later checked and found to be very close to the actual number. With knowledge of this method Nala was subsequently able to regain his kingdom.

The earliest writing on statistics was found in a 9th century book entitled: "Manuscript on Deciphering Cryptographic Messages", written by Al-Kindi (801–873 CE). In his book, Al-Kindi gave a detailed description of how to use statistics and frequency analysis to decipher encrypted messages, this was the birth of both statistics and cryptanalysis.

The Trial of the Pyx is a test of the purity of the coinage of the Royal Mint which has been held on a regular basis since the 12th century. The Trial itself is based on statistical sampling methods. After minting a series of coins - originally from ten pounds of silver - a single coin was placed in the Pyx - a box in Westminster Abbey. After a given period - now once a year - the coins are removed and weighed. A sample of coins removed from the box are then tested for purity.

The Nuova Cronica, a 14th century history of Florence by the Florentine banker and official Giovanni Villani, includes much statistical information on population, ordinances, commerce and trade, education, and religious facilities and has been described as the first introduction of statistics as a positive element in history, though neither the term nor the concept of statistics as a specific field yet existed. But this was proven to be incorrect after the rediscovery of Al-Kindi's book on frequency analysis. The arithmetic mean, although a concept known to the Greeks, was not generalised to more than two values until the 16th century. The invention of the decimal system by Simon Stevin in 1585 seems likely to have facilitated these calculations. This method was first adopted in astronomy by Tycho Brahe who was attempting to reduce the errors in his estimates of the locations of various celestial bodies.

The idea of the median originated in Edward Wright's book on navigation (Certaine Errors in Navigation) in 1599 in a section concerning the determination of location with a compass. Wright felt that this value was the most likely to be the correct value in a series of observations.

John Graunt in his book Natural and Political Observations Made upon the Bills of Mortality estimated the population of London in 1662 from parish records. He knew that there were around 13,000 funerals per year in London and that three people died per eleven families per year. He estimated from the parish records that the average family size was 8 and calculated that the population of London was about 384,000. Laplace in 1802 estimated the population of France with a similar method.

The mathematical methods of statistics emerged from probability theory, which can be dated to the correspondence between Pierre de Fermat and Blaise Pascal (1654). Christiaan Huygens (1657) gave the earliest known scientific treatment of the subject. Jakob Bernoulli's Ars Conjectandi (posthumous, 1713) and Abraham de Moivre's The Doctrine of Chances (1718) treated the subject as a branch of mathematics. In his book Bernoulli introduced the idea of representing complete certainty as one and probability as a number between zero and one.

Galileo struggled with the problem of errors in observations and had vaguely formulated the principle that the most likely values of the unknowns would be those that made the errors in all the equations reasonably small. The formal study of theory of errors may be traced back to Roger Cotes' Opera Miscellanea (posthumous, 1722). Tobias Mayer, in his study of the libration of the moon (Kosmographische Nachrichten, Nuremberg, 1750), invented the first formal method for estimating the unknown quantities by generalized the averaging of observations under identical circumstances to the averaging of groups of similar equations.

The first example of what later became known as the normal curve was studied by Abraham de Moivre who plotted this curve on November 12, 1733. de Moive was studying the number of heads that occurred when a 'fair' coin was tossed.

A memoir - An attempt to show the advantage arising by taking the mean of a number of observations in practical astronomy - prepared by Thomas Simpson in 1755 (printed 1756) first applied the theory to the discussion of errors of observation. The reprint (1757) of this memoir lays down the axioms that positive and negative errors are equally probable, and that there are certain assignable limits within which all errors may be supposed to fall; continuous errors are discussed and a probability curve is given. Simpson discussed several possible distributions of error. He first considered the uniform distribution and then the discrete symmetric triangular distribution followed by the continuous symmetric triangle distribution..

Ruðer Boškoviæ in 1755 based in his work on the shape of the earth proposed in his book De Litteraria expeditione per pontificiam ditionem ad dimetiendos duos meridiani gradus a PP. Maire et Boscovicli that the true value of a series of observations would be that which minimises the sum of absolute errors. In modern terminology this value is the median.

Johann Heinrich Lambert in his 1765 book Anlage zur Architectonic proposed the semicircle as a distribution of errors:

$$f(x) = \frac{1}{2}\sqrt{(1-x^2)}$$

with $-1 \leq x \leq 1$.

Pierre-Simon Laplace (1774) made the first attempt to deduce a rule for the combination of observations from the principles of the theory of probabilities. He represented the law of probability of errors by a curve and deduced a formula for the mean of three observations.

Laplace in 1774 noted that the frequency of an error could be expressed as an exponential function of its magnitude once its sign was disregarded. This distribution is now known as the Laplace distribution.

Lagrange proposed a parabolic distribution of errors in 1776:

$$f(x) = \frac{3}{4}(1-x^2)$$

with $-1 \leq x \leq 1$.

Laplace in 1778 published his second law of errors wherein he noted that the frequency of an error was proportional to the exponential of the square of its magnitude. This was subsequently rediscovered by Gauss (possibly in 1795) and is now best known as the normal distribution which is of central importance in statistics. This distribution was first referred to as the normal distribution by Pierce in 1873 who was studying measurement errors when an object was dropped onto a wooden base. He chose the term normal because of its frequent occurrence in naturally occurring variables.

Lagrange also suggested in 1781 two other distributions for errors - a cosine distribution

$$f(x) = \frac{\pi}{4}cos(\frac{\pi x}{2})$$

with $-1 \leq x \leq 1$ and a logarithmic distribution

$$f(x) = \frac{1}{2}\frac{1}{|x|}$$

with $-1 \leq x \leq 1$ where | | is the absolute value of x.

Laplace gave (1781) a formula for the law of facility of error (a term due to Joseph Louis Lagrange, 1774), but one which led to unmanageable equations. Daniel Bernoulli (1778) introduced the principle of the maximum product of the probabilities of a system of concurrent errors.

Laplace, in an investigation of the motions of Saturn and Jupiter in 1787, generalized Mayer's method by using different linear combinations of a single group of equations.

In 1802 Laplace estimated the population of France to be 28,328,612. He calculated this figure using the number of births in the previous year and census data for three communities.

The census data of these communities showed that they had 2,037,615 persons and that the number of births were 71,866. Assuming that these samples were representative of France, Laplace produced his estimate for the entire population.

The method of least squares, which was used to minimize errors in data measurement, was published independently by Adrien-Marie Legendre (1805), Robert Adrain (1808), and Carl Friedrich Gauss (1809).

Gauss had used the method in his famous 1801 prediction of the location of the dwarf planet Ceres. The observations that Gauss based his calculations on were made by the Italian monk Piazzi. Further proofs were given by Laplace (1810, 1812), Gauss (1823), Ivory (1825, 1826), Hagen (1837), Bessel (1838), Donkin (1844, 1856), Herschel (1850), Crofton (1870), and Thiele (1880, 1889).

The term probable error (der wahrscheinliche Fehler) - the median deviation from the mean - was introduced in 1815 by the German astronomer Frederik Wilhelm Bessel.

Antoine Augustin Cournot in 1843 was the first to use the term median (valeur médiane) for the value that divides a probability distribution into two equal halves.

Other contributors to the theory of errors were Ellis (1844), De Morgan (1864), Glaisher (1872), and Giovanni Schiaparelli (1875). Peters's (1856) formula for *r*, the "probable error" of a single observation was widely used and inspired early robust statistics.

In the 19th century authors on statistical theory included Laplace, S. Lacroix (1816), Littrow (1833), Dedekind (1860), Helmert (1872), Laurant (1873), Liagre, Didion, De Morgan, Boole, Edgeworth, and K. Pearson.

Gustav Theodor Fechner used the median (Centralwerth) in sociological and psychological phenomena. It had earlier been used only in astronomy and related fields. Francis Galton used the English term median for the first time in 1881 having earlier used the terms middle-most value in 1869 and the medium in 1880.

Adolphe Quetelet (1796–1874), another important founder of statistics, introduced the notion of the "average man" (l'homme moyen) as a means of understanding complex social phenomena such as crime rates, marriage rates, and suicide rates.

The first tests of the normal distribution were invented by the German statistician Wilhelm Lexis in the 1870s. The only data sets available to him that he was able to show were normally distributed were birth rates.

Francis Galton studied a variety of human characteristics - height, weight, eyelash length among others - and found that many of these could be fitted to a normal curve distribution.

Francis Galton in 1907 submitted a paper to Nature on the usefulness of the median. He examined the accuracy of 787 guesses of the weight of an ox at a country fair. The actual weight was 1208 pounds: the median guess was 1198. The guesses were markedly non-normally distributed.

The Norwegian Anders Nicolai Kiær introduced the concept of stratified sampling in 1895. Arthur Lyon Bowley introduced random sampling in 1906. Jerzy Neyman in 1934 showed that stratified random sampling was in general a better method of estimation than purposive (quota) sampling.

The 5% level of significance appears to have been introduced by Fisher in 1925. Fisher stated that deviations exceeding twice the standard deviation are regarded as significant. Before this deviations exceeding three times the probable error were considered significant.

For a symmetrical distribution the probable error is half the interquartile range. The upper quartile of a standard normal distribution lies between 0.66 and 0.67 its probable error is approximately 2/3 of a standard deviation. It appears that Fisher's 5% criterion was rooted in previous practice.

In 1929 Wilson and Hilferty re examined Pierce's data from 1873 and discovered that it was not actually normally distributed.

Design of Experiments

In 1747, while serving as surgeon on HM Bark Salisbury, James Lind carried out a controlled experiment to develop a cure for scurvy. In this study his subjects' cases "were as similar as I could have them", that is he provided strict entry requirements to reduce extraneous variation. The men were paired, which provided blocking. From a modern perspective, the main thing that is missing is randomized allocation of subjects to treatments.

James Lind is today often described as a one-factor-at-a-time experimenter. One-factor-at-a-time (OFAT) experimen-tation reached its zenith with Thomas Edison's "trial and error" methods.

A theory of statistical inference was developed by Charles S. Peirce in "Illustrations of the Logic of Science" (1877–1878) and –A Theory of Probable Inference" (1883), two publications that emphasized the importance of randomization-based inference in statistics. In another study, Peirce randomly assigned volunteers to a blinded, repeated-measures design to evaluate their ability to discriminate weights. Peirce's experiment inspired other researchers in psychology and education, which developed a research tradition of randomized experiments in laboratories and specialized textbooks in the 1800s. Peirce also contributed the first English-language publication on an optimal design for regression-models in 1876. A pioneering optimal design for polynomial regression was suggested by Gergonne in 1815. In 1918 Kirstine Smith published optimal designs for polynomials of degree six (and less).

The use of a sequence of experiments, where the design of each may depend on the results of previous experiments, including the possible decision to stop experimenting, was pioneered by Abraham Wald in the context of sequential tests of statistical hypotheses. Surveys are available of optimal sequential designs, and of adaptive designs. One specific type of sequential design is the "two-armed bandit", generalized to the multi-armed bandit, on which early work was done by Herbert Robbins in 1952.

The term "design of experiments" (DOE) derives from early statistical work performed by Sir Ronald Fisher. He was described by Anders Hald as "a genius who almost single-handedly created the foundations for modern statistical science." Fisher initiated the principles of design of experiments and elaborated on his studies of "analysis of variance". Perhaps even more important, Fisher began his systematic approach to the analysis of real data as the springboard for the development of new statistical methods. He began to pay particular attention to the labour involved in the necessary computations performed by hand, and developed methods that were as practical as they were founded in rigour. In 1925, this work culminated in the publication of his first book, Statistical Methods for Research Workers. This went into many editions and translations in later years, and became a standard reference work for scientists in many disciplines.

A methodology for designing experiments was proposed by Ronald A. Fisher, in his innovative book The Design of Experiments (1935) which also became a standard. As an example, he described how to test the hypothesis that a certain lady could distinguish by flavour alone whether the milk or the tea was first placed in the cup. While this sounds like a frivolous application, it allowed him to illustrate the most important ideas of experimental design.

Agricultural science advances served to meet the combination of larger city populations and fewer farms. But for crop scientists to take due account of widely differing geographical growing climates and needs, it was important to differentiate local growing conditions. To extrapolate experiments on local crops to a national scale, they had to extend crop sample testing economically to overall populations. As statistical methods advanced (primarily the efficacy of designed experiments instead of one-factor-at-a-time experimentation), representative factorial design of experiments began to enable the meaningful extension, by inference, of experimental sampling results to the population as a whole. But it was hard to decide how representative was the crop sample chosen. Factorial design methodology showed how to estimate and correct for any random variation within the sample and also in the data collection procedures.

Inference

Charles S. Peirce (1839—1914) formulated frequentist theories of estimation and hypothesis-testing in (1877—1878) and (1883), in which he introduced "confidence". Peirce also introduced blinded, controlled randomized experiments with a repeated measures design. Peirce invented an optimal design for experiments on gravity.

Bayesian Statistics

The term Bayesian refers to Thomas Bayes (1702–1761), who proved a special case of what is now called Bayes' theorem. However it was Pierre-Simon Laplace (1749–1827) who introduced a general version of the theorem and applied it to celestial mechanics, medical statistics, reliability, and jurisprudence. When insufficient knowledge was available to specify an informed prior, Laplace used uniform priors, according to his "principle of insufficient reason". Laplace assumed uniform priors for mathematical simplicity rather than for philosophical reasons. Laplace also introduced primitive versions of conjugate priors and the theorem of von Mises and Bernstein, according to which the posteriors corresponding to initially differing priors ultimately agree, as the number of observations increases. This early Bayesian inference, which used uniform priors following Laplace's principle of insufficient reason, was called "inverse probability" (because it infers backwards from observations to parameters, or from effects to causes).

After the 1920s, inverse probability was largely supplanted by a collection of methods that were developed by Ronald A. Fisher, Jerzy Neyman and Egon Pearson. Their methods came to be called frequentist statistics. Fisher rejected the Bayesian view, writing that "the theory of inverse probability is founded upon an error, and must be wholly rejected". At the end of his life, however, Fisher expressed greater respect for the essay of Bayes, which Fisher believed to have anticipated his own, fiducial approach to probability; Fisher still maintained that Laplace's views on probability were "fallacious rubbish". Neyman started out as a "quasi-Bayesian", but subsequently developed confidence intervals (a key method in frequentist statistics) because "the whole theory would look nicer if it were built from the start without reference to Bayesianism and priors". The word Bayesian appeared in the 1930s, and by the 1960s it became the term preferred by those dissatisfied with the limitations of frequentist statistics.

In the 20th century, the ideas of Laplace were further developed in two different directions, giving rise to objective and subjective currents in Bayesian practice. In the objectivist stream, the statistical analysis depends on only the model assumed and the data analysed. No subjective decisions need to be involved. In contrast, "subjectivist" statisticians deny the possibility of fully objective analysis for the general case.

In the further development of Laplace's ideas, subjective ideas predate objectivist positions. The idea that 'probability' should be interpreted as 'subjective degree of belief in a proposition' was proposed, for example, by John Maynard Keynes in the early 1920s. This idea was taken further by Bruno de Finetti in Italy (Fondamenti Logici del Ragionamento Probabilistico, 1930) and Frank Ramsey in Cambridge (The Foundations of Mathematics, 1931). The approach was devised to solve problems with the frequentist definition of probability but also with the earlier, objectivist approach of Laplace. The subjective Bayesian methods were further developed and popularized in the 1950s by L.J. Savage. Objective Bayesian inference was further developed due to Harold Jeffreys, whose seminal book "Theory of probability" first appeared in 1939. In 1957, Edwin Jaynes promoted the concept of maximum entropy for constructing priors, which is an important principle in the formulation of objective methods, mainly for discrete problems. In 1965, Dennis Lindley's 2-volume work "Introduction to Probability and Statistics from a Bayesian Viewpoint" brought Bayesian methods to a wide audience. In 1979, José-Miguel Bernardo introduced reference analysis, which offers a general applicable framework for objective analysis. Other well-known proponents of Bayesian probability theory include I.J. Good, B.O. Koopman, Howard Raiffa, Robert Schlaifer and Alan Turing. In the 1980s, there was a dramatic growth in research and applications of Bayesian methods, mostly attributed to the discovery of Markov chain Monte Carlo methods, which removed many of the computational problems, and an increasing interest in nonstandard, complex applications. Despite growth of Bayesian research, most undergraduate teaching is still based on frequentist statistics. Nonetheless, Bayesian methods are widely accepted and used, such as for example in the field of machine learning.

Statistics Today

During the 20th century, the creation of precise instruments for agricultural research, public health concerns (epidemiology, biostatistics, etc.), industrial quality control, and economic and social purposes (unemployment rate, econometry, etc.) necessitated substantial advances in statistical practices.

Today the use of statistics has broadened far beyond its origins. Individuals and organizations use statistics to understand data and make informed decisions throughout the natural and social sciences, medicine, business, and other areas.

Statistics is generally regarded not as a subfield of mathematics but rather as a distinct, albeit allied, field. Many universities maintain separate mathematics and statistics departments. Statistics is also taught in departments as diverse as psychology, education, and public health.

Overview

In applying statistics to a scientific, industrial, or societal problem, it is necessary to begin with a population or process to be studied. Populations can be diverse topics such as "all persons living in a country" or "every atom composing a crystal". A population can also be composed of observations of a process at various times, with the data from each observation serving as a different member of the overall group. Data collected about this kind of "population" constitutes what is called a time series.

For practical reasons, a chosen subset of the population called a sample is studied — as opposed to compiling data about the entire group (an operation called census). Once a sample that is representative of the population is determined, data is collected for the sample members in an observational or experimental setting. This data can then be subjected to statistical analysis, serving two related purposes: description and inference.

- Descriptive statistics summarize the population data by describing what was observed in the sample numerically or graphically. Numerical descriptors include mean and standard deviation for continuous data types (like heights or weights), while frequency and percentage are more useful in terms of describing categorical data (like race).
- Inferential statistics uses patterns in the sample data to draw inferences about the population represented, accounting for randomness. These inferences may take the form of: answering yes/no questions about the data (hypothesis testing), estimating numerical characteristics of the data (estimation), describing associations within the data (correlation) and modelling relationships within the data (for example, using regression analysis). Inference can extend to forecasting, prediction and estimation of unobserved values either in or associated with the population being studied; it can include extrapolation and interpolation of time series or spatial data, and can also include data mining.

The concept of correlation is particularly noteworthy for the potential confusion it can cause. Statistical analysis of a data set often reveals that two variables (properties) of the population under consideration tend to vary together, as if they were connected. For example, a study of annual income that also looks at age of death might find that poor people tend to have shorter lives than affluent people. The two variables are said to be correlated; however, they may or may not be the cause of one another. The correlation phenomena could be caused by a third, previously unconsidered phenomenon, called a lurking variable or confounding variable. For this reason, there is no way to immediately infer the existence of a causal relationship between the two variables.

For a sample to be used as a guide to an entire population, it is important that it is truly a representative of that overall population. Representative sampling assures that the inferences and conclusions can be safely extended from the sample to the population as a whole. A major problem lies in determining the extent to which the sample chosen is actually representative. Statistics offers methods to estimate and correct for any random trending within the sample and data collection procedures. There are also methods of experimental design for experiments that can lessen these issues at the outset of a study, streng-thening its capability to discern truths about the population.

Randomness is studied using the mathematical discipline of probability theory. Probability is used in "mathematical statistics" (alternatively, "statistical theory") to study the sampling distributions of sample statistics and, more generally, the properties of statistical procedures. The use of any statistical method is valid when the system or population under consideration satisfies the assumptions of the method.

Misuse of statistics can produce subtle, but serious errors in description and interpretation — subtle in the sense that even experienced professionals make such errors, and serious in the sense that they can lead to devastating decision errors. For instance, social policy, medical practice, and the reliability of structures like bridges all rely on the proper use of statistics.

Even when statistical techniques are correctly applied, the results can be difficult to interpret for those lacking expertise. The statistical significance of a trend in the data — which measures the extent to which a trend could be caused by random variation in the sample — may or may not agree with an intuitive sense of its significance. The set of basic statistical skills (and skepticism) that people need to deal with information in their everyday lives properly is referred to as statistical literacy.

Statistical Methods

Experimental and Observational Studies

A common goal for a statistical research project is to investigate causality, and in particular to draw a conclusion on the effect of changes in the values of predictors or independent variables on dependent variables or response. There are two major types of causal statistical studies: experimental studies and observational studies. In both types of studies, the effect of differences of an independent variable (or variables) on the behaviour of the dependent variable are observed. The difference between the two types lies in how the study is actually conducted. Each can be very effective. An experimental study involves taking measurements of the system under study, manipulating the system, and then taking additional measurements using the same procedure to determine if the manipulation has modified the values of the measurements. In contrast, an observational study does not involve experimental manipulation. Instead, data are gathered and correlations between predictors and response are investigated.

Experiments

The basic steps of a statistical experiment are:

1. Planning the research, including finding the number of replicates of the study, using the following information: preliminary estimates regarding the size of treatment effects, alternative hypotheses, and the estimated experimental variability. Consideration of the selection of experimental subjects and the ethics of research is necessary. Statisticians recommend that experiments compare (at least) one new treatment with a standard treatment or control, to allow an unbiased estimate of the difference in treatment effects.
2. Design of experiments, using blocking to reduce the influence of confounding variables, and randomized assignment of treatments to subjects to allow unbiased estimates of treatment effects and experimental error. At this stage, the experimenters and statisticians write the experimental protocol that shall guide the performance of the experiment and that specifies the primary analysis of the experimental data.
3. Performing the experiment following the experimental protocol and analysing the data following the experimental protocol.
4. Further examining the data set in secondary analyses, to suggest new hypotheses for future study.
5. Documenting and presenting the results of the study.

Experiments on human behaviour have special concerns. The famous Hawthorne study examined changes to the working environment at the Hawthorne plant of the Western Electric Company. The researchers were interested in determining whether increased illumination would increase the productivity of the assembly line workers.

The researchers first measured the productivity in the plant, then modified the illumination in an area of the plant and checked if the changes in illumination affected productivity. It turned out that productivity indeed improved (under the experimental conditions).

However, the study is heavily criticized today for errors in experimental procedures, specifically for the lack of a control group and blindness. The Hawthorne effect refers to finding that an outcome (in this case, worker productivity) changed due to observation itself. Those in the Hawthorne study became more productive not because the lighting was changed but because they were being observed.

Observational Study

An example of an observational study is one that explores the correlation between smoking and lung cancer. This type of study typically uses a survey to collect observations about the area of interest and then performs statistical analysis. In this case, the researchers would collect observations of both smokers and non-smokers, perhaps through a case-control study, and then look for the number of cases of lung cancer in each group.

Level of Measurement

The "levels of measurement", or scales of measure are expressions that typically refer to the theory of scale types developed by the psychologist Stanley Smith Stevens. Stevens proposed his theory in a 1946 Science article titled "On the theory of scales of measurement".

In that article, Stevens claimed that all measurement in science was conducted using four different types of scales that he called "nominal", "ordinal", "interval" and "ratio", unifying both qualitative (which are described by his "nominal" scale) and quantitative (to a different degree, all the rest of his scales).

Nominal Scale

Only the most simple operations, such as equivalence and set membership, are possible between the data collected at this scale of measurement. Examples include both dichotomous nominal data, such as 'male' vs. 'female' when measuring gender, 'sedimentary' vs. 'non-sedimentary' when measuring rocks, etc, and non-dichotomous consisting of multiple values, such as 'British', 'American', 'Australian' etc. when measuring nationality. Higher operations which imply order, such as 'greater-than' or 'lower-than', are not possible for such data.

Neither the mean nor the median can be calculated, the central tendency can be given only by the mode.

This is the reason why the data collected at the nominal scale are sometimes called qualitative data and are sometimes treated as having nothing in common with the quantitative data. Nonetheless, even at this level regression analysis is possible, using dummy variables; for example, gender can be treated as a dummy variable equaling 0 for subjects of male gender and 1 for subjects of female gender. They can be used either as an independent variable (explanatory variable) in an ordinary least squares regression, or as dependent variables in the probit or logistic regression.

Categorical Variables

If dichotomous data happen to be randomly distributed, they are called binary, which is characterized by Bernoulli distribution. The binomial distribution is useful for data comprised of successes and failures. If non-dichotomous data happen to be randomly distributed, they are called multi-way (or K-way for some specific value of K), which is characterized by a categorical distribution. Both are called categorical variables.

Interval Scale

Quantitative attributes are all measurable on interval scales, as any difference between the levels of an attribute can be multiplied by any real number to exceed or equal another difference. A highly familiar example of interval scale measurement is temperature with the Celsius scale. In this particular scale, the unit of measurement is 1/100 of the temperature difference between the freezing and boiling points of water under a pressure of 1 atmosphere. Time can be an interval scale, when measured from an arbitrary epoch as it often is. The "zero point" on an interval scale is arbitrary; and negative values can be used.

The formal mathematical term is an affine space (in this case an affine line). Variables measured at the interval level are called "interval variables" or sometimes "scaled variables" as they have units of measurement.

Ratios between numbers on the scale are not meaningful, so operations such as multiplication and division cannot be carried out directly. But ratios of differences can be expressed; for example, one difference can be twice another.

The central tendency of a variable measured at the interval level can be represented by its mode, its median, or its arithmetic mean.

Statistical dispersion can be measured in most of the usual ways, which just involved differences or averaging, such as range, interquartile range, and standard deviation.

Since one cannot divide, one cannot define measures that require a ratio, such as studentized range or coefficient of variation. More subtly, while one can define moments about the origin, only central moments are useful, since the choice of origin is arbitrary and not meaningful.

One can define standardized moments, since ratios of differences are meaningful, but one cannot define coefficient of variation, since the mean is a moment about the origin, unlike the standard deviation, which is (the square root of) a central moment.

Ratio Scale

Most measurement in the physical sciences and engineering is done on ratio scales. Mass, length, duration, plane angle, energy and electric charge are examples of physical measures that are ratio scales. The scale type takes its name from the fact that measurement is the estimation of the ratio between a magnitude of a continuous quantity and a unit magnitude of the same kind (Michell, 1997, 1999). Informally, the distinguishing feature of a ratio scale is the possession of a zero value. For example, the Kelvin temperature scale has a non-arbitrary zero point of absolute zero, which is denoted 0K and is equal to -273.15 degrees Celsius. This zero point is accurately representing the particles that compose matter at this temperature having zero kinetic energy.

Examples of ratio scale measurement in the behavioural sciences are all but non-existent. Luce (2000) argues that an example of ratio scale measurement in psychology can be found in rank and sign dependent expected utility theory. All statistical measures can be used for a variable measured at the ratio level, as all necessary mathematical operations are defined. The central tendency of a variable measured at the ratio level can be represented by, in addition to its mode, its median, or its arithmetic mean, also its geometric mean or harmonic mean. In addition to the measures of statistical dispersion defined for interval variables, such as range and standard deviation, for ratio variables one can also define measures that require a ratio, such as studentized range or coefficient of variation.

Debate on Classification Scheme

There has been, and continues to be, debates about the merits of the classifications, particularly in the cases of the nominal and ordinal classifications (Michell, 1986). Thus, while Stevens' classification is widely adopted, it is by no means universally accepted.

Duncan (1986) observed that Stevens' classification nominal measurement is contrary to his own definition of measurement. Stevens (1975) said on his own definition of measurement that "the assignment can be any consistent rule. The only rule not allowed would be random assignment, for randomness amounts in effect to a nonrule". However, so-called nominal measurement involves arbitrary assignment, and the "permissible transformation" is any number for any other. This is one of the points made in Lord's (1953) satirical paper On the Statistical Treatment of Football Numbers.

Among those who accept the classification scheme, there is also some controversy in behavioural sciences over whether the mean is meaningful for ordinal measurement. In terms of measurement theory, it is not, because the arithmetic operations are not made on numbers that are measurements in units, and so the results of computations do not give numbers in units. However, many behavioural scientists use means for ordinal data anyway. This is often justified on the basis that ordinal scales in behavioural science are really somewhere between true ordinal and interval scales; although the interval difference between two ordinal ranks is not constant, it is often of the same order of magnitude. For example, applications of measurement models in educational contexts often indicate that total scores have a fairly linear relationship with measurements across a range of an assessment. Thus, some argue, that so long as the unknown interval difference between ordinal scale ranks is not too variable, interval scale statistics such as means can meaningfully be used on ordinal scale variables. Statistical analysis software such as PSPP require the user to select the appropriate measurement class for each variable.

This ensures that subsequent user errors cannot inad-vertently perform meaningless analyses (for example correlation analysis with a variable on a nominal level).

L. L. Thurstone made progress towards developing a justification for obtaining interval-level measurements based on the law of comparative judgement. For a common application of the law. Further progress was made by Georg Rasch (1960), who developed the probabilistic Rasch model that provides a theoretical basis and justification for obtaining interval-level measurements from counts of observations such as total scores on assessments.

Another issue is derived from Nicholas R. Chrisman's article "Rethinking Levels of Measurement for Cartography", in which he introduces an expanded list of levels of measurement to account for various measurements that do not necessarily fit with the traditional notion of levels of measurement. Measurements bound to a range and repeat (like degrees in a circle, time, etc.), graded membership categories, and other types of measurement do not fit to Steven's original work, leading to the introduction of 6 new levels of measurement leading to: (1) Nominal, (2) Graded membership, (3) Ordinal, (4) Interval, (5) Log-Interval, (6) Extensive Ratio, (7) Cyclical Ratio, (8) Derived Ratio, (9) Counts and finally (10) Absolute. The extended levels of measurement are rarely used outside of academic geography.

Scale Types and Stevens' "Operational theory of Measurement"

The theory of scale types is the intellectual handmaiden to Stevens' "operational theory of measurement", which was to become definitive within psychology and the behavioural sciences, despite Michell's characterization as its being quite at odds with measurement in the natural sciences (Michell, 1999). Essentially, the operational theory of measurement was a reaction to the conclusions of a committee established in 1932 by the British Association for the Advancement of Science to investigate the possibility of genuine scientific measurement in the psychological and behavioural sciences.

This committee, which became known as the Ferguson committee, published a Final Report (Ferguson, et al., 1940, p. 245) in which Stevens' sone scale (Stevens & Davis, 1938) was an object of criticism:

> *"...any law purporting to express a quantitative relation between sensation intensity and stimulus intensity is not merely false but is in fact meaningless unless and until a meaning can be given to the concept of addition as applied to sensation."*

That is, if Stevens' sone scale was genuinely measuring the intensity of auditory sensations, then evidence for such sensations as being quantitative attributes must be produced. The evidence needed was the presence of additive structure - a concept comprehensively treated by the German mathematician Otto Hölder (Hölder, 1901). Given the physicist and measurement theorist Norman Robert Campbell dominated the Ferguson committee's deliberations, the committee concluded that measurement in the social sciences was impossible due to the lack of concatenation operations.

This conclusion was later rendered false by the discovery of the theory of conjoint measurement by Debreu (1960) and independently by Luce & Tukey (1964).

However, Stevens' reaction was not to conduct experiments to test for the presence of additive structure in sensations, but instead to render the conclusions of the Ferguson committee null and void by proposing a new theory of measurement:

> *"Paraphrasing N.R. Campbell (Final Report, p.340), we may say that measurement, in the broadest sense, is defined as the assignment of numerals to objects and events according to rules (Stevens, 1946, p.677)."*

Stevens was greatly influenced by the ideas of another Harvard academic, the Nobel laureate physicist Percy Bridgman (1927), whose doctrine of operationism Stevens used to define measurement. In Stevens' definition for example, it is the use of a tape measure that defines length (the object of measurement) as being measurable (and so by implication quantitative). Critics of operationism object that it confuses the relations between two objects or events for properties of one of those of objects or events (Hardcastle, 1995; Michell, 1999; Moyer, 1981a,b; Rogers, 1989).

The Canadian measurement theorist William Rozeboom (1966) was an early and trenchant critic of Stevens' theory of scale types. But it was not until much later with the work of mathematical psychologists Theodore Alper (1985, 1987), Louis Narens (1981a, b) and R. Duncan Luce (1986, 1987, 2001) did the concept of scale types receive the mathematical rigour that it lacked at its inception. As Luce (1997, p. 395) bluntly stated:

> *" S.S. Stevens (1946, 1951, 1975) claimed that what counted was having an interval or ratio scale. Subsequent research has given meaning to this assertion, but given his attempts to invoke scale type ideas it is doubtful if he understood it himself...no measurement theorist I know accepts Stevens' broad definition of measurement...in our view, the only sensible meaning for 'rule' is empirically testable laws about the attribute.*

Key Terms Used in Statistics

Null Hypothesis

Interpretation of statistical information can often involve the development of a null hypothesis in that the assumption is that whatever is proposed as a cause has no effect on the variable being measured. The best illustration for a novice is the predicament encountered by a jury trial. The null hypothesis, H*0*, asserts that the defendant is innocent, whereas the alternative hypothesis, H*1*, asserts that the defendant is guilty.

The indictment comes because of suspicion of the guilt. The H*0* (status quo) stands in opposition to H*1* and is maintained unless H*1* is supported by evidence "beyond a reasonable doubt". However," failure to reject H*0*– in this case does not imply innocence, but merely that the evidence was insufficient to convict. So the jury does not necessarily accept H*0* but fails to reject H*0*. While one can not "prove" a null hypothesis one can test how close it is to being true with a power test, which tests for type II errors.

Error

Working from a null hypothesis two basic forms of error are recognized:

- Type I errors where the null hypothesis is falsely rejected giving a "false positive".
- Type II errors where the null hypothesis fails to be rejected and an actual difference between populations is missed giving a "false negative".

Error also refers to the extent to which individual observations in a sample differ from a central value, such as the sample or population mean. Many statistical methods seek to minimize the mean-squared error, and these are called "methods of least squares."

Measurement processes that generate statistical data are also subject to error. Many of these errors are classified as random (noise) or systematic (bias), but other important types of errors (e.g., blunder, such as when an analyst reports incorrect units) can also be important.

Interval Estimation

In statistics, interval estimation is the use of sample data to calculate an interval of possible (or probable) values of an unknown population parameter, in contrast to point estimation, which is a single number. Neyman (1937) identified interval estimation ("estimation by interval") as distinct from point estimation ("estimation by unique estimate").

In doing so, he recognised that then-recent work quoting results in the form of an estimate plus-or-minus a standard deviation indicated that interval estimation was actually the problem statisticians really had in mind.

The most prevalent forms of interval estimation are:

- Confidence intervals (a frequentist method); and
- Credible intervals (a Bayesian method).

Other common approaches to interval estimation, which are encompassed by statistical theory, are:

- Tolerance intervals
- Prediction intervals - used mainly in Regression Analysis
- Likelihood intervals

There is a third approach to statistical inference, namely fiducial inference, that also considers interval estimation. Non-statistical methods that can lead to interval estimates include fuzzy logic. An interval estimate is one type of outcome of a statistical analysis. Some other types of outcome are point estimates and decisions.

Discussion

The scientific problems associated with interval estimation may be summarised as follows:

- When interval estimates are reported, they should have a commonly-held interpretation in the scientific community and more widely. In this regard, credible intervals are held to be most readily understood by the general public. Interval estimates derived from fuzzy logic have much more application-specific meanings.
- For commonly occurring situations there should be sets of standard procedures that can be used, subject to the checking and validity of any required assumptions. This applies for both confidence intervals and credible intervals.
- For more novel situations there should be guidance on how interval estimates can be formulated. In this regard confidence intervals and credible intervals have a similar standing but there are differences:
- Credible intervals can readily deal with prior information, while confidence intervals cannot.
- Confidence intervals are more flexible and can be used practically in more situations than credible intervals: one area

where credible intervals suffer in comparison is in dealing with non-parametric models.

- There should be ways of testing the performance of interval estimation procedures. This arises because many such procedures involve approximations of various kinds and there is a need to check that the actual performance of a procedure is close to what is claimed. The use of stochastic simulations makes this is straightforward in the case of confidence intervals, but it is somewhat more problematic for credible intervals where prior information needs to taken properly into account. Checking of credible intervals can be done for situations representing no-prior-information but the check involves checking the long-run frequency properties of the procedures.

Severini (1991) discusses conditions under which credible intervals and confidence intervals will produce similar results, and also discusses both the coverage probabilities of credible intervals and the posterior probabilities associated with confidence intervals.

Behrens–Fisher Problem

The Behrens–Fisher problem. This has played an important role in the development of the theory behind applicable statistical methodologies. This problem is one of the simplest to state but which is not easily solved. The task of specifying interval estimates for this problem is one where a frequentist approach fails to provide an exact solution, although some approximations are available.

The Bayesian approach also fails to provide an answer that can be expressed as straightforward simple formulae, but modern computational methods of Bayesian analysis do allow essentially exact solutions to be found. Thus study of the problem can be used to elucidate the differences between the frequentist and Bayesian approaches to interval estimation.

Does Order of Procedure Affect Statistical Significance?

Order refers to which comes first: the test data or the specification of the hypotheses to be tested. When the hypotheses come first the test is "prospective" and when the data come first the test is "retrospective". Traditionally, prospective tests have been required. However, there is a well-known generally accepted hypothesis test in which the data preceded the hypotheses. In that study the statistical significance was calculated the same as it would have been had the hypotheses preceded the data. A related question in use of statistics in the physical sciences is whether probability theory applies to the known past in the same way that it applies to the unknown future. Although these questions have been discussed, there are few references in this area of statistics.

It hardly seems reasonable to accord the same status to a hypothesis that explains the results of an experiment after the results are known as to a hypothesis that predicts the results of an experiment before they are known. This is because it is well known that predicting an event before it occurs is more difficult than explaining it after it occurs.

4

Regression Analysis

In statistics, regression analysis is a statistical technique for estimating the relationships among variables. It includes many techniques for modelling and analysing several variables, when the focus is on the relationship between a dependent variable and one or more independent variables.

More specifically, regression analysis helps one understand how the typical value of the dependent variable changes when any one of the independent variables is varied, while the other independent variables are held fixed.

Most commonly, regression analysis estimates the conditional expectation of the dependent variable given the independent variables — that is, the average value of the dependent variable when the independent variables are fixed. Less commonly, the focus is on a quantile, or other location parameter of the conditional distribution of the dependent variable given the independent variables.

In all cases, the estimation target is a function of the independent variables called the regression function. In regression analysis, it is also of interest to characterize the variation of the dependent variable around the regression function, which can be described by a probability distribution.

Regression analysis is widely used for prediction and forecasting, where its use has substantial overlap with the field of machine learning.

Regression analysis is also used to understand which among the independent variables are related to the dependent variable, and to explore the forms of these relationships.

In restricted circumstances, regression analysis can be used to infer causal relationships between the independent and dependent variables. However this can lead to illusions or false relationships, so caution is advisable.

A large body of techniques for carrying out regression analysis has been developed. Familiar methods such as linear regression and ordinary least squares regression are parametric, in that the regression function is defined in terms of a finite number of unknown parameters that are estimated from the data. Nonparametric regression refers to techniques that allow the regression function to lie in a specified set of functions, which may be infinite-dimensional.

The performance of regression analysis methods in practice depends on the form of the data generating process, and how it relates to the regression approach being used. Since the true form of the data-generating process is generally not known, regression analysis often depends to some extent on making assumptions about this process.

These assumptions are sometimes testable if a large amount of data is available. Regression models for prediction are often useful even when the assumptions are moderately violated, although they may not perform optimally. However, in many applications, especially with small effects or questions of causality based on observational data, regression methods give misleading results.

History

The earliest form of regression was the method of least squares, which was published by Legendre in 1805, and by Gauss in 1809. Legendre and Gauss both applied the method to the problem of determining, from astronomical observations, the orbits of bodies about the Sun (mostly comets, but also later the then newly discovered minor planets). Gauss published a further development of the theory of least squares in 1821, including a version of the Gauss–Markov theorem.

The term "regression" was coined by Francis Galton in the nineteenth century to describe a biological phenomenon. The phenomenon was that the heights of descendants of tall ancestors tend to regress down towards a normal average (a phenomenon also known as regression towards the mean). For Galton, regression had only this biological meaning, but his work was later extended by Udny Yule and Karl Pearson to a more general statistical context.

In the work of Yule and Pearson, the joint distribution of the response and explanatory variables is assumed to be Gaussian. This assumption was weakened by R.A. Fisher in his works of 1922 and 1925. Fisher assumed that the conditional distribution of the response variable is Gaussian, but the joint distribution need not be. In this respect, Fisher's assumption is closer to Gauss's formulation of 1821.

In the 1950s and 1960s, economists used electromechanical desk calculators to calculate regressions. Before 1970, it sometimes took up to 24 hours to receive the result from one regression. Regression methods continue to be an area of active research. In recent decades, new methods have been developed for robust regression, regression involving correlated responses such as time series and growth curves, regression in which the predictor or response variables are curves, images, graphs, or other complex data objects, regression methods accommodating various types of missing data, nonparametric regression, Bayesian methods for regression, regression in which the predictor variables are measured with error, regression with more predictor variables than observations, and causal inference with regression.

Assumptions

Standard linear regression models with standard estimation techniques make a number of assumptions about the predictor variables, the response variables and their relationship. Numerous extensions have been developed that allow each of these assumptions to be relaxed (i.e. reduced to a weaker form), and in some cases eliminated entirely.

Some methods are general enough that they can relax multiple assumptions at once, and in other cases this can be achieved by combining different extensions. Generally these extensions make the estimation procedure more complex and time-consuming, and may also require more data in order to get an accurate model. The following are the major assumptions made by standard linear regression models with standard estimation techniques (e.g. ordinary least squares):

Weak exogeneity: This essentially means that the predictor variables x can be treated as fixed values, rather than random variables. This means, for example, that the predictor variables are assumed to be error-free, that is they are not contaminated with measurement errors. Although not realistic in many settings, dropping this assumption leads to significantly more difficult errors-in-variables models.

Linearity: This means that the mean of the response variable is a linear combination of the parameters (regression coefficients) and the predictor variables. Note that this assumption is much less restrictive than it may at first seem. Because the predictor variables are treated as fixed values, linearity is really only a restriction on the parameters. The predictor variables themselves can be arbitrarily transformed, and in fact multiple copies of the same underlying predictor variable can be added, each one transformed differently. This trick is used, for example, in polynomial regression, which uses linear regression to fit the response variable as an arbitrary polynomial function (up to a given rank) of a predictor variable.

This makes linear regression an extremely powerful inference method. In fact, models such as polynomial regression are often "too powerful", in that they tend to overfit the data. As a result, some kind of regularization must typically be used to prevent unreasonable solutions coming out of the estimation process. Common examples are ridge regression and lasso regression. Bayesian linear regression can also be used, which by its nature is more or less immune to the problem of overfitting. (In fact, ridge regression and lasso regression can both be viewed as special cases of Bayesian linear regression, with particular types of prior distributions placed on the regression coefficients.)

Constant variance (aka homoscedasticity). This means that different response variables have the same variance in their errors, regardless of the values of the predictor variables. In practice this assumption is invalid (i.e. the errors are heteroscedastic) if the response variables can vary over a wide scale. In order to determine for heterogeneous error variance, or when a pattern of residuals violates model assumptions of homoscedasticity (error is equally variable around the 'best-fitting line' for all points of x), it is prudent to look for a "fanning effect" between residual error and predicted values. This is to say there will be a systematic change in the absolute or squared residuals when plotted against the predicting outcome.

Error will not be evenly distributed across the regression line. Heteroscedasticity will result in the averaging over of distinguishable variances around the points to get a single variance that is inaccurately representing all the variances of the line. In effect, residuals appear clustered and spread apart on their predicted plots for larger and smaller values for points along the linear regression line, and the mean squared error for the model will be wrong. Typically, for example, a response variable whose mean is large will have a greater variance than one whose mean is small.

For example, a given person whose income is predicted to be \$100,000 may easily have an actual income of \$80,000 or \$120,000 (a standard deviation of around \$20,000), while another person with a predicted income of \$10,000 is unlikely to have the same \$20,000 standard deviation, which would imply their actual income would vary anywhere between -\$10,000 and \$30,000. (In fact, as this shows, in many cases – often the same cases where the assumption of normally distributed errors fails – the variance or standard deviation should be predicted to be proportional to the mean, rather than constant.)

Simple linear regression estimation methods give less precise parameter estimates and misleading inferential quantities such as standard errors when substantial heteroscedasticity is present. However, various estimation techniques (e.g. weighted least squares and heteroscedasticity-consistent standard errors) can handle heteroscedasticity in a quite general way.

Bayesian linear regression techniques can also be used when the variance is assumed to be a function of the mean. It is also possible in some cases to fix the problem by applying a transformation to the response variable (e.g. fit the logarithm of the response variable using a linear regression model, which implies – as noted above – that the response variable has a log-normal distribution rather than a normal distribution).

Independence of errors: This assumes that the errors of the response variables are uncorrelated with each other. (Actual statistical independence is a stronger condition than mere lack of correlation and is often not needed, although it can be exploited if it is known to hold.) Some methods (e.g. generalized least squares) are capable of handling correlated errors, although they typically require significantly more data unless some sort of regularization is used to bias the model towards assuming uncorrelated errors. Bayesian linear regression is a general way of handling this issue.

Lack of multicollinearity in the predictors. For standard least squares estimation methods, the design matrix X must have full column rank p, i.e. be invertible; otherwise, we have a condition known as multicollinearity in the predictor variables. This can be triggered by having two or more perfectly correlated predictor variables (e.g. if the same predictor variable is mistakenly given twice, either without transforming one of the copies or by transforming one of the copies linearly).

It can also happen if there is too little data available compared to the number of parameters to be estimated (e.g. fewer data points than regression coefficients). In the case of multicollinearity, the parameter vector β will be non-identifiable — it has no unique solution. At most we will be able to identify some of the parameters, i.e. narrow down its value to some linear subspace of R^p. Methods for fitting linear models with multicollinearity have been developed; some require additional assumptions such as "effect sparsity" — that a large fraction of the effects are exactly zero. Note that the more computationally expensive iterated algorithms for parameter estimation, such as those used in generalized linear models, do not suffer from this problem — and in fact it's quite normal to when handling categorically-valued predictors to introduce a separate indicator variable predictor for each possible category, which inevitably introduces multicollinearity.

Beyond these assumptions, several other statistical properties of the data strongly influence the performance of different estimation methods:

- The statistical relationship between the error terms and the regressors plays an important role in determining whether an estimation procedure has desirable sampling properties such as being unbiased and consistent.
- The arrangement, or probability distribution of the predictor variables x has a major influence on the precision of estimates of β. Sampling and design of experiments are highly-developed subfields of statistics that provide guidance for collecting data in such a way to achieve a precise estimate of β.

Unpaired and Paired two-sample t-tests

Two-sample t-tests for a difference in mean involve independent samples, paired samples and overlapping samples. Paired t-tests are a form of blocking, and have greater power than unpaired tests when the paired units are similar with respect to "noise factors" that are independent of membership in the two groups being compared. In a different context, paired t-tests can be used to reduce the effects of confounding factors in an observational study.

Independent Samples

The independent samples t-test is used when two separate sets of independent and identically distributed samples are obtained, one from each of the two populations being compared. For example, suppose we are evaluating the effect of a medical treatment, and we enroll

100 subjects into our study, then randomize 50 subjects to the treatment group and 50 subjects to the control group. In this case, we have two independent samples and would use the unpaired form of the t-test.

The randomization is not essential here—if we contacted 100 people by phone and obtained each person's age and gender, and then used a two-sample t-test to see whether the mean ages differ by gender, this would also be an independent samples t-test, even though the data are observational.

Paired Samples

Paired samples t-tests typically consist of a sample of matched pairs of similar units, or one group of units that has been tested twice (a "repeated measures" t-test).

A typical example of the repeated measures t-test would be where subjects are tested prior to a treatment, say for high blood pressure, and the same subjects are tested again after treatment with a blood-pressure lowering medication. By comparing the same patient's numbers before and after treatment, we are effectively using each patient as their own control.

That way the correct rejection of the null hypothesis (here: of no difference made by the treatment) can become much more likely, with statistical power increasing simply because the random between-patient variation has now been eliminated. Note however that an increase of statistical power comes at a price: more tests are required, each subject having to be tested twice. Because half of the sample now depends on the other half, the paired version of Student's t-test has only 'n/2 - 1' degrees of freedom (with 'n' being the total number of observations). Pairs become individual test units, and the sample has to be doubled to achieve the same number of degrees of freedom. A paired samples t-test based on a "matched-pairs sample" results from an unpaired sample that is subsequently used to form a paired sample, by using additional variables that were measured along with the variable of interest.

The matching is carried out by identifying pairs of values consisting of one observation from each of the two samples, where the pair is similar in terms of other measured variables.

This approach is sometimes used in observational studies to reduce or eliminate the effects of confounding factors. Paired samples t-tests are often referred to as –dependent samples t-tests (as are t-tests on overlapping samples).

Overlapping Samples

An overlapping samples t-test is used when there are paired samples with data missing in one or the other samples (e.g., due to selection of "Don't know" options in questionnaires are because respondents are randomly assigned to a subset question). These tests are widely used in commercial survey research (e.g., by polling companies) and are available in many standard crosstab software packages.

Calculations

Explicit expressions that can be used to carry out various t-tests are given below. In each case, the formula for a test statistic that either exactly follows or closely approximates a t-distribution under the null hypothesis is given. Also, the appropriate degrees of freedom are given in each case. Each of these statistics can be used to carry out either a one-tailed test or a two-tailed test.

Once a t value is determined, a p-value can be found using a table of values from Student's t-distribution. If the calculated p-value is below the threshold chosen for statistical significance (usually the 0.10, the 0.05, or 0.01 level), then the null hypothesis is rejected in favour of the alternative hypothesis.

One-sample t-test

In testing the null hypothesis that the population mean is equal to a specified value $\mu 0$, one uses the statistic

$$t = \frac{\overline{x} - \mu_0}{s / \sqrt{n}}$$

where $\overline{x}$ is the sample mean, s is the sample standard deviation of the sample and n is the sample size. The degrees of freedom used in this test is n – 1.

Slope of a Regression Line

Suppose one is fitting the model

$$Y_i = \alpha + \beta x_i + \varepsilon_i,$$

where x_i, $i = 1, ..., n$ are known, α and β are unknown, and εi are independent identically normally distributed random errors with expected value 0 and unknown variance σ^2, and Yi, i = 1, ..., n are observed. It is desired to test the null hypothesis that the slope β is equal to some specified value $\beta 0$ (often taken to be 0, in which case the hypothesis is that x and y are unrelated).

Let

$\hat{\alpha}, \hat{\beta}$ = least-squares estimators,

$SE_{\hat{\alpha}}, SE_{\hat{\beta}}$ = the standard errors of least-squares estimators.

Then

$$t_{\text{score}} = \frac{\hat{\beta} - \beta_0}{SE_{\hat{\beta}}}$$

has a t-distribution with n – 2 degrees of freedom if the null hypothesis is true. The standard error of the slope coefficient:

$$SE_{\hat{\beta}} = \frac{\sqrt{\frac{1}{n-2}\sum_{i=1}^{n}(Y_i - \hat{y}_i)^2}}{\sqrt{\sum_{i=1}^{n}(x_i - \bar{x})^2}}$$

can be written in terms of the residuals. Let

$\hat{\varepsilon}_i = Y_i - \hat{y}_i = Y_i - (\hat{\alpha} + \hat{\beta}x_i)$ = residuals = estimated errors,

SSR $= \sum_{i=1}^{n} \hat{\varepsilon}_i^{\,2}$ = sum of squares of residuals.

Then t_{score} is given by:

$$t_{\text{score}} = \frac{(\hat{\beta} - \beta_0)\sqrt{n-2}}{\sqrt{\text{SSR} / \sum_{i=1}^{n}(x_i - \bar{x})^2}}.$$

Harmonic Mean

In mathematics, the harmonic mean (sometimes called the subcontrary mean) is one of several kinds of average. Typically, it is appropriate for situations when the average of rates is desired. It is the special case (M^{-1}) of the power mean. As it tends strongly towards the least elements of the list, it may (compared to the arithmetic mean) mitigate the influence of large outliers and increase the influence of small values.

Definition

Discrete Distribution

The harmonic mean H of the positive real numbers $x_1, x_2, \ldots, x_n$ is defined to be the reciprocal of the arithmetic mean of the reciprocals of $x_1, x_2, \ldots, x_n$:

$$H = \left(\frac{1}{n}\cdot\sum_{i=1}^{n} x_i^{-1}\right)^{-1} = \frac{1}{\frac{1}{n}\cdot\left(\frac{1}{x_1}+\frac{1}{x_2}+\cdots+\frac{1}{x_n}\right)} = \frac{n}{\frac{1}{x_1}+\frac{1}{x_2}+\cdots+\frac{1}{x_n}}.$$

Example

The harmonic mean of 1, 2, and 4 is

$$\frac{3}{\frac{1}{1}+\frac{1}{2}+\frac{1}{4}} = \frac{1}{\frac{1}{3}(\frac{1}{1}+\frac{1}{2}+\frac{1}{4})} = \frac{12}{7} = 1.\overline{714285}$$

Continuous Distribution

For a continuous distribution the harmonic mean is

$$H = \frac{1}{\int \frac{1}{x} f(x)dx}$$

Weighted Harmonic Mean

If a set of weights $w_1, ..., w_n$ is associated with the dataset $x_1, ..., x_n$, the weighted harmonic mean is defined by

$$\frac{\sum_{i=1}^{n} w_i}{\sum_{i=1}^{n} \frac{w_i}{x_i}}.$$

The harmonic mean is a special case where all of the weights are equal to 1. It is also equivalent to any weighted harmonic mean where all weights are equal.

Recursive Calculation

It is possible to recursively calculate the harmonic mean (H) of n variates. This method may be of use in computations.

$$H(x_1, x_2, x_3, ...) = \frac{n}{\sum \frac{1}{x_i}} = \left(\frac{1}{n}x_1^{-1} + \frac{n-1}{n}H(x_2, x_3, ...)^{-1}\right)^{-1}$$

Harmonic Mean of two Numbers

For the special case of just two numbers x_1 and x_2, the harmonic mean can be written $H = \frac{2x_1x_2}{x_1 + x_2}$.

In this special case, the harmonic mean is related to the arithmetic mean $A = \frac{x_1 + x_2}{2}$ and the geometric mean $G = \sqrt{x_1 x_2}$, by

$$H = \frac{G^2}{A}.$$

So

$$G = \sqrt{AH}$$

meaning the two numbers' geometric mean equals the geometric mean of their arithmetic and harmonic means. As noted above this relationship between the three Pythagorean means is not limited to n equals 1 or 2; there is a relationship for all n. However, for n = 1 all means are equal and for $n = 2$ we have the above relationship between the means. For arbitrary $n \geq 2$ we may generalize this formula, as noted above, by interpreting the third equation for the harmonic mean differently. The generalized relationship was already explained above. If one carefully observes the third equation one will notice it also works for $n = 1$. That is, it predicts the equivalence between the harmonic and geometric means but it falls short by not predicting the equivalence between the harmonic and arithmetic means.

The general formula, which can be derived from the third formula for the harmonic mean by the reinterpretation as explained in relationship with other means, is

$$H(x_1, \ldots, x_n) = \frac{(G(x_1, \ldots, x_n))^n}{A(x_2 x_3 \cdots x_n, x_1 x_3 \cdots x_n, \ldots, x_1 x_2 \cdots x_{n-1})}$$

$$= \frac{(G(x_1, \ldots, x_n))^n}{A\left(\frac{\prod_{i=1}^{n} x_i}{x_1}, \frac{\prod_{i=1}^{n} x_i}{x_2}, \ldots, \frac{\prod_{i=1}^{n} x_i}{x_n}\right)}.$$

Notice that for n = 2 we have

$$H(x_1, x_2) = \frac{(G(x_1, x_2))^2}{A(x_2, x_1)} = \frac{(G(x_2, x_1))^2}{A(x_2, x_1)}$$

where we used the fact that the arithmetic mean evaluates to the same number independent of the order of the terms. This equation can be reduced to the original equation if we reinterpret this result in terms of the operators themselves. If we do this we get the symbolic equation

$$H = \frac{G^2}{A}$$

because each function was evaluated at

$$(x_1, x_2).$$

Relationship with Other Means

If a set of non-identical numbers is subjected to a mean-preserving spread — that is, two or more elements of the set are "spread apart" from each other while leaving the arithmetic mean unchanged — then the harmonic mean always decreases.

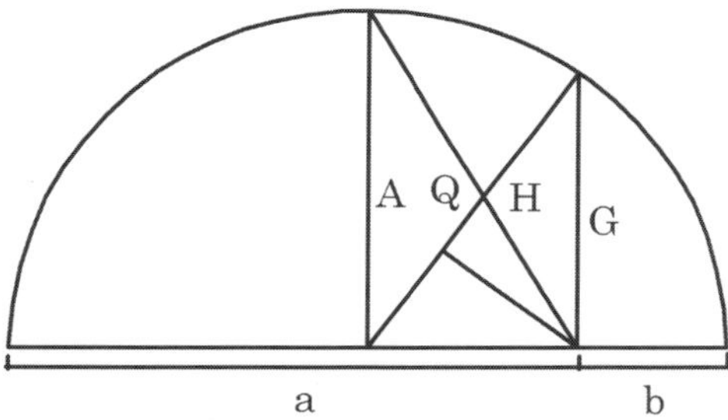

Figufre: *A geometric construction of the three Pythagorean means of two numbers, a and b. Harmonic mean is denoted by H in purple colour. The Q denotes a fourth mean, the quadratic mean.*

Let r be a non zero real number and let the rth power mean (M^r) of a series of real variables (a*1*, a*2*, a*3*, ...) be defined as

$$M^r(a_1, a_2, a_3, \ ....) = \left(\frac{1}{n}\sum(a_i)^r\right)^{\frac{1}{r}}.$$

For r = -1, 1 and 2 we have the harmonic, the arithmetic and the quadratic means respectively. Define r = 0, -– and +– to be the geometric mean, the minimum of the variates and the maximum of the variates respectively. Then for any two real numbers s and t such that s < t we have

$$M^s(a_1, a_2, a_3, ...) \leq M^t(a_1, a_2, a_3, ...).$$

with equality only if all the a*i* are equal.

Let R be the quadratic mean (or root mean square). Then

$$\frac{2R + H}{3} \leq A.$$

Inequalities

For a set of real variables lying within the interval [m, M] it has been shown that

$$A - H \geq \frac{s^2}{2M}$$

where A is the arithmetic mean, H is the harmonic mean, M is the maximum of the interval and s^2 is the variance of the set.

Several other inequalities are also known:

$$\frac{m(A-m)(A-H)}{H-m} \leq s^2 \leq \frac{M(A-H)(M-A)}{M-H}$$

$$\frac{(M-s)^2}{M(M-2s)} \leq \frac{A}{H} \leq \frac{(m+s)^2}{m(m+2s)}$$

$$\frac{(M-m)s^2}{M(M-m)-s^2} \leq A-H \leq \frac{(M-m)s^2}{m(M-m)+s^2}$$

Examples

Geometry

In any triangle, the radius of the incircle is one-third the harmonic mean of the altitudes. For any point P on the minor arc BC of the circumcircle of an equilateral triangle ABC, with distances q and t from B and C respectively, and with the intersection of PA and BC being at a distance y from point P, we have that y is half the harmonic mean of q and t.

In a right triangle with legs a and b and altitude h from the hypotenuse to the right angle, h^2 is half the harmonic mean of a^2 and b^2.

Let t and s (t > s) be the sides of the two inscribed squares in a right triangle with hypotenuse c. Then s^2 equals half the harmonic mean of c^2 and t^2.

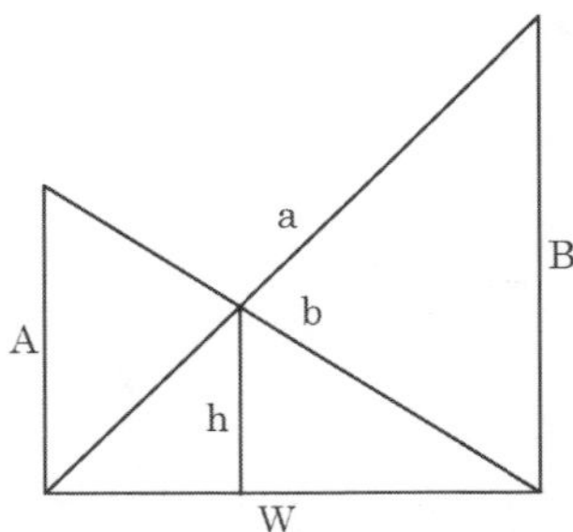

Figure: *Crossed ladders. h is half the harmonic mean of A and B*

Let a trapezoid have vertices A, B, C, and D in sequence and have parallel sides AB and CD. Let E be the intersection of the diagonals, and let F be on side DA and G be on side BC such that FEG is parallel to AB and CD. Then FG is the harmonic mean of AB and DC. (This is provable using similar triangles.)

In the crossed ladders problem, two ladders lie oppositely across an alley, each with feet at the base of one sidewall, with one leaning against a wall at height A and the other leaning against the opposite wall at height B, as shown. The ladders cross at a height of h above the alley floor. Then h is half the harmonic mean of A and B. This result still holds if the walls are slanted but still parallel and the "heights" A, B, and h are measured as distances from the floor along lines parallel to the walls. In an ellipse, the semi-latus rectum (the distance from a focus to the ellipse along a line parallel to the minor axis) is the harmonic mean of the maximum and minimum distances of the ellipse from a focus.

Trigonometry

In the case of the double-angle tangent identity, if the tangent of an angle A is given as a / b then the tangent of 2A is the product of (1) the harmonic mean of the numerator and denominator of tan A; and (2) the reciprocal of the denominator less the numerator of tan A.

In symbols if a and b are real numbers and

$\tan A = \frac{a}{b}$ the double angle formula for the tangent can be written as

$$\tan 2A = H(a,b) \cdot \frac{1}{b-a} = \frac{2ab}{a+b} \cdot \frac{1}{b-a}$$

where H(a, b) is the harmonic mean of a and b.

Example

Let $\tan A = \frac{3}{7}$

The harmonic mean of 3 and 7 is $H(3,7) = \frac{42}{10} = 4.2$

The most familiar form of the double angle formula is

$$\tan 2A = \frac{2 \cdot \frac{3}{7}}{1 - (\frac{3}{7})^2} = \frac{21}{20};$$

The double angle formula can also be written as

$$\frac{2\cdot3\cdot7}{3+7}\cdot\frac{1}{7-3}=\frac{42}{10}\cdot\frac{1}{4}=\frac{21}{20}=1.05$$

Algebra

The harmonic mean also features in elementary algebra when considering problems of working in parallel.

Example

If a gas powered pump can drain a pool in 4 hours and a battery powered pump can drain the same pool in 6 hours, then it will take both pumps $(6\cdot4)/(6+4)=\frac{1}{2}H(4,6)=2.4$ hours to drain the pool working together.

Physics

In certain situations, especially many situations involving rates and ratios, the harmonic mean provides the truest average. For instance, if a vehicle travels a certain distance at a speed x (e.g. 60 kilometres per hour) and then the same distance again at a speed y (e.g. 40 kilometres per hour), then its average speed is the harmonic mean of x and y (48 kilometres per hour), and its total travel time is the same as if it had traveled the whole distance at that average speed. However, if the vehicle travels for a certain amount of time at a speed x and then the same amount of time at a speed y, then its average speed is the arithmetic mean of x and y, which in the above example is 50 kilometres per hour.

The same principle applies to more than two segments: given a series of sub-trips at different speeds, if each sub-trip covers the same distance, then the average speed is the harmonic mean of all the sub-trip speeds, and if each sub-trip takes the same amount of time, then the average speed is the arithmetic mean of all the sub-trip speeds. (If neither is the case, then a weighted harmonic mean or weighted arithmetic mean is needed.)

Similarly, if one connects two electrical resistors in parallel, one having resistance x (e.g. 60Ω) and one having resistance y (e.g. 40Ω), then the effect is the same as if one had used two resistors with the same resistance, both equal to the harmonic mean of x and y (48Ω): the equivalent resistance in either case is 24Ω (one-half of the harmonic mean).

However, if one connects the resistors in series, then the average resistance is the arithmetic mean of x and y (with total resistance equal to the sum of x and y). And, as with previous example, the same principle applies when more than two resistors are connected, provided that all are in parallel or all are in series. The weighted harmonic mean is the correct approach to determine the average specific gravity of a mixture when the composition by weight is known. Note however that this is only correct for ideal solutions.

Other Sciences

In computer science, specifically information retrieval and machine learning, the harmonic mean of the precision and the recall is often used as an aggregated performance score for the evaluation of algorithms and systems: the F-score (or F-measure). In hydrology the harmonic mean is used to average hydraulic conductivity values for flow that is perpendicular to layers (e.g. geologic or soil) while flow parallel to layers uses the arithmetic mean. This apparent difference in averaging is explained by the fact that hydrology uses conductivity, which is the inverse of resistivity.

In population genetics the harmonic mean is used when calculating the effects of fluctuations in generation size on the effective breeding population. This is to take into account the fact that a very small generation is effectively like a bottleneck and means that a very small number of individuals are contributing disproportionately to the gene pool which can result in higher levels of inbreeding.

When considering fuel economy in automobiles two measures are commonly used – miles per gallon (mpg), and litres per 100 km.

As the dimensions of these quantities are the inverse of each other (one is distance per volume, the other volume per distance) when taking the mean value of the fuel-economy of a range of cars one measure will produce the harmonic mean of the other – i.e. converting the mean value of fuel economy expressed in litres per 100 km to miles per gallon will produce the harmonic mean of the fuel economy expressed in miles-per-gallon.

Finance

The harmonic mean is the preferable method for averaging multiples, such as the price/earning ratio, in which price is in the numerator. If these ratios are averaged using an arithmetic mean (a common error), high data points are given greater weights than low data points. The harmonic mean, on the other hand, gives equal weight to each data point.

Statistics

For a random sample the harmonic mean is calculated as above. Both the mean and the variance may be infinite (if it includes at least one term of the form 1/0).

Theoretical Value

The variance of the harmonic mean is

$$\mathrm{Var}\left(\frac{1}{x}\right) = \frac{m\left[\mathrm{E}(1/x-1)\right]}{nm^2}$$

where m is the arithmetic mean of the reciprocals, x are the variates, n is the population size and E is the expectation operator. Asymptotically E(1 / x) is distributed normally.

The mean of the sample m is also distributed normally with variance s^2.

$$s^2 = \frac{m[\mathrm{E}(1/x-1)]}{m^2 n}$$

Delta Method

Assuming that the variance is not infinite and that the central limit theorem applies to the sample then using the delta method, the variance is

$$\mathrm{Var}(H) = \frac{1}{n}\frac{s^2}{m^4}$$

where H is the harmonic mean, m is the arithmetic mean of the reciprocals

$$m = \frac{1}{n}\sum\frac{1}{x}.$$

s^2 is the variance of the reciprocals of the data

$$s^2 = \mathrm{Var}\left(\frac{1}{x}\right)$$

and n is the number of data points in the sample.

Jackknife Method

A jackknife method of estimating the variance is possible if the mean is known. This method is the usual 'delete 1' rather than the 'delete m' version. This method first requires the computation of the mean of the sample (m)

$$m = \frac{n}{\sum \frac{1}{x}}$$

where x are the sample values.

A series of value wi is then computed where

$$w_i = \frac{n-1}{\sum_{j \neq i} \frac{1}{x}}.$$

The mean (h) of the wi is then taken:

$$h = \frac{1}{n} \sum w_i$$

The variance of the mean is

$$\frac{n-1}{n} \sum (m-h)^2.$$

Significance testing and confidence intervals for the mean can then be estimated with the t test.

Size Biased Sampling

Assume a random variate has a distribution $f(x)$. Assume also that the likelihood of a variate being chosen is proportional to its value. This is known as length based or size biased sampling.

Let μ be the mean of the population. Then the probability density function $f^*(x)$ of the size biased population is

$$f^*(x) = \frac{xf(x)}{\mu}$$

The expectation of this length biased distribution $E^*(x)$ is

$$E^*(x) = \mu \left[1 + \frac{\sigma^2}{\mu^2} \right]$$

where σ^2 is the variance.

The expectation of the harmonic mean is the same as the non length biased version E(x)

$$E^*\left(\frac{1}{x}\right) = E\left(\frac{1}{x}\right)$$

The problem of length biased sampling arises in a number of areas including textile manufacture pedigree analysis and survival analysis. Akman et al have developed a test for the detection of length based bias in samples.

Shifted Variables

If X is a positive random variable and q > 0 then for all ε > 0

$$\mathrm{Var}\left[\frac{1}{(X+\epsilon)^q}\right] < \mathrm{Var}\left(\frac{1}{X^q}\right).$$

Moments

Assuming that X and E(X) are > 0 then

$$\mathrm{E}\left[\frac{1}{X}\right] \geq \frac{1}{\mathrm{E}(X)}$$

This follows from Jensen's inequality.

Gurland has shown that for a distribution that takes only positive values, for any n > 0

$$\mathrm{E}(X^{-1}) \geq \frac{\mathrm{E}(X^{n-1})}{\mathrm{E}(X^n)}.$$

Under some conditions

$$\mathrm{E}(a+X)^{-n} \sim \mathrm{E}(a+X^{-n})$$

where ~ means approximately.

Lognormal Distribution

The harmonic mean (H) of a lognormal distribution is

$$H = \exp\left(\mu - \frac{1}{2}\sigma^2\right)$$

where μ is the arithmetic mean and σ^2 is the variance of the distribution.

The harmonic and arithmetic means are related

$$\frac{\mu}{H} = 1 + C_v$$

where Cv is the coefficient of variation.

The geometric (G), arithmetic and harmonic means are related

$$H\mu = G^2$$

Sampling Properties

Assuming that the variates (x) are drawn from a lognormal distribution there are several possible estimators for H:

$$H_1 = \frac{n}{\sum(\frac{1}{x})}$$

$$H_2 = \frac{[\exp(\frac{1}{n}\sum \log_e(x))]^2}{\frac{1}{n}\sum(x)}$$

$$H_3 = \exp\left(m - \frac{1}{2}s^2\right)$$

where $$m = \frac{1}{n}\sum \log_e(x)$$

$$s^2 = \frac{1}{n}\sum(\log_e(x) - m)^2$$

Of these H*3* is probably the best estimator for samples of 25 or more.

Bias and Variance Estimators

A first order approximation to the bias and variance of H*1* are

$$\text{bias}[H_1] = \frac{HC_v}{n}$$

$$\text{Var}[H_1] = \frac{H^2C_v}{n}$$

where C*v* is the coefficient of variation.

Similarly a first order approximation to the bias and variance of H_3 are

$$\frac{H\log_e(1+C_v)}{2n}\left[1+\frac{1+C_v^2}{2}\right]$$

$$\frac{H\log_e(1+C_v)}{n}\left[1+\frac{1+C_v^2}{4}\right]$$

It has been found in numerical experiments that H*3* is generally a superior estimator of the harmonic mean than H*1*. H*2* produces estimates that are largely similar to H*1*.

Pareto Distribution

The harmonic mean of a type 1 Pareto distribution is

$$H = k\left(1 + \frac{1}{\alpha}\right)$$

where k is the scale parameter and α is the shape parameter.

Compound Annual Growth Rate

Compounded Annual Growth rate (CAGR) is a business and investing specific term for the smoothed annualized gain of an investment over a given time period. CAGR is not an accounting term, but remains widely used, particularly in growth industries or to compare the growth rates of two investments because CAGR dampens the effect of volatility of periodic returns that can render arithmetic means irrelevant. CAGR is often used to describe the growth over a period of time of some element of the business, for example revenue, units delivered, registered users, etc.

Formula

$$\text{CAGR}(t_0, t_n) = \left(V(t_n) / V(t_0)\right)^{\frac{1}{t_n - t_0}} - 1$$

- $V(t_0)$: start value, $V(t_n)$: finish value, $t_n - t_0$: number of years.
- Actual or normalized values may be used for calculation as long as they retain the same mathematical proportion.
- The CAGR can also be calculated as the geometric mean of 1 plus each year's return minus 1. For example, +3% becomes 1.03, and -2% becomes 0.98.

Example

Suppose the revenues of a company for four years, V(t) in above formula, have been:

Year	**2004**	**2005**	**2006**	**2007**
Revenues	100	115	150	200

$$t_n - t_0 \, 2007 - 2004 = 3$$

Then the CAGR of revenues over the three-year period from the end of 2004 to the end of 2007 is:

$$\text{CAGR}(0,3) = \left(\frac{200}{100}\right)^{\frac{1}{3}} - 1 = 0.2599 = 25.99\%$$

Verification: If you multiply the initial value by (1 + CAGR) three times (because we calculated for 3 years) you will get exactly the final value again. This is:

$$V(t_n) = V(t_0) \times (1 + \text{CAGR})^n$$

For n = 3:

$$= V(t_0) \times (1 + \text{CAGR}) \times (1 + \text{CAGR}) \times (1 + \text{CAGR})$$

$$= 100 \times 1.2599 \times 1.2599 \times 1.2599 = 200$$

For comparison: the Arithmetic Mean Return (AMR) would be the sum of annual revenue changes (compared with the previous year) divided by number of years, or:

$$\text{AMR} = \bar{x} = \frac{1}{n}\sum_{i=1}^{n} x_i = \frac{1}{n}(x_1 + \cdots + x_n)$$

$$= \frac{15\% + 30.4\% + 33.3\%}{3} = 26.26\%.$$

In contrast to CAGR, you cannot obtain $V(t_n)$ by multiplying the initial value, $V(t_0)$, three times by (1 + AMR) (unless all annual growth rates are the same). The Arithmetic Return (AR) or simple return would be the ending value minus beginning value divided by the beginning value:

$$\text{AR} = \frac{V_f - V_i}{V_i} = \frac{200 - 100}{100} = 100\%.$$

Applications

These are some of the common CAGR applications:

- Calculating and communicating the average returns of investment funds
- Demonstrating and comparing the performance of investment advisors
- Comparing the historical returns of stocks with bonds or with a savings account
- Forecasting future values based on the CAGR of a data series (you find future values by multiplying the last datum of the series by (1 + CAGR) as many times as years required). As every forecasting method, this method has a calculation error associated.
- Analysing and communicating the behaviour, over a series of years, of different business measures such as sales, market share, costs, customer satisfaction, and performance.

Inequality of Arithmetic and Geometric Means

In mathematics, the inequality of arithmetic and geometric means, or more briefly the AM–GM inequality, states that the arithmetic mean of a list of non-negative real numbers is greater than or equal to the geometric mean of the same list; and further, that the two means are equal if and only if every number in the list is the same.

Background

The arithmetic mean, or less precisely the average, of a list of n numbers $x_1, x_2, \ldots, x_n$ is the sum of the numbers divided by n:

$$\frac{x_1 + x_2 + \cdots + x_n}{n}.$$

The geometric mean is similar, except that it is only defined for a list of nonnegative real numbers, and uses multiplication and a root in place of addition and division:

$$\sqrt[n]{x_1 \cdot x_2 \cdots x_n}.$$

If $x_1, x_2, \ldots, x_n > 0$, this is equal to the exponential of the arithmetic mean of the natural logarithms of the numbers:

$$\exp\left(\frac{\ln x_1 + \ln x_2 + \cdots + \ln x_n}{n}\right).$$

The Inequality

Restating the inequality using mathematical notation, we have that for any list of n nonnegative real numbers $x_1, x_2, \ldots, x_n$,

$$\frac{x_1 + x_2 + \cdots + x_n}{n} \geq \sqrt[n]{x_1 \cdot x_2 \cdots x_n},$$

and that equality holds if and only if $x_1 = x_2 = \cdots = x_n$.

Geometric Interpretation

In two dimensions, $2x_1 + 2x_2$ is the perimeter of a rectangle with sides of length x_1 and x_2. Similarly, $4-x_1x_2$ is the perimeter of a square with the same area. Thus for $n = 2$ the AM–GM inequality states that only the square has the smallest perimeter amongst all rectangles of equal area.

The full inequality is an extension of this idea to n dimensions. Every vertex of an n-dimensional box is connected to n edges. If these edges' lengths are $x_1, x_2, \ldots, x_n$, then $x_1 + x_2 + \cdots + x_n$ is the total length of edges incident to the vertex. There are 2 vertices, so we multiply this by 2^n; since each edge, however, meets two vertices, every edge is counted twice.

Therefore we divide by 2 and conclude that there are $2^{n-1}n$ edges. There are equally many edges of each length and n lengths; hence there are 2^{n-1} edges of each length and the total edge-length is $2^{n-1}(x_1 + x_2 + \cdots + x_n)$. On the other hand,

$$2^{n-1}n\sqrt[n]{x_1 x_2 \cdots x_n}$$

is the total length of edges connected to a vertex on an n-dimensional cube of equal volume. Since the inequality says

$$\frac{x_1 + x_2 + \cdots + x_n}{n} \geq \sqrt[n]{x_1 x_2 \cdots x_n},$$

we get

$$2^{n-1}(x_1 + x_2 + \cdots + x_n) \geq 2^{n-1}n\sqrt[n]{x_1 x_2 \cdots x_n}$$

with equality if and only if $x_1 = x_2 = \cdots = x_n$.

Thus the AM–GM inequality states that only the n-cube has the smallest sum of lengths of edges connected to each vertex amongst all n-dimensional boxes with the same volume.

Proofs of the AM–GM inequality

There are several ways to prove the AM–GM inequality; for example, it can be inferred from Jensen's inequality, using the concave function ln(x). It can also be proven using the rearrangement inequality. Considering length and required prerequisites, the elementary proof by induction given below is probably the best recommendation for first reading.

Idea of the First two Proofs

We have to show that

$$\frac{x_1 + x_2 + \cdots + x_n}{n} \geq \sqrt[n]{x_1 x_2 \cdots x_n}$$

with equality only when all numbers are equal. If $x_i \neq x_j$, then replacing both x_i and x_j by $(x_i + x_j)/2$ will leave the arithmetic mean on the left-hand side unchanged, but will increase the geometric mean on the right-hand side because

$$\left(\frac{x_i + x_j}{2}\right)^2 - x_i x_j = \left(\frac{x_i - x_j}{2}\right)^2 > 0.$$

Thus right-hand side will be largest — so the idea — when all x_is are equal to the arithmetic mean

$$\alpha = \frac{x_1 + x_2 + \ldots + x_n}{n},$$

thus as this is then the largest value of right-hand side of the expression, we have

$$\frac{x_1 + x_2 + \ldots + x_n}{n} = \alpha = \sqrt[n]{\alpha\alpha\ldots\alpha} \geq \sqrt[n]{x_1 x_2 \ldots x_n}.$$

This is a valid proof for the case $n = 2$, put the procedure of taking iteratively pairwise averages may fail to produce n equal numbers in the case $n \geq 3$. An example of this case is $x_1 = x_2 \neq x_3$: Averaging two different numbers produces two equal numbers, but the third one is still different. Therefore, we never actually get an inequality involving the geometric mean of three equal numbers. Hence, an additional trick or a modified argument is necessary to turn the above idea into a valid proof for the case $n \geq 3$.

Proof by Cauchy Using Forward-backward-induction

The following proof by cases relies directly on well-known rules of arithmetic but employs the rarely used technique of forward-backward-induction. It is essentially from Augustin Louis Cauchy and can be found in his Cours d'analyse.

The Case Where all the Terms are Equal

If all the terms are equal:

$$x_1 = x_2 = \cdots = x_n,$$

then their sum is nx_1, so their arithmetic mean is x_1; and their product is x_1^n, so their geometric mean is x_1; therefore, the arithmetic mean and geometric mean are equal, as desired.

Proof Using Jensen's Inequality

Using the finite form of Jensen's inequality for the natural logarithm, we can prove the inequality between the weighted arithmetic mean and the weighted geometric mean stated above.

Since an x*k* with weight w*k* = 0 has no influence on the inequality, we may assume in the following that all weights are positive. If all x*k* are equal, then equality holds.

Therefore, it remains to prove strict inequality if they are not all equal, which we will assume in the following, too. If at least one x*k* is zero (but not all), then the weighted geometric mean is zero, while the weighted arithmetic mean is positive, hence strict inequality holds. Therefore, we may assume also that all x*k* are positive.

Since the natural logarithm is strictly concave, the finite form of Jensen's inequality and the functional equations of the natural logarithm imply

$$\ln\left(\frac{w_1x_1+\cdots+w_nx_n}{w}\right) > \frac{w_1}{w}\ln x_1+\cdots+\frac{w_n}{w}\ln x_n = \ln\sqrt[w]{x_1^{w_1}x_2^{w_2}\cdots x_n^{w_n}}.$$

Since the natural logarithm is strictly increasing,

$$\frac{w_1x_1+\cdots+w_nx_n}{w} > \sqrt[w]{x_1^{w_1}x_2^{w_2}\cdots x_n^{w_n}}.$$

5

Measures of Location and Dispersion

The median is one of a number of ways of summarising the typical values associated with members of a statistical population; thus, it is a possible location parameter. When the median is used as a location parameter in descriptive statistics, there are several choices for a measure of variability: the range, the interquartile range, the mean absolute deviation, and the median absolute deviation. Since the median is the same as the second quartile, its calculation is illustrated in the article on quartiles.

For practical purposes, different measures of location and dispersion are often compared on the basis of how well the corresponding population values can be estimated from a sample of data. The median, estimated using the sample median, has good properties in this regard. While it is not usually optimal if a given population distribution is assumed, its properties are always reasonably good.

For example, a comparison of the efficiency of candidate estimators shows that the sample mean is more statistically efficient than the sample median when data are uncontaminated by data from heavy-tailed distributions or from mixtures of distributions, but less efficient otherwise, and that the efficiency of the sample median is higher than that for a wide range of distributions.

Medians of Probability Distributions

For any probability distribution on the real line R with cumulative distribution function F, regardless of whether it is any kind of continuous probability distribution, in particular an absolutely continuous distribution (and therefore has a probability density function), or a discrete probability distribution, a median is by definition any real number m that satisfies the inequalities

$$P(X \le m) \ge \frac{1}{2} \text{ and } P(X \ge m) \ge \frac{1}{2}$$

or, equivalently, the inequalities

$$\int_{-\infty}^{m} dF(x) \ge \frac{1}{2} \text{ and } \int_{m}^{\infty} dF(x) \ge \frac{1}{2}$$

in which a Lebesgue–Stieltjes integral is used. For an absolutely continuous probability distribution with probability density function f, the median satisfies

$$P(X \le m) = P(X \ge m) = \int_{-\infty}^{m} f(x)dx = \frac{1}{2}.$$

Any probability distribution on R has at least one median, but there may be more than one median. Where exactly one median exists, statisticians speak of "the median" correctly; even when the median is not unique, some statisticians speak of "the median" informally.

Medians of Particular Distributions

The medians of certain types of distributions can be easily calculated from their parameters:

- The median of a normal distribution with mean μ and variance σ^2 is μ. In fact, for a normal distribution, mean = median = mode.
- The median of a uniform distribution in the interval $[a, b]$ is $(a + b) / 2$, which is also the mean.
- The median of a Cauchy distribution with location parameter x*0* and scale parameter *y* is *x0*, the location parameter.
- The median of an exponential distribution with rate parameter λ is the natural logarithm of 2 divided by the rate parameter: $\lambda^{-1}\ln 2$.
- The median of a Weibull distribution with shape parameter k and scale parameter λ is $\lambda(\ln 2)^{1/k}$.

Medians in Descriptive Statistics

The median is used primarily for skewed distributions, which it summarizes differently than the arithmetic mean. Consider the multiset { 1, 2, 2, 2, 3, 14 }. The median is 2 in this case, as is the mode, and it might be seen as a better indication of central tendency than the arithmetic mean of 4.

Calculation of medians is a popular technique in summary statistics and summarizing statistical data, since it is simple to understand and easy to calculate, while also giving a measure that is more robust in the presence of outlier values than is the mean.

Medians for Populations

An Optimality Property

The mean absolute error of a real variable c with respect to the random variable X is

$$E(|X-c|)$$

Provided that the probability distribution of X is such that the above expectation exists, then m is a median of X if and only if m is a minimizer of the mean absolute error with respect to X. In particular, m is a sample median if and only if m minimizes the arithmetic mean of the absolute deviations.

Unimodal Distributions

It can be shown for a unimodal distribution that the mean and the median lie within $(3/5)^{1/2}$ times the standard deviation of each other. In symbols

$$\frac{|\tilde{x}-\bar{x}|}{\sigma} \leq (3/5)^{1/2}$$

where | | is the absolute value.

A similar relation holds between the mode and the median. In this case the mode and the median lie within $3^{1/2}$ times the standard deviation of each other.

$$\frac{|\tilde{x}-\text{mode}|}{\sigma} \leq 3^{1/2}$$

An Inequality Relating Means and Medians

If the distribution has finite variance, then the distance between the median and the mean is bounded by one standard deviation.

This bound was proved by Mallows, who used Jensen's inequality twice, as follows.

We have

$$|\mu - m| = |\mathrm{E}(X - m)| \le \mathrm{E}\left(|X - m|\right)$$
$$\le \mathrm{E}\left(|X - \mu|\right)$$
$$\le \sqrt{\mathrm{E}((X - \mu)^2)} = \sigma.$$

The first and third inequalities come from Jensen's inequality applied to the absolute-value function and the square function, which are each convex. The second inequality comes from the fact that a median minimizes the absolute deviation function

$$a \mapsto \mathrm{E}(|X - a|).$$

This proof can easily be generalized to obtain a multivariate version of the inequality, as follows:

$$\|\mu - m\| = \|\mathrm{E}(X - m)\| \le \mathrm{E}\,\| X - m \|$$
$$\le \mathrm{E}(\|X - \mu\|)$$
$$\le \sqrt{\mathrm{E}(\| X - \mu \|^2)} = \sqrt{\mathrm{trace}(\mathrm{var}(X))}$$

where m is a spatial median, that is, a minimizer of the function $a \mapsto \mathrm{E}(\|X - a\|)$. The spatial median is unique when the data-set's dimension is two or more. An alternative proof uses the one-sided Chebyshev inequality; it appears in an inequality on location and scale parameters.

Jensen's Inequality for Medians

Jensen's inequality states that for any random variable x with a ûnite expectation E(X) and for any convex function f then

$$f(E(x)) \le E(f(x))$$

It has been shown that if x is a real variable with a unique median m and f is a C function then

$$f(m) \le \mathrm{Median}(f(x))$$

A C function is a real valued function, defined on the set of real numbers R, with the property that for any real t

$$f^{-1}((-\infty, t]) = \{x \in R \mid f(x) \le t\}$$

is a closed interval, a singleton or an empty set.

Multivariate Median

Previously, this article discussed the concept of a univariate median for a one-dimensional object (population, sample). When the dimension is two or higher, there are multiple concepts that extend the definition of the univariate median; each such multivariate median agrees with the univariate median when the dimension is exactly one. In higher dimensions, however, there are several multivariate medians.

Marginal Median

The marginal median is defined for vectors defined with respect to a fixed set of coordinates. A marginal median is defined to be the vector whose components are univariate medians. The marginal median is easy to compute, and its properties were studied by Puri and Sen.

Spatial Median (L1 median)

In a normed vector space of dimension two or greater, the "spatial median" minimizes the expected distance

$$a \mapsto \mathrm{E}(\|X - a\|),$$

where X and a are vectors, if this expectation has a finite minimum; another definition is better suited for general probability-distributions. The spatial median is unique when the data-set's dimension is two or more. It is a robust and highly efficient estimator of the population spatial-median (also called the "L1 median").

Other Multivariate Medians

An alternative to the spatial median is defined in a similar way, but based on a different loss function, and is called the Geometric median. The centerpoint is another generalization to higher dimensions that does not relate to a particular metric.

Other Median-related Concepts

Pseudo-median

For univariate distributions that are symmetric about one median, the Hodges–Lehmann estimator is a robust and highly efficient estimator of the population median; for non-symmetric distributions, the Hodges–Lehmann estimator is a robust and highly efficient estimator of the population pseudo-median, which is the median of a symmetrized distribution and which is close to the population median. The Hodges–Lehmann estimator has been generalized to multivariate distributions.

Variants of Regression

The Theil–Sen estimator is a method for robust linear regression based on finding medians of slopes.

Median Gilter

In the context of image processing of monochrome raster images there is a type of noise, known as the salt and pepper noise, when each pixel independently becomes black (with some small probability) or white (with some small probability), and is unchanged otherwise (with the probability close to 1). An image constructed of median values of neighbourhoods (like 3×3 square) can effectively reduce noise in this case.

Cluster Analysis

In cluster analysis, the k-medians clustering algorithm provides a way of defining clusters, in which the criterion of maximising the distance between cluster-means that is used in k-means clustering, is replaced by maximising the distance between cluster-medians.

Median-unbiased Estimators

Any mean-unbiased estimator minimizes the risk (expected loss) with respect to the squared-error loss function, as observed by Gauss. A median-unbiased estimator minimizes the risk with respect to the absolute-deviation loss function, as observed by Laplace. Other loss functions are used in statistical theory, particularly in robust statistics.

The theory of median-unbiased estimators was revived by George W. Brown in 1947:

An estimate of a one-dimensional parameter θ will be said to be median-unbiased if, for fixed θ, the median of the distribution of the estimate is at the value θ; i.e., the estimate underestimates just as often as it overestimates. This requirement seems for most purposes to accomplish as much as the mean-unbiased requirement and has the additional property that it is invariant under one-to-one transformation.

Further properties of median-unbiased estimators have been reported. In particular, median-unbiased estimators exist in cases where mean-unbiased and maximum-likelihood estimators do not exist. Median-unbiased estimators are invariant under one-to-one transformations.

History

The idea of the median originated in Edward Wright's book on navigation (Certaine Errors in Navigation) in 1599 in a section concerning the determination of location with a compass. Wright felt that this value was the most likely to be the correct value in a series of observations. In 1757, Roger Joseph Boscovich developed a regression method based on the L1 norm and therefore implicitly on the median.

The distribution of both the sample mean and the sample median were determined by Laplace in the early 1800s.

Antoine Augustin Cournot in 1843 was the first to use the term median (valeur médiane) for the value that divides a probability distribution into two equal halves. Gustav Theodor Fechner used the median (Centralwerth) in sociological and psychological phenomena. It had earlier been used only in astronomy and related fields. Gustav Fechner popularized the median into the formal analysis of data, although it had been used previously by Laplace.

Francis Galton used the English term median in 1881, having earlier used the terms middle-most value in 1869 and the medium in 1880.

Mode (Statistics)

The mode is the value that appears most often in a set of data. Like the statistical mean and median, the mode is a way of expressing, in a single number, important information about a random variable or a population. The numerical value of the mode is the same as that of the mean and median in a normal distribution, and it may be very different in highly skewed distributions.

The mode is not necessarily unique, since the same maximum frequency may be attained at different values. The most extreme case occurs in uniform distributions, where all values occur equally frequently.

The mode of a discrete probability distribution is the value x at which its probability mass function takes its maximum value. In other words, it is the value that is most likely to be sampled.

The mode of a continuous probability distribution is the value x at which its probability density function has its maximum value, so, informally speaking, the mode is at the peak.

As noted above, the mode is not necessarily unique, since the probability mass function or probability density function may take the same maximum value at several points *x1, x2*, etc.

The above definition tells us that only global maxima are modes. Slightly confusingly, when a probability density function has multiple local maxima it is common to refer to all of the local maxima as modes of the distribution. Such a continuous distribution is called multimodal (as opposed to unimodal).

In symmetric unimodal distributions, such as the normal (or Gaussian) distribution (the distribution whose density function, when graphed, gives the famous "bell curve"), the mean (if defined), median and mode all coincide. For samples, if it is known that they are drawn from a symmetric distribution, the sample mean can be used as an estimate of the population mode.

Mode of a Sample

The mode of a sample is the element that occurs most often in the collection. For example, the mode of the sample [1, 3, 6, 6, 6, 6, 7, 7, 12, 12, 17] is 6. Given the list of data [1, 1, 2, 4, 4] the mode is not unique - the dataset may be said to be bimodal, while a set with more than two modes may be described as multimodal.

For a sample from a continuous distribution, such as [0.935..., 1.211..., 2.430..., 3.668..., 3.874...], the concept is unusable in its raw form, since no two values will be exactly the same, so each value will occur precisely once. In order to estimate the mode, the usual practice is to discretize the data by assigning frequency values to intervals of equal distance, as for making a histogram, effectively replacing the values by the midpoints of the intervals they are assigned to. The mode is then the value where the histogram reaches its peak. For small or middle-sized samples the outcome of this procedure is sensitive to the choice of interval width if chosen too narrow or too wide; typically one should have a sizable fraction of the data concentrated in a relatively small number of intervals (5 to 10), while the fraction of the data falling outside these intervals is also sizable. An alternate approach is kernel density estimation, which essentially blurs point samples to produce a continuous estimate of the probability density function which can provide an estimate of the mode.

The following MATLAB (or Octave) code example computes the mode of a sample:

```
X = sort(x);
indices = find(diff([X; realmax]) > 0); % indices where repeated
          values change
[modeL,i] =max (diff([0; indices]));   % longest persistence length
          of repeated values
mode = X(indices(i));
```

The algorithm requires as a first step to sort the sample in ascending order. It then computes the discrete derivative of the sorted list, and finds the indices where this derivative is positive. Next it computes the discrete derivative of this set of indices, locating the maximum of this derivative of indices, and finally evaluates the sorted sample at the point where that maximum occurs, which corresponds to the last member of the stretch of repeated values.

Standard Deviation

In statistics and probability theory, standard deviation (represented by the symbol sigma, σ) shows how much variation or "dispersion" exists from the average (mean, or expected value). A low standard deviation indicates that the data points tend to be very close to the mean; high standard deviation indicates that the data points are spread out over a large range of values.

The standard deviation of a random variable, statistical population, data set, or probability distribution is the square root of its variance. It is algebraically simpler though practically less robust than the average absolute deviation. A useful property of standard deviation is that, unlike variance, it is expressed in the same units as the data.

In addition to expressing the variability of a population, standard deviation is commonly used to measure confidence in statistical conclusions. For example, the margin of error in polling data is determined by calculating the expected standard deviation in the results if the same poll were to be conducted multiple times.

The reported margin of error is typically about twice the standard deviation -— the radius of a 95 percent confidence interval. In science, researchers commonly report the standard deviation of experimental data, and only effects that fall far outside the range of standard deviation are considered statistically significant – normal random error or variation in the measurements is in this way distinguished from causal variation. Standard deviation is also important in finance, where the standard deviation on the rate of return on an investment is a measure of the volatility of the investment.

When only a sample of data from a population is available, the population standard deviation can be estimated by a modified quantity called the sample standard deviation, explained below.

Basic Examples

Consider a population consisting of the following eight values:

2, 4, 4, 4, 5, 5, 7, 9.

These eight data points have the mean (average) of 5:

$$\frac{2+4+4+4+5+5+7+9}{8} = 5.$$

To calculate the population standard deviation, first compute the difference of each data point from the mean, and square the result of each:

$$\begin{array}{ll}(2-5)^2 = (-3)^2 = 9 & (5-5)^2 = 0^2 = 0 \\ (4-5)^2 = (-1)^2 = 1 & (5-5)^2 = 0^2 = 0 \\ (4-5)^2 = (-1)^2 = 1 & (7-5)^2 = 2^2 = 4 \\ (4-5)^2 = (-1)^2 = 1 & (9-5)^2 = 4^2 = 16.\end{array}$$

Next, compute the average of these values, and take the square root:

$$\sqrt{\frac{(9+1+1+1+0+0+4+16)}{8}} = 2.$$

This quantity is the population standard deviation; it is equal to the square root of the variance. The formula is valid *only* if the eight values we began with form the *complete* population. If they instead were a random sample, drawn from some larger, "parent" population, then we should have divided by 7 (which is $n - 1$) instead of 8 (which is n) in the denominator of the last formula, and then the quantity thus obtained would have been called the sample standard deviation.

A slightly more complicated real life example, the average height for adult men in the United States is about 70–, with a standard deviation of around 3–. This means that most men (about 68%, assuming a normal distribution) have a height within 3– of the mean (67––73–) — one standard deviation — and almost all men (about 95%) have a height within 6– of the mean (64––76–) — two standard deviations. If the standard deviation were zero, then all men would be exactly 70– tall. If the standard deviation were 20–, then men would have much more variable heights, with a typical range of about 50––90–. Three standard deviations account for 99.7% of the sample population being studied, assuming the distribution is normal (bell-shaped).

Definition of Population Values

Let X be a random variable with mean value μ:

$$\mathrm{E}[X] = \mu.$$

Here the operator E denotes the average or expected value of X. Then the standard deviation of X is the quantity

$$\sigma = \sqrt{\operatorname{E}[(X-\mu)^2]} = \sqrt{\operatorname{E}[X^2] - (\operatorname{E}[X])^2}.$$

That is, the standard deviation σ (sigma) is the square root of the variance of X, i.e., it is the square root of the average value of $(X - \mu)^2$.

The standard deviation of a (univariate) probability distribution is the same as that of a random variable having that distribution. Not all random variables have a standard deviation, since these expected values need not exist. For example, the standard deviation of a random variable that follows a Cauchy distribution is undefined because its expected value μ is undefined.

Identities and Mathematical Properties

The standard deviation is invariant under changes in location, and scales directly with the scale of the random variable. Thus, for a constant c and random variables X and Y:

$$\operatorname{stdev}(c) = 0$$
$$\operatorname{stdev}(X + c) = \operatorname{stdev}(X),$$
$$\operatorname{stdev}(cX) = |c| \operatorname{stdev}(X).$$

The standard deviation of the sum of two random variables can be related to their individual standard deviations and the covariance between them:

$$\operatorname{stdev}(X+Y) = \sqrt{\operatorname{var}(X) + \operatorname{var}(Y) + 2\operatorname{cov}(X,Y)}.$$

where $\operatorname{var} = \operatorname{stdev}^2$ and cov stand for variance and covariance, respectively.

The calculation of the sum of squared deviations can be related to moments calculated directly from the data. The standard deviation of the sample can be computed as:

$$\operatorname{stdev}(X) = \sqrt{E[(X-E(X))^2]} = \sqrt{E[X^2] - (E[X])^2}.$$

The sample standard deviation can be computed as:

$$\operatorname{stdev}(X) = \sqrt{\frac{N}{N-1}}\sqrt{E[(X-E(X))^2]}.$$

For a finite population with equal probabilities at all points, we have

$$\sqrt{\frac{1}{N}\sum_{i=1}^{N}(x_i - \overline{x})^2} = \sqrt{\frac{1}{N}\left(\sum_{i=1}^{N} x_i^2\right) - \overline{x}^2} = \sqrt{\frac{1}{N}\sum_{i=1}^{N} x_i^2 - \left(\frac{1}{N}\sum_{i=1}^{N} x_i\right)^2}.$$

This means that the standard deviation is equal to the square root of (the average of the squares less the square of the average).

Interpretation and Application

A large standard deviation indicates that the data points are far from the mean and a small standard deviation indicates that they are clustered closely around the mean.

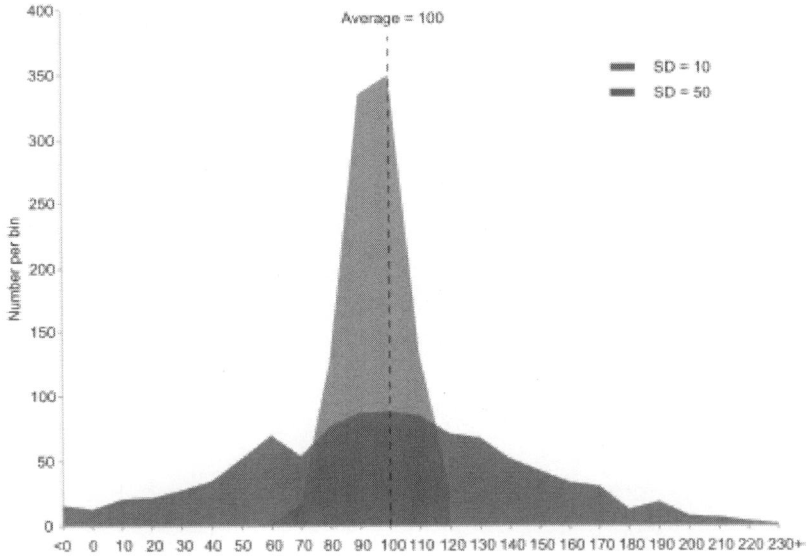

Figure: *Example of two sample populations with the same mean and different standard deviations. Red population has mean **100** and SD **10**; blue population has mean **100** and SD **50**.*

For example, each of the three populations {0, 0, 14, 14}, {0, 6, 8, 14} and {6, 6, 8, 8} has a mean of 7. Their standard deviations are 7, 5, and 1, respectively. The third population has a much smaller standard deviation than the other two because its values are all close to 7. It will have the same units as the data points themselves. If, for instance, the data set {0, 6, 8, 14} represents the ages of a population of four siblings in years, the standard deviation is 5 years. As another example, the population {1000, 1006, 1008, 1014} may represent the distances traveled by four athletes, measured in metres. It has a mean of 1007 metres, and a standard deviation of 5 metres.

Standard deviation may serve as a measure of uncertainty. In physical science, for example, the reported standard deviation of a group of repeated measurements gives the precision of those measurements.

When deciding whether measurements agree with a theoretical prediction, the standard deviation of those measurements is of crucial importance: if the mean of the measurements is too far away from the prediction (with the distance measured in standard deviations), then the theory being tested probably needs to be revised. This makes sense since they fall outside the range of values that could reasonably be expected to occur, if the prediction were correct and the standard deviation appropriately quantified.

While the standard deviation does measure how far typical values tend to be from the mean, other measures are available. An example is the mean absolute deviation, which might be considered a more direct measure of average distance, compared to the root mean square distance inherent in the standard deviation.

Application Examples

The practical value of understanding the standard deviation of a set of values is in appreciating how much variation there is from the "average" (mean).

Climate

As a simple example, consider the average daily maximum temperatures for two cities, one inland and one on the coast. It is helpful to understand that the range of daily maximum temperatures for cities near the coast is smaller than for cities inland.

Thus, while these two cities may each have the same average maximum temperature, the standard deviation of the daily maximum temperature for the coastal city will be less than that of the inland city as, on any particular day, the actual maximum temperature is more likely to be farther from the average maximum temperature for the inland city than for the coastal one.

Particle Physics

Particle physics uses a standard of "5 sigma" for the declaration of a discovery. At five-sigma there is only one chance in nearly two million that a random fluctuation would yield the result. This level of certainty prompted the announcement that a particle consistent with the Higgs boson has been discovered in two independent experiments at CERN.

Sports

Another way of seeing it is to consider sports teams. In any set of categories, there will be teams that rate highly at some things and poorly at others. Chances are, the teams that lead in the standings will not show such disparity but will perform well in most categories. The lower the standard deviation of their ratings in each category, the more balanced and consistent they will tend to be. Teams with a higher standard deviation, however, will be more unpredictable. For example, a team that is consistently bad in most categories will have a low standard deviation. A team that is consistently good in most categories will also have a low standard deviation. However, a team with a high standard deviation might be the type of team that scores a lot (strong offence) but also concedes a lot (weak defence), or, vice versa, that might have a poor offence but compensates by being difficult to score on.

Trying to predict which teams, on any given day, will win, may include looking at the standard deviations of the various team "stats" ratings, in which anomalies can match strengths vs. weaknesses to attempt to understand what factors may prevail as stronger indicators of eventual scoring outcomes.

In racing, a driver is timed on successive laps. A driver with a low standard deviation of lap times is more consistent than a driver with a higher standard deviation. This information can be used to help understand where opportunities might be found to reduce lap times.

Finance

In finance, standard deviation is often used as a measure of the risk associated with price-fluctuations of a given asset (stocks, bonds, property, etc.), or the risk of a portfolio of assets (actively managed mutual funds, index mutual funds, or ETFs). Risk is an important factor in determining how to efficiently manage a portfolio of investments because it determines the variation in returns on the asset and/or portfolio and gives investors a mathematical basis for investment decisions (known as mean-variance optimization). The fundamental concept of risk is that as it increases, the expected return on an investment should increase as well, an increase known as the "risk premium." In other words, investors should expect a higher return on an investment when that investment carries a higher level of risk or uncertainty. When evaluating investments, investors should estimate both the expected return and the uncertainty of future returns. Standard deviation provides a quantified estimate of the uncertainty of future returns.

For example, let's assume an investor had to choose between two stocks. Stock A over the past 20 years had an average return of 10 percent, with a standard deviation of 20 percentage points (pp) and Stock B, over the same period, had average returns of 12 percent but a higher standard deviation of 30 pp. On the basis of risk and return, an investor may decide that Stock A is the safer choice, because Stock B's additional two percentage points of return is not worth the additional 10 pp standard deviation (greater risk or uncertainty of the expected return). Stock B is likely to fall short of the initial investment (but also to exceed the initial investment) more often than Stock A under the same circumstances, and is estimated to return only two percent more on average.

In this example, Stock A is expected to earn about 10 percent, plus or minus 20 pp (a range of 30 percent to -10 percent), about two-thirds of the future year returns. When considering more extreme possible returns or outcomes in future, an investor should expect results of as much as 10 percent plus or minus 60 pp, or a range from 70 percent to –50 percent, which includes outcomes for three standard deviations from the average return (about 99.7 percent of probable returns).

However , there is another example showing the negative relation between standard deviation and the expected return.

Calculating the average (or arithmetic mean) of the return of a security over a given period will generate the expected return of the asset. For each period, subtracting the expected return from the actual return results in the difference from the mean. Squaring the difference in each period and taking the average gives the overall variance of the return of the asset. The larger the variance, the greater risk the security carries. Finding the square root of this variance will give the standard deviation of the investment tool in question.

Population standard deviation is used to set the width of Bollinger Bands, a widely adopted technical analysis tool. For example, the upper Bollinger Band is given as $x + n\sigma$. The most commonly used value for n is 2; there is about a five percent chance of going outside, assuming a normal distribution of returns.

Rules for Normally Distributed Data

The central limit theorem says that the distribution of an average of many independent, identically distributed random variables tends towards the famous bell-shaped normal distribution with a probability density function of:

$$f(x;\mu,\sigma^2) = \frac{1}{\sigma\sqrt{2\pi}} e^{-\frac{1}{2}\left(\frac{x-\mu}{\sigma}\right)^2}$$

where μ is the expected value of the random variables, σ equals their distribution's standard deviation divided by $n^{1/2}$, and n is the number of random variables. The standard deviation therefore is simply a scaling variable that adjusts how broad the curve will be, though it also appears in the normalizing constant.

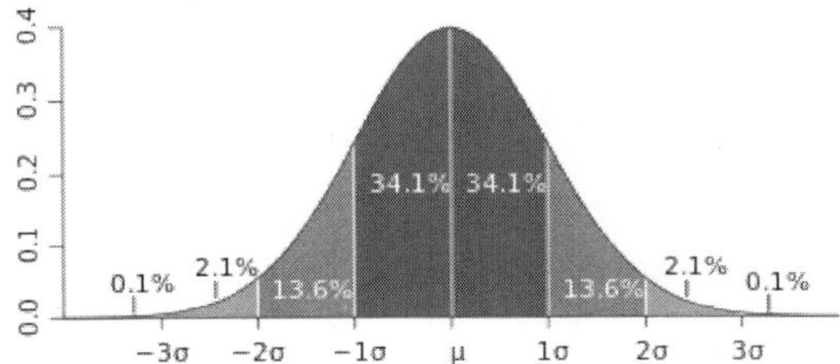

Figure: *Dark blue is less than one standard deviation from the mean. For the normal distribution, this accounts for 68.27 percent of the set; while two standard deviations from the mean (medium and dark blue) account for 95.45 percent; three standard deviations (light, medium, and dark blue) account for 99.73 percent; and four standard deviations account for 99.994 percent. The two points of the curve that are one standard deviation from the mean are also the inflection points.*

If a data distribution is approximately normal, then the proportion of data values within z standard deviations of the mean is defined by:

$$\text{Proportion} = \operatorname{erf}\left(\frac{z}{\sqrt{2}}\right)$$

where *erf* is the error function. If a data distribution is approximately normal then about 68 percent of the data values are within one standard deviation of the mean (mathematically, $\mu \pm \sigma$, where μ is the arithmetic mean), about 95 percent are within two standard deviations ($\mu \pm 2\sigma$), and about 99.7 percent lie within three standard deviations ($\mu \pm 3\sigma$). This is known as the *68-95-99.7 rule*, or *the empirical rule.*

Relationship Between Standard Deviation and Mean

The mean and the standard deviation of a set of data are usually reported together. In a certain sense, the standard deviation is a "natural" measure of statistical dispersion if the center of the data is measured about the mean.

This is because the standard deviation from the mean is smaller than from any other point. The precise statement is the following: suppose *x1*, ..., x_n are real numbers and define the function:

$$\sigma(r) = \sqrt{\frac{1}{N-1}\sum_{i=1}^{N}(x_i - r)^2}$$

Using calculus or by completing the square, it is possible to show that $\sigma(r)$ has a unique minimum at the mean:

$$r = \overline{x}.$$

Variability can also be measured by the coefficient of variation, which is the ratio of the standard deviation to the mean. It is a dimensionless number.

Often, we want some information about the precision of the mean we obtained. We can obtain this by determining the standard deviation of the sampled mean. The standard deviation of the mean is related to the standard deviation of the distribution by:

$$\sigma_{\text{mean}} = \frac{1}{\sqrt{N}}\sigma$$

where N is the number of observations in the sample used to estimate the mean. This can easily be proven with:

$$\begin{aligned} \text{var}(X) &\equiv \sigma_X^2 \\ \text{var}(X_1 + X_2) &\equiv \text{var}(X_1) + \text{var}(X_2) \\ \text{var}(cX_1) &\equiv c^2\,\text{var}(X_1) \end{aligned}$$

hence

$$\begin{aligned} \text{var(mean)} &= \text{var}\left(\frac{1}{N}\sum_{i=1}^{N}X_i\right) = \frac{1}{N^2}\text{var}\left(\sum_{i=1}^{N}X_i\right) \\ &= \frac{1}{N^2}\sum_{i=1}^{N}\text{var}(X_i) = \frac{N}{N^2}\text{var}(X) = \frac{1}{N}\text{var}(X). \end{aligned}$$

Resulting in:

$$\sigma_{\text{mean}} = \frac{\sigma}{\sqrt{N}}..$$

Rapid Calculation Methods

The following two formulas can represent a running (continuous) standard deviation. A set of three power sums *s0*, *s1*, *s2* are each computed over a set of N values of x, denoted as *x1*, ..., x_N:

$$s_j = \sum_{k=1}^{N} x_k^j.$$

Note that *s0* raises x to the zero power, and since x^0 is always 1, *s0* evaluates to N.

Given the results of these three running summations, the values *s0, s1, s2* can be used at any time to compute the *current* value of the running standard deviation:

$$\sigma = \frac{\sqrt{s_0 s_2 - s_1^2}}{s_0}$$

Similarly for sample standard deviation,

$$s = \sqrt{\frac{s_0 s_2 - s_1^2}{s_0(s_0 - 1)}}.$$

In a computer implementation, as the three s_j sums become large, we need to consider round-off error, arithmetic overflow, and arithmetic underflow. The method below calculates the running sums method with reduced rounding errors.

This is a "one pass" algorithm for calculating variance of n samples without the need to store prior data during the calculation. Applying this method to a time series will result in successive values of standard deviation corresponding to n data points as n grows larger with each new sample, rather than a constant-width sliding window calculation.

For $k = 0, \ldots, n$:

$$A_0 = 0$$

$$A_k = A_{k-1} + \frac{x_k - A_{k-1}}{k}$$

where A is the mean value.

$$Q_0 = 0$$

$$Q_k = Q_{k-1} + \frac{k-1}{k}(x_k - A_{k-1})^2 = Q_{k-1} + (x_k - A_{k-1})(x_k - A_k)$$

Sample variance:

$$s_n^2 = \frac{Q_n}{n-1}$$

Standard variance:

$$\sigma_n^2 = \frac{Q_n}{n}$$

Interquartile Range

In descriptive statistics, the interquartile range (IQR), also called the midspread or middle fifty, is a measure of statistical dispersion, being equal to the difference between the upper and lower quartiles, IQR = $Q3 - Q1$

Use

Unlike (total) range, the interquartile range is a robust statistic, having a breakdown point of 25%, and is thus often preferred to the total range. The IQR is used to build box plots, simple graphical representations of a probability distribution. For a symmetric distribution (where the median equals the midhinge, the average of the first and third quartiles), half the IQR equals the median absolute deviation (MAD). The median is the corresponding measure of central tendency.

Interdecile Range

In statistics, the interdecile range is the difference between the first and the ninth deciles (10% and 90%). The interdecile range is a measure of statistical dispersion of the values in a set of data, similar to the range and the interquartile range.

Range (statistics)

In the descriptive statistics, the range of a set of data is the difference between the largest and smallest values. It is the size of the smallest interval which contains all the data and provides an indication of statistical dispersion.

It is measured in the same units as the data. Since it only depends on two of the observations, it is most useful in representing the dispersion of small data sets.

Independent Identically Distributed Continuous Random Variables

For n independent and identically distributed continuous random variables $X1, X2, \ldots, X_n$ with cumulative distribution function G(x) and probability density function g(x) the range of the X_i is the range of a sample of size n from a population with distribution function $G(x)$.

Distribution

The range has cumulative distribution function

$$F(t) = n\int_{-\infty}^{\infty} g(x)[G(x+t) - G(x)]^{n-1}\,\mathrm{d}x.$$

Gumbel notes that the "beauty of this formula is completely marred by the facts that, in general, we cannot express $G(x + t)$ by $G(x)$, and that the numerical integration is lengthy and tiresome."

If the distribution of each X_i is limited to the right (or left) then the asymptotic distribution of the range is equal to the asymptotic distribution of the largest (smallest) value.

For more general distributions the asymptotic distribution can be expressed as a Bessel function.

Moments

The mean range is given by

$$n\int_0^1 x(G)[G^{n-1} - (1-G)^{n-1}]\mathrm{d}G$$

where $x(G)$ is the inverse function. In the case where each of the X_i has a standard normal distribution, the mean range is given by

$$\int_{-\infty}^{\infty} (1-(1-\Phi(x))^n - \Phi(x)^n)\mathrm{d}x.$$

Independent Nonidentically Distributed Continuous Random Variables

For n nonidentically distributed independent continuous random variables $X1, X2, \ldots, X_n$ with cumulative distribution functions $G1(x)$, $G2(x), \ldots, G_n(x)$ and probability density functions $g1(x), g2(x), \ldots, g_n(x)$, the range has cumulative distribution function

$$\mathrm{F}(t) = \sum_{i=1}^{n} \int_{-\infty}^{\infty} g_i(x) \prod_{j=1, j\neq i}^{n} \left[G_j(x+t) - G_j(x)\right] dx.$$

Independent Identically Distributed Discrete Random Variables

For n independent and identically distributed discrete random variables $X1, X2, \ldots, X_n$ with cumulative distribution function $G(x)$ and probability mass function $g(x)$ the range of the X_i is the range of a sample of size n from a population with distribution function $G(x)$. We can assume without loss of generality that the support of each X_i is $\{1,2,3,\ldots,N\}$ where N is a positive integer or infinity.

Related Quantities

The range is a simple function of the sample maximum and minimum and these are specific examples of order statistics. In particular, the range is a linear function of order statistics, which brings it into the scope of L-estimation.

Median Absolute Deviation

In statistics, the median absolute deviation (MAD) is a robust measure of the variability of a univariate sample of quantitative data. It can also refer to the population parameter that is estimated by the MAD calculated from a sample.

For a univariate data set *X1*, *X2*, ..., X_n, the MAD is defined as the median of the absolute deviations from the data's median:

$$\text{MAD} = \text{median}_i\left(\left|X_i - \text{median}_j(X_j)\right|\right),$$

that is, starting with the residuals (deviations) from the data's median, the MAD is the median of their absolute values.

Example

Consider the data (1, 1, 2, 2, 4, 6, 9). It has a median value of 2. The absolute deviations about 2 are (1, 1, 0, 0, 2, 4, 7) which in turn have a median value of 1 (because the sorted absolute deviations are (0, 0, 1, 1, 2, 4, 7)). So the median absolute deviation for this data is 1.

Uses

The median absolute deviation is a measure of statistical dispersion. Moreover, the MAD is a robust statistic, being more resilient to outliers in a data set than the standard deviation. In the standard deviation, the distances from the mean are squared, so large deviations are weighted more heavily, and thus outliers can heavily influence it. In the MAD, the deviations of a small number of outliers are irrelevant.

Because the MAD is a more robust estimator of scale than the sample variance or standard deviation, it works better with distributions without a mean or variance, such as the Cauchy distribution.

The Population MAD

The population MAD is defined analogously to the sample MAD, but is based on the complete distribution rather than on a sample. For a symmetric distribution with zero mean, the population MAD is the 75th percentile of the distribution.

Unlike the variance, which may be infinite or undefined, the population MAD is always a finite number. For example, the standard Cauchy distribution has undefined variance, but its MAD is 1.

The earliest known mention of the concept of the MAD occurred in 1816, in a paper by Carl Friedrich Gauss on the determination of the accuracy of numerical observations.

Distance Correlation

In statistics and in probability theory, distance correlation is a measure of statistical dependence between two random variables or two random vectors of arbitrary, not necessarily equal dimension. Its important property is that this measure of dependence is zero if and only if the random variables are statistically independent. This measure is derived from a number of other quantities that are used in its specification, specifically: distance variance, distance standard deviation and distance covariance. These take the same roles as the ordinary moments with corresponding names in the specification of the Pearson product-moment correlation coefficient.

These distance-based measures can be put into an indirect relationship to the ordinary moments by an alternative formulation (described below) using ideas related to Brownian motion, and this has led to the use of names such as Brownian covariance and Brownian distance covariance.

Background

The classical measure of dependence, the Pearson correlation coefficient, is mainly sensitive to a linear relationship between two variables. Distance correlation was introduced in 2005 by Gabor J Szekely in several lectures to address this deficiency of Pearson's correlation, namely that it can easily be zero for dependent variables. Correlation = 0 (uncorrelatedness) does not imply independence while distance correlation = 0 does imply independence. The first results on distance correlation were published in 2007 and 2009. It was proved that distance covariance is the same as the Brownian covariance. These measures are examples of energy distances.

Coefficient of Variation

In probability theory and statistics, the coefficient of variation (CV) is a normalized measure of dispersion of a probability distribution. It is also known as unitized risk or the variation coefficient. The absolute value of the CV is sometimes known as relative standard deviation (RSD), which is expressed as a percentage.

Definition

The coefficient of variation (CV) is defined as the ratio of the standard deviation α to the mean μ:

$$c_v = \frac{\sigma}{\mu}$$

which is the inverse of the signal-to-noise ratio. It shows the extent of variability in relation to mean of the population.

The coefficient of variation should be computed only for data measured on a ratio scale, as these are measurements that can only take non-negative values. The coefficient of variation may not have any meaning for data on an interval scale.

For example, most temperature scales are interval scales (e.g., Celsius, Fahrenheit etc.), they can take both positive and negative values. The Kelvin scale has an absolute null value, and no negative values can naturally occur. Hence, the Kelvin scale is a ratio scale. While the standard deviation (SD) can be derived on both the Kelvin and the Celsius scale (with both leading to the same SDs), the CV is only relevant as a measure of relative variability for the Kelvin scale.

Often, laboratory values that are measured based on chromatographic methods are log-normally distributed. In this case, the CV would be constant over a large range of measurements, while SDs would vary depending on typical values that are being measured.

Estimation

When only a sample of data from a population is available, the population CV can be estimated using the ratio of the sample standard deviation *s*to the sample mean $\bar{x}$:

$$\widehat{c_v} = \frac{s}{\bar{x}}$$

But this estimator, when applied to a small or moderately sized sample, tends to be too low: it is a biased estimator. For normally distributed data, an unbiased estimator for a sample of size n is:

$$\widehat{c_v}^* = \left(1 + \frac{1}{4n}\right)\widehat{c_v}$$

If it is assumed that the data are log-normally distributed, a more accurate estimate, derived from the properties of the log-normal distribution, is defined as:

$$\widehat{c_{v\,ln}} = \sqrt{e^{s_{ln}^{\,2}} - 1}$$

where s_{ln} is the sample standard deviation of the data after a natural log transformation. (In the event that measurements are recorded using any other logarithmic base, b, their standard deviation s_b is converted to base e using $s_{ln} = s_b ln(b)$, and the formula for $\widehat{c_{v\,ln}}$ remains the same.) This estimate is sometimes referred to as the "geometric coefficient of variation" in order to distinguish it from the simple estimate above. However, "geometric coefficient of variation" has also been defined as:

$$GCV = e^{s_{ln}} - 1$$

This term was intended to be *analogous* to the coefficient of variation, for describing multiplicative variation in log-normal data, but this definition of GCV has no theoretical basis as an estimate of c_v itself.

For many practical purposes (such as sample size determination and calculation of confidence intervals) it is s_{ln} which is of most use in the context of log-normally distributed data. If necessary, this can be derived from an estimate of or GCV by inverting the corresponding formula.

Comparison to Standard Deviation

Advantages

The coefficient of variation is useful because the standard deviation of data must always be understood in the context of the mean of the data. In contrast, the actual value of the CV is independent of the unit in which the measurement has been taken, so it is a dimensionless number. For comparison between data sets with different units or widely different means, one should use the coefficient of variation instead of the standard deviation.

Disadvantages

- When the mean value is close to zero, the coefficient of variation will approach infinity and is therefore sensitive to small changes in the mean. This is often the case if the values do not originate from a ratio scale.
- Unlike the standard deviation, it cannot be used directly to construct confidence intervals for the mean.

Applications

The coefficient of variation is also common in applied probability fields such as renewal theory, queueing theory, and reliability theory. In these fields, the exponential distribution is often more important than the normal distribution. The standard deviation of an exponential distribution is equal to its mean, so its coefficient of variation is equal to 1. Distributions with CV < 1 (such as an Erlang distribution) are considered low-variance, while those with CV > 1 (such as a hyper-exponential distribution) are considered high-variance. Some formulas in these fields are expressed using the squared coefficient of variation, often abbreviated SCV. In modelling, a variation of the CV is the CV(RMSD). Essentially the CV(RMSD) replaces the standard deviation term with the Root Mean Square Deviation (RMSD).

Quartile Coefficient of Dispersion

In statistics, the quartile coefficient of dispersion is a descriptive statistic which measures dispersion and which is used to make comparisons within and between data sets. The statistic is easily computed using the first (*Q1*) and third (*Q3*) quartiles for each data set. The quartile coefficient of dispersion is

$$\frac{Q_3 - Q_1}{Q_3 + Q_1}.$$

Consider the following two data sets:

Data set A: 2, 4, 6, 8, 10, 12, 14.

n = 7, range = 12, mean = 8, median = 8, *Q1* = 4, *Q3* = 12

coefficient of dispersion = 0.5

Data set B: 1.8, 2, 2.1, 2.4, 2.6, 2.9, 3

n = 7, range = 1.2, mean = 2.4, median = 2.4, *Q1* = 2, *Q3* = 2.9

coefficient of dispersion = 0.18

The quartile coefficient of dispersion of data set A is 2.7 times as great (0.5 / 0.18) as that of data set B.

6

Statistical Significance

Statistical significance is a statistical assessment of whether observations reflect a pattern rather than just chance. The fundamental challenge is that any partial picture of a given hypothesis, poll or question is subject to random error. In statistical testing, a result is deemed statistically significant if it is so extreme (without external variables which would influence the correlation results of the test) that such a result would be expected to arise simply by chance only in rare circumstances. Hence the result provides enough evidence to reject the hypothesis of 'no effect'.

For example, tossing 3 coins and obtaining 3 heads would not be considered an extreme result. However, tossing 10 coins and finding that all 10 land the same way up would be considered an extreme result: for fair coins the probability of having the first coin matched by all 9 others is $\left(\frac{1}{2}\right)^9 \approx 0.002$ which is rare. The result may therefore be considered statistically significant evidence that the coins are not fair. When used in statistics, the word significant does not mean important or meaningful, as it does in everyday speech.

Researchers focusing solely on whether individual test results are significant or not may miss important response patterns which individually fall under the threshold set for tests of significance. Therefore along with tests of significance, it is preferable to examine effect-size statistics, which describe how large the effect is and the uncertainty around that estimate, so that the practical importance of the effect may be gauged by the reader.

The calculated statistical significance of a result is in principle only valid if the hypothesis was specified before any data were examined. If, instead, the hypothesis was specified after some of the data were examined, and specifically tuned to match the direction in which the early data appeared to point, the calculation would overestimate statistical significance.

An alternative (but nevertheless related) statistical hypothesis testing framework is the Neyman–Pearson frequentist school which requires both a null and an alternative hypothesis to be defined and investigates the repeat sampling properties of the procedure, i.e. the probability that a decision to reject the null hypothesis will be made when it is in fact true and should not have been rejected (this is called a "false positive" or Type I error) and the probability that a decision will be made to accept the null hypothesis when it is in fact false (Type II error). Fisherian p-values are philosophically different from Neyman–Pearson Type I errors. This confusion is unfortunately propagated by many statistics textbooks.

Use in Practice

The significance level is usually denoted by the Greek symbol α (lowercase alpha). Popular levels of significance are 10% (0.1), 5% (0.05), 1% (0.01), 0.5% (0.005), and 0.1% (0.001). If a test of significance gives a p-value lower than the significance level α, the null hypothesis is rejected. Such results are informally referred to as 'statistically significant'. For example, if someone argues that "there's only one chance in a thousand this could have happened by coincidence", a 0.001 level of statistical significance is being implied. The lower the significance level chosen, the stronger the evidence required. The choice of significance level is somewhat arbitrary, but for many applications, a level of 5% is chosen by convention.

In some situations it is convenient to express the statistical significance as $1 - \alpha$. In general, when interpreting a stated significance, one must be careful to note what, precisely, is being tested statistically.

Different levels of α trade off countervailing effects. Smaller levels of α increase confidence in the determination of significance, but run an increased risk of failing to reject a false null hypothesis (a Type II error, or "false negative determination"), and so have less statistical power. The selection of the level α thus inevitably involves a compromise between significance and power, and consequently between the Type I error and the Type II error. More powerful experiments – usually experiments with more subjects or replications – can obviate this choice to an arbitrary degree.

Graphically, statistical significance is often indicated by the use of star symbols (*). The number of stars usually indicates the significance level: one star (*) for 0.05, two (**) for 0.01, and three (***) for 0.001 or 0.005. These star symbols may also be used on graphics, such as bar charts, to indicate a significant effect, such as a significant difference in the mean value between two populations (e.g. here).

In Terms of σ (sigma)

In some fields, for example nuclear and particle physics, it is common to express statistical significance in units of the standard deviation σ of a normal distribution. A statistical significance of "$n\sigma$" can be converted into a value of α by use of the cumulative distribution function Φ of the standard normal distribution, through the relation:

$$\alpha = 2(1 - \Phi(n)),$$

(this formula varies depending on whether a one-tailed or a two-tailed test is appropriate)

or via use of the error function:

$$\alpha = 1 - \operatorname{erf}\left(n / \sqrt{2}\right).$$

Tabulated values of these functions are often found in statistics text books. The use of σ implicitly assumes a normal distribution of measurement values. For example, if a theory predicts a parameter to have a value of, say, 109 ± 3, and one measures the parameter to be 100, then one might report the measurement as a –3σ deviation" from the theoretical prediction. In terms of α, this statement is equivalent to saying that "assuming the theory is true, the likelihood of obtaining the experimental result by coincidence is 0.27%– (since 1 – erf(3/–2) = 0.0027) (again depending on whether a one-tailed test or two-tailed test is appropriate).

Fixed significance levels such as those mentioned above may be regarded as useful in exploratory data analyses. However, modern practice is to quote the p-value explicitly, where the outcome of a test is essentially the final outcome of an experiment or other study. And, importantly, it should be stated whether the p-value is judged to be significant. This allows the maximum information to be transferred from a summary of the study into meta-analyses.

Pitfalls and Criticism

The scientific literature contains extensive discussion of the concept of statistical significance and in particular of its potential misuse and abuse.

Signal–noise ratio Conceptualisation of Significance

Statistical significance can be considered to be the confidence one has in a given result. In a comparison study, it is dependent on the relative difference between the groups compared, the amount of measurement and the noise associated with the measurement. In other words, the confidence one has in a given result being non-random (i.e. it is not a consequence of chance) depends on the signal-to-noise ratio (SNR) and the sample size.

Expressed mathematically, the confidence that a result is not by random chance is given by the following formula by Sackett:

$$\text{confidence} = \frac{\text{signal}}{\text{noise}} \times \sqrt{\text{sample size}}.$$

For clarity, the above formula is presented in tabular form below.

Table: *Dependence of confidence with noise, signal and sample size (tabular form)*

Parameter	*Parameter increases*	*Parameter decreases*
Noise	Confidence decreases	Confidence increases
Signal	Confidence increases	Confidence decreases
Sample size	Confidence increases	Confidence decreases

In words, the dependence of confidence is high if the noise is low and/or the sample size is large and/or the effect size (signal) is large. The confidence of a result (and its associated confidence interval) is not dependent on effect size alone. If the sample size is large and the noise is low a small effect size can be measured with great confidence. Whether a small effect size is considered important is dependent on the context of the events compared.

In medicine, small effect sizes (reflected by small increases of risk) are often considered clinically relevant and are frequently used to guide treatment decisions if there is great confidence in them. Whether a given treatment is considered a worthy endeavour is dependent on the risks, benefits and costs.

Analysis of Variance

In statistics, analysis of variance (ANOVA) is a collection of statistical models, and their associated procedures, in which the observed variance in a particular variable is partitioned into components attributable to different sources of variation. In its simplest form, ANOVA provides a statistical test of whether or not the means of several groups are all equal, and therefore generalizes t-test to more than two groups. Doing multiple two-sample t-tests would result in an increased chance of committing a type I error. For this reason, ANOVAs are useful in comparing two, three, or more means.

Background and Terminology

ANOVA is a particular form of statistical hypothesis testing heavily used in the analysis of experimental data. A statistical hypothesis test is a method of making decisions using data. A test result (calculated from the null hypothesis and the sample) is called statistically significant if it is deemed unlikely to have occurred, assuming the truth of the null hypothesis. A statistically significant result (when a probability (p-value) is less than a threshold (significance level)) justifies the rejection of the null hypothesis.

In the typical application of ANOVA, the null hypothesis is that all groups are simply random samples of the same population. This implies that all treatments have the same effect (perhaps none). Rejecting the null hypothesis implies that different treatments result in altered effects.

By construction, hypothesis testing limits the rate of Type I errors (false positives leading to false scientific claims) to a significance level. Experimenters also wish to limit Type II errors (false negatives resulting in missed scientific discoveries). The Type II error rate is a function of several things including sample size (positively correlated with experiment cost), significance level (when the standard of proof is high, the chances of overlooking a discovery are also high) and effect size (when the effect is obvious to the casual observer, Type II error rates are low).

The terminology of ANOVA is largely from the statistical design of experiments. The experimenter adjusts factors and measures responses in an attempt to determine an effect. Factors are assigned to experimental units by a combination of randomization and blocking to ensure the validity of the results. Blinding keeps the weighing impartial. Responses show a variability that is partially the result of the effect and is partially random error.

ANOVA is the synthesis of several ideas and it is used for multiple purposes. As a consequence, it is difficult to define concisely or precisely. "Classical ANOVA for balanced data does three things at once:

1. As exploratory data analysis, an ANOVA is an organization of an additive data decomposition, and its sums of squares indicate the variance of each component of the decomposition (or, equivalently, each set of terms of a linear model).

2. Comparisons of mean squares, along with F-tests ... allow testing of a nested sequence of models.
3. Closely related to the ANOVA is a linear model fit with coefficient estimates and standard errors." In short, ANOVA is a statistical tool used in several ways to develop and confirm an explanation for the observed data.
4. It is computationally elegant and relatively robust against violations to its assumptions.
5. ANOVA provides industrial strength (multiple sample comparison) statistical analysis.
6. It has been adapted to the analysis of a variety of experimental designs.

As a result: ANOVA "has long enjoyed the status of being the most used (some would say abused) statistical technique in psychological research." ANOVA "is probably the most useful technique in the field of statistical inference." ANOVA is difficult to teach, particularly for complex experiments, with split-plot designs being notorious. In some cases the proper application of the method is best determined by problem pattern recognition followed by the consultation of a classic authoritative text.

Fixed Effects Model

In econometrics and statistics, a fixed effects model is a statistical model that represents the observed quantities in terms of explanatory variables that are treated as if the quantities were non-random. This is in contrast to random effects models and mixed models in which either all or some of the explanatory variables are treated as if they arise from random causes. Note that the biostatistics definitions differ, as biostatisticians refer to the population-average and subject-specific effects as "fixed" and "random" effects respectively. Often the same structure of model, which is usually a linear regression model, can be treated as any of the three types depending on the analyst's viewpoint, although there may be a natural choice in any given situation. In panel data analysis, the term fixed effects estimator (also known as the within estimator) is used to refer to an estimator for the coefficients in the regression model. If we assume fixed effects, we impose time independent effects for each entity that are possibly correlated with the regressors.

Qualitative Description

Such models assist in controlling for unobserved heterogeneity when this heterogeneity is constant over time and correlated with independent variables. This constant can be removed from the data through differencing, for example by taking a first difference which will remove any time invariant components of the model.

There are two common assumptions made about the individual specific effect, the random effects assumption and the fixed effects assumption. The random effects assumption (made in a random effects model) is that the individual specific effects are uncorrelated with the independent variables.

The fixed effect assumption is that the individual specific effect is correlated with the independent variables. If the random effects assumption holds, the random effects model is more efficient than the fixed effects model. However, if this assumption does not hold (i.e., if the Durbin–Watson test fails), the random effects model is not consistent.

Steps in Fixed Effects Model for Sample Data

1. Calculate group and grand means
2. Calculate k=number of groups, n=number of observations per group, *N*=total number of observations (*k x n*)
3. Calculate SS-total (or total variance) as: (Each score - Grand mean)^2 then summed
4. Calculate SS-treat (or treatment effect) as: (Each group mean-Grand mean)^2 then summed *x n*
5. Calculate *SS*-error (or error effect) as (Each score - Its group mean)^2 then summed
6. Calculate *df*-total: *N*-1, df-treat: *k*-1 and df-error k(n-1)
7. Calculate Mean Square MS-treat: SS-treat/df-treat, then MS-error: SS-error/df-error
8. Calculate obtained f value: MS-treat/MS-error
9. Use F-table or probability function, to look up critical f value with a certain significance level
10. Conclude as to whether treatment effect significantly affects the variable of interest

Random Effects Model

In statistics, a random effect(s) model, also called a variance components model, is a kind of hierarchical linear model. It assumes that the dataset being analysed consists of a hierarchy of different populations whose differences relate to that hierarchy. In econometrics, random effects models are used in the analysis of hierarchical or panel data when one assumes no fixed effects (i.e. no individual effects).

The fixed effects model is a special case of the random effects model. Note that the biostatistics definitions differ, as biostatisticians respectively refer to the population-average and subject-specific effects as "fixed" and "random" effects.

Simple Example

Suppose m large elementary schools are chosen randomly from among thousands in a large country. Suppose also that n pupils of the same age are chosen randomly at each selected school. Their scores on a standard aptitude test are ascertained. Let Y_{ij} be the score of the jth pupil at the ith school. A simple way to model the relationships of these quantities is

$$Y_{ij} = \mu + U_i + W_{ij},$$

where μ is the average test score for the entire population. In this model U_i is the school-specific random effect: it measures the difference between the average score at school *i* and the average score in the entire country and it is "random" because the school has been randomly selected from a larger population of schools. The term, W_{ij} is the individual-specific error. That is, it is the deviation of the *j*-th pupil's score from the average for the i-th school. Again this is regarded as random because of the random selection of pupils within the school, even though it is a fixed quantity for any given pupil.

The model can be augmented by including additional explanatory variables, which would capture differences in scores among different groups. For example:

$$Y_{ij} = \mu + \beta_1 \text{Sex}_{ij} + \beta_2 \text{Race}_{ij} + \beta_3 \text{ParentsEduc}_{ij} + U_i + W_{ij},$$

where Sex_{ij} is the dummy variable for boys/girls, Race_{ij} is the dummy variable for white/black pupils, and ParentsEduc*ij* records the average education level of child's parents. This is a mixed model, not a purely random effects model.

Variance Components

The variance of Y_{ij} is the sum of the variances τ^2 and σ^2 of U_i and W*ij* respectively.

Let

$$\bar{Y}_{i\cdot} = \frac{1}{n}\sum_{j=1}^{n} Y_{ij}$$

be the average, not of all scores at the ith school, but of those at the ith school that are included in the random sample. Let

$$\overline{Y}_{..} = \frac{1}{mn}\sum_{i=1}^{m}\sum_{j=1}^{n} Y_{ij}$$

be the "grand average".

Let

$$SSW = \sum_{i=1}^{m}\sum_{j=1}^{n}(Y_{ij} - \overline{Y}_{i\cdot})^2$$

$$SSB = n\sum_{i=1}^{m}(\overline{Y}_{i\cdot} - \overline{Y}_{..})^2$$

be respectively the sum of squares due to differences within groups and the sum of squares due to difference between groups. Then it can be shown that

$$\frac{1}{m(n-1)}E(SSW) = \sigma^2$$

and

$$\frac{1}{(m-1)n}E(SSB) = \frac{\sigma^2}{n} + \tau^2.$$

These "expected mean squares" can be used as the basis for estimation of the "variance components" σ^2 and τ^2.

Unbiasedness

In general, random effects is efficient, and should be used (over fixed effects) if the assumptions underlying it are believed to be satisfied. For RE to work in the school example it is necessary that the school-specific effects be orthogonal to the other covariates of the model. This can be tested by running random effects, then fixed effects, and doing a Hausman specification test. If the test rejects, then random effects is biased and fixed effects is the correct estimation procedure.

Assumptions of ANOVA

The analysis of variance has been studied from several approaches, the most common of which uses a linear model that relates the response to the treatments and blocks. Even when the statistical model is nonlinear, it can be approximated by a linear model for which an analysis of variance may be appropriate.

Textbook Analysis Using a Normal Distribution

The analysis of variance can be presented in terms of a linear model, which makes the following assumptions about the probability distribution of the responses:

- Independence of observations – this is an assumption of the model that simplifies the statistical analysis.
- Normality – the distributions of the residuals are normal.
- Equality (or "homogeneity") of variances, called homoscedasticity — the variance of data in groups should be the same.

The separate assumptions of the textbook model imply that the errors are independently, identically, and normally distributed for fixed effects models, that is, that the errors (ε 's) are independent and

$$\varepsilon \sim N(0, \sigma^2).$$

Randomization-based Analysis

In a randomized controlled experiment, the treatments are randomly assigned to experimental units, following the experimental protocol. This randomization is objective and declared before the experiment is carried out. The objective random-assignment is used to test the significance of the null hypothesis, following the ideas of C. S. Peirce and Ronald A. Fisher. This design-based analysis was discussed and developed by Francis J. Anscombe at Rothamsted Experimental Station and by Oscar Kempthorne at Iowa State University. Kempthorne and his students make an assumption of unit treatment additivity, which is discussed in the books of Kempthorne and David R. Cox.

Derived Linear Model

Kempthorne uses the randomization-distribution and the assumption of unit treatment additivity to produce a derived linear model, very similar to the textbook model discussed previously. The test statistics of this derived linear model are closely approximated by the test statistics of an appropriate normal linear model, according to approximation theorems and simulation studies. However, there are differences. For example, the randomization-based analysis results in a small but (strictly) negative correlation between the observations. In the randomization-based analysis, there is no assumption of a normal distribution and certainly no assumption of independence. On the contrary, the observations are dependent!

The randomization-based analysis has the disadvantage that its exposition involves tedious algebra and extensive time. Since the randomization-based analysis is complicated and is closely approximated by the approach using a normal linear model, most teachers emphasize the normal linear model approach. Few statisticians object to model-based analysis of balanced randomized experiments.

Statistical Models for Observational Data

However, when applied to data from non-randomized experiments or observational studies, model-based analysis lacks the warrant of randomization. For observational data, the derivation of confidence intervals must use subjective models, as emphasized by Ronald A. Fisher and his followers. In practice, the estimates of treatment-effects from observational studies generally are often inconsistent. In practice, "statistical models" and observational data are useful for suggesting hypotheses that should be treated very cautiously by the public.

Summary of Assumptions

The normal-model based ANOVA analysis assumes the independence, normality and homogeneity of the variances of the residuals. The randomization-based analysis assumes only the homogeneity of the variances of the residuals (as a consequence of unit-treatment additivity) and uses the randomization procedure of the experiment. Both these analyses require homoscedasticity, as an assumption for the normal-model analysis and as a consequence of randomization and additivity for the randomization-based analysis.

However, studies of processes that change variances rather than means (called dispersion effects) have been successfully conducted using ANOVA. There are no necessary assumptions for ANOVA is its full generality, but the F-test used for ANOVA hypothesis testing has assumptions and practical limitations which are of continuing interest.

Problems which do not satisfy the assumptions of ANOVA can often be transformed to satisfy the assumptions. The property of unit-treatment additivity is not invariant under a "change of scale", so statisticians often use transformations to achieve unit-treatment additivity. If the response variable is expected to follow a parametric family of probability distributions, then the statistician may specify (in the protocol for the experiment or observational study) that the responses be transformed to stabilize the variance. Also, a statistician may specify that logarithmic transforms be applied to the responses, which are believed to follow a multiplicative model. According to Cauchy's functional equation theorem, the logarithm is the only continuous transformation that transforms real multiplication to addition.

Characteristics of ANOVA

ANOVA is used in the analysis of comparative experiments, those in which only the difference in outcomes is of interest. The statistical significance of the experiment is determined by a ratio of two variances. This ratio is independent of several possible alterations to the experimental observations: Adding a constant to all observations does not alter significance. Multiplying all observations by a constant does not alter significance. So ANOVA statistical significance results are independent of constant bias and scaling errors as well as the units used in expressing observations. In the era of mechanical calculation it was common to subtract a constant from all observations (when equivalent to dropping leading digits) to simplify data entry. This is an example of data coding.

Logic of ANOVA

The calculations of ANOVA can be characterized as computing a number of means and variances, dividing two variances and comparing the ratio to a handbook value to determine statistical significance. Calculating a treatment effect is then trivial, "the effect of any treatment is estimated by taking the difference between the mean of the observations which receive the treatment and the general mean."

Partition of Sums of Squares

The partition of sums of squares is a concept that permeates much of inferential statistics and descriptive statistics. More properly, it is the partitioning of sums of squared deviations or errors. Mathematically, the sum of squared deviations is an unscaled, or unadjusted measure of dispersion (also called variability). When scaled for the number of degrees of freedom, it estimates the variance, or spread of the observations about their mean value. Partitioning of the sum of squared deviations into various components allows the overall variability in a dataset to be ascribed to different types or sources of variability, with the relative importance of each being quantified by the size of each component of the overall sum of squares.

Background

The distance from any point in a collection of data, to the mean of the data, is the deviation. This can be written as $y_i - \overline{y}$, where y_i is the ith data point, and $\bar{y}$ is the estimate of the mean. If all such deviations are squared, then summed, as in:

$$\sum_{i=1}^{n}(y_i - \bar{y})^2,$$

this gives the "sum of squares" for these data.

When more data are added to the collection the sum of squares will increase, except in unlikely cases such as the new data being equal to the mean. So usually, the sum of squares will grow with the size of the data collection. That is a manifestation of the fact that it is unscaled.

In many cases, the number of degrees of freedom is simply the number of data in the collection, minus one. We write this as $n - 1$, where n is the number of data.

Scaling (also known as normalizing) means adjusting the sum of squares so that it does not grow as the size of the data collection grows. This is important when we want to compare samples of different sizes, such as a sample of 100 people compared to a sample of 20 people. If the sum of squares was not normalized, its value would always be larger for the sample of 100 people than for the sample of 20 people. To scale the sum of squares, we divide it by the degrees of freedom, i.e., calculate the sum of squares per degree of freedom, or variance. Standard deviation, in turn, is the square root of the variance.

Partitioning the Sum of Squares in Linear Eegression

Theorem. Given a linear regression model

$$y_i = \beta_0 + \beta_1 x_{i1} + \cdots + \beta_p x_{ip} + \varepsilon_i$$

including a constant based on a sample

$$(y_i, x_{i1}, \ldots, x_{ip}), i = 1, \ldots, n$$

containing n observations, the total sum of squares

$$\sum_{i=1}^{n}(y_i - \bar{y})^2$$

(TSS) can be partitioned as follows into the explained sum of squares (ESS) and the residual sum of squares (RSS):

$$\text{TSS} = \text{ESS} + \text{RSS},$$

where this equation is equivalent to each of the following forms:

$$\begin{aligned}\|y-\bar{y}1\|^2 &= \|\hat{y}-\bar{y}1\|^2+\|\hat{\varepsilon}\|^2, \quad 1=(1,1,\ldots,1)^T,\\ \sum_{i=1}^{n}(y_i-\bar{y})^2 &= \sum_{i=1}^{n}(\hat{y}_i-\bar{y})^2+\sum_{i=1}^{n}(y_i-\hat{y}_i)^2,\\ \sum_{i=1}^{n}(y_i-\bar{y})^2 &= \sum_{i=1}^{n}(\hat{y}_i-\bar{y})^2+\sum_{i=1}^{n}\hat{\varepsilon}_i^2.\end{aligned}$$

Proof

$$\begin{aligned}\sum_{i=1}^{n}(y_i-\bar{y})^2 &= \sum_{i=1}^{n}(y_i-\bar{y}+\hat{y}_i-\hat{y}_i)^2=\sum_{i=1}^{n}((\hat{y}_i-\bar{y})+\underbrace{(y_i-\hat{y}_i)}_{\hat{\varepsilon}_i})^2\\ &= \sum_{i=1}^{n}((\hat{y}_i-\bar{y})^2+2\hat{\varepsilon}_i(\hat{y}_i-\bar{y})+\hat{\varepsilon}_i^2)\\ &= \sum_{i=1}^{n}(\hat{y}_i-\bar{y})^2+\sum_{i=1}^{n}\hat{\varepsilon}_i^2+2\sum_{i=1}^{n}\hat{\varepsilon}_i(\hat{y}_i-\bar{y})\\ &= \sum_{i=1}^{n}(\hat{y}_i-\bar{y})^2+\sum_{i=1}^{n}\hat{\varepsilon}_i^2+2\sum_{i=1}^{n}\hat{\varepsilon}_i(\hat{\beta}_0+\hat{\beta}_1x_{i1}+\cdots+\hat{\beta}_px_{ip}-\bar{y})\\ &= \sum_{i=1}^{n}(\hat{y}_i-\bar{y})^2+\sum_{i=1}^{n}\hat{\varepsilon}_i^2+2(\hat{\beta}_0-\bar{y})\underbrace{\sum_{i=1}^{n}\hat{\varepsilon}_i}_{0}+2\hat{\beta}_1\underbrace{\sum_{i=1}^{n}\hat{\varepsilon}_ix_{i1}}_{0}+\cdots+2\hat{\beta}_p\underbrace{\sum_{i=1}^{n}\hat{\varepsilon}_ix_{ip}}_{0}\\ &= \sum_{i=1}^{n}(\hat{y}_i-\bar{y})^2+\sum_{i=1}^{n}\hat{\varepsilon}_i^2=\mathrm{ESS}+\mathrm{RSS}\end{aligned}$$

The requirement that the model includes a constant or equivalently that the design matrix contains a column of ones ensures that

$$\sum_{i=1}^{n}\hat{\varepsilon}_i=0.$$

Some readers may find the following version of the proof, set in vector form, more enlightening:

$$\begin{aligned}SS_{\text{total}}=(\mathrm{y}-\bar{y}1)^2 &= (\mathrm{y}-\bar{y}1+\hat{\mathrm{y}}-\hat{\mathrm{y}})^2,\\ &= ((\hat{\mathrm{y}}-\bar{y}1)+(\mathrm{y}-\hat{\mathrm{y}}))^2,\\ &= (\hat{\mathrm{y}}-\bar{y}1)^2+\hat{\varepsilon}^2+2\hat{\varepsilon}^T(\hat{\mathrm{y}}-\bar{y}1),\\ &= SS_{\text{regression}}+SS_{\text{error}}+2\hat{\varepsilon}^T(X\hat{\beta}-\bar{y}1),\\ &= SS_{\text{regression}}+SS_{\text{error}}+2(\hat{\varepsilon}^TX)\hat{\beta}-2\bar{y}\hat{\varepsilon}^T1,\\ &= SS_{\text{regression}}+SS_{\text{error}}.\end{aligned}$$

The elimination of terms in the last line, used the fact that

$$\hat{\varepsilon}^TX=(\mathrm{y}-\hat{\mathrm{y}})^TX=\mathrm{y}^T\left(I-X(X^TX)^{-1}X^T\right)X=\mathrm{y}^T(X-X)=0.$$

Further Partitioning

Note that the residual sum of squares can be further partitioned as the lack-of-fit sum of squares plus the sum of squares due to pure error.

F-test

An F-test is any statistical test in which the test statistic has an F-distribution under the null hypothesis. It is most often used when comparing statistical models that have been fitted to a data set, in order to identify the model that best fits the population from which the data were sampled. Exact F-tests mainly arise when the models have been fitted to the data using least squares. The name was coined by George W. Snedecor, in honour of Sir Ronald A. Fisher. Fisher initially developed the statistic as the variance ratio in the 1920s.

Common Examples of F-tests

Examples of F-tests include:

- The hypothesis that the means of several normally distributed populations, all having the same standard deviation, are equal. This is perhaps the best-known F-test, and plays an important role in the analysis of variance (ANOVA).
- The hypothesis that a proposed regression model fits the data well.
- The hypothesis that a data set in a regression analysis follows the simpler of two proposed linear models that are nested within each other.
- Scheffé's method for multiple comparisons adjustment in linear models.

F-test of the Equality of Two Variances

This F-test is sensitive to non-normality. In the analysis of variance (ANOVA), alternative tests include Levene's test, Bartlett's test, and the Brown–Forsythe test. However, when any of these tests are conducted to test the underlying assumption of homoscedasticity (i.e. homogeneity of variance), as a preliminary step to testing for mean effects, there is an increase in the experiment-wise Type I error rate.

7

Mean Difference

The mean difference is a measure of statistical dispersion equal to the average absolute difference of two independent values drawn from a probability distribution. A related statistic is the relative mean difference, which is the mean difference divided by the arithmetic mean. An important relationship is that the relative mean difference is equal to twice the Gini coefficient, which is defined in terms of the Lorenz curve.

The mean difference is also known as the absolute mean difference and the Gini mean difference. The mean difference is sometimes denoted by Δ or as MD. The mean deviation is a different measure of dispersion.

Calculation: For a population of size n, with a sequence of values y_i, $i = 1$ to n:

$$MD = \frac{1}{n^2} \Sigma_{i=1}^{n} \Sigma_{j=1}^{n} \mid y_i - y_j \mid .$$

For a discrete probability function $f(y)$, where y_i, $i = 1$ to n, are the values with nonzero probabilities:

$$MD = \Sigma_{i=1}^{n} \Sigma_{j=1}^{n} f(y_i) f(y_j) \mid y_i - y_j \mid .$$

For a probability density function $f(x)$:

$$MD = \int_{-\infty}^{\infty} \int_{-\infty}^{\infty} f(x) f(y) \mid x - y \mid dx dy.$$

For a cumulative distribution function F(x) with quantile function F(x):

$$MD = \int_{0}^{1} \int_{0}^{1} \mid F(x) - F(y) \mid dx dy.$$

Relative Mean Difference

When the probability distribution has a finite and nonzero arithmetic mean, the relative mean difference, sometimes denoted by " or RMD, is defined by

$$RMD = \frac{MD}{\text{arithmetic mean}}.$$

The relative mean difference quantifies the mean difference in comparison to the size of the mean and is a dimensionless quantity. The relative mean difference is equal to twice the Gini coefficient which is defined in terms of the Lorenz curve.

This relationship gives complementary perspectives to both the relative mean difference and the Gini coefficient, including alternative ways of calculating their values.

Properties

The mean difference is invariant to translations and negation, and varies proportionally to positive scaling. That is to say, if X is a random variable and c is a constant:

- MD(X + c) = MD(X),
- MD(-X) = MD(X), and
- MD(c X) = $|c|$ MD(X).

The relative mean difference is invariant to positive scaling, commutes with negation, and varies under translation in proportion to the ratio of the original and translated arithmetic means. That is to say, if X is a random variable and c is a constant:

- RMD(X + c) = RMD(X) · mean(X)/(mean(X) + c) = RMD(X) / (1+c / mean(X)) for c ¹ -mean(X),
- RMD(-X) = -RMD(X), and
- RMD(c X) = RMD(X) for $c > 0$.

If a random variable has a positive mean, then its relative mean difference will always be greater than or equal to zero. If, additionally, the random variable can only take on values that are greater than or equal to zero, then its relative mean difference will be less than 2.

Compared to Standard Deviation

Both the standard deviation and the mean difference measure dispersion—how spread out are the values of a population or the probabilities of a distribution. The mean difference is not defined in terms of a specific measure of central tendency, whereas the standard deviation is defined in terms of the deviation from the arithmetic mean.

Because the standard deviation squares its differences, it tends to give more weight to larger differences and less weight to smaller differences compared to the mean difference. When the arithmetic mean is finite, the mean difference will also be finite, even when the standard deviation is infinite. The examples for some specific comparisons. The recently introduced distance standard deviation plays similar role than the mean difference but the distance standard deviation works with centered distances.

Sample Estimators

For a random sample S from a random variable X, consisting of n values y_i, the statistic

$$MD(S) = \frac{\sum_{i=1}^{n}\sum_{j=1}^{n}|y_i - y_j|}{n(n-1)}$$

is a consistent and unbiased estimator of MD(X). The statistic:

$$RMD(S) = \frac{\sum_{i=1}^{n}\sum_{j=1}^{n}|y_i - y_j|}{(n-1)\sum_{i=1}^{n} y_i}$$

is a consistent estimator of RMD(X), but is not, in general, unbiased.

Confidence intervals for RMD(X) can be calculated using bootstrap sampling techniques.

There does not exist, in general, an unbiased estimator for RMD(X), in part because of the difficulty of finding an unbiased estimation for multiplying by the inverse of the mean. For example, even where the sample is known to be taken from a random variable $X(p)$ for an unknown p, and $X(p)$ - 1 has the Bernoulli distribution, so that $\Pr(X(p) = 1) = 1 - p$ and $\Pr(X(p) = 2) = p$, then

$\text{RMD}(X(p)) = 2p(1 - p)/(1 + p)$.

But the expected value of any estimator $R(S)$ of RMD($X(p)$) will be of the form:

$$\text{E}(R(S)) = \sum_{i=0}^{n} p^i (1-p)^{n-i} r_i,$$

where the r i are constants. So $E(R(S))$ can never equal $RMD(X(p))$ for all p between 0 and 1.

Gini Coefficient

The Gini coefficient (also known as the Gini index or Gini ratio) is a measure of statistical dispersion developed by the Italian statistician and sociologist Corrado Gini and published in his 1912 paper "Variability and Mutability" (Italian: *Variabilità e mutabilità*).

The Gini coefficient measures the inequality among values of a frequency distribution (for example levels of income). A Gini coefficient of zero expresses perfect equality, where all values are the same (for example, where everyone has an exactly equal income). A Gini coefficient of one (100 on the percentile scale) expresses maximal inequality among values (for example where only one person has all the income).

It has found application in the study of inequalities in disciplines as diverse as sociology, economics, health science, ecology, chemistry, engineering and agriculture.

Gini coefficient is commonly used as a measure of inequality of income or wealth. For OECD countries, in the late 2000s, considering the effect of taxes and transfer payments, the income Gini coefficient ranged between 0.24 to 0.49, with Slovenia the lowest and Chile the highest.

The countries in Africa had the highest pre-tax Gini coefficients in 2008-2009, with South Africa the world's highest at 0.7. The global income inequality Gini coefficient in 2005, for all human beings taken together, has been estimated to be between 0.61 and 0.68 by various sources.

A Gini coefficient is a controversial measure of income inequality. Not only does its value depend on income inequality within a country, its value depends on other factors, such as the demographic structure. Countries with an aging population, or with a baby boom, experience increasing pre-tax Gini coefficient even if real income distribution for working adults remain constant. Scholars have devised over a dozen methods to calculate Gini, each of which gives a different value.

Definition

The graph shows that the Gini coefficient is equal to the area marked A divided by the sum of the areas marked A and B. that is, Gini = A / (A + B). It is also equal to $2*A$ due to fact that $A + B$ = 0.5 (since the axes scale from 0 to 1).

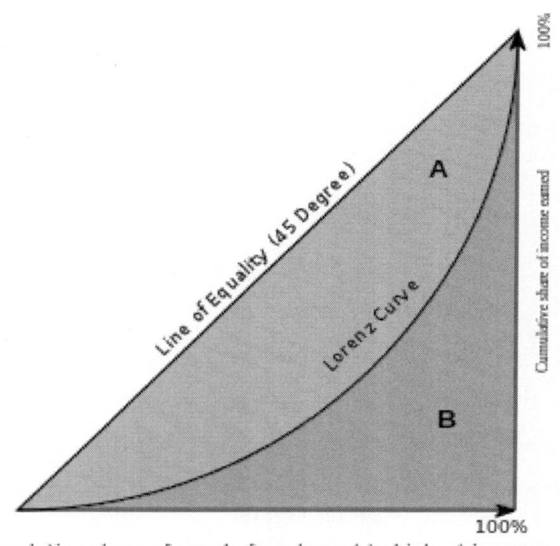

Figure: *Graphical representation of the Gini coefficient*

The Gini coefficient is usually defined mathematically based on the Lorenz curve, which plots the proportion of the total income of the population (y axis) that is cumulatively earned by the bottom x% of the population. The line at 45 degrees thus represents perfect equality of incomes. The Gini coefficient can then be thought of as the ratio of the area that lies between the line of equality and the Lorenz curve (marked A in the diagram) over the total area under the line of equality (marked A and B in the diagram); i.e., $G = A/(A + B)$.

The Gini coefficient can theoretically range from 0 to 1; it is sometimes expressed as a percentage ranging between 0 and 100. In practice, both extreme values are not quite reached.

A low Gini coefficient indicates a more equal distribution, with 0 corresponding to complete equality, while higher Gini coefficients indicate more unequal distribution, with 1 corresponding to complete inequality. To be validly computed, no negative goods can be distributed. Thus, if the Gini coefficient is being used to describe household income inequality, then no household can have a negative income. When used as a measure of income inequality, the most unequal society will be one in which a single person receives 100% of the total income and the remaining people receive none ($G = 1$); and the most equal society will be one in which every person receives the same income ($G = 0$).

An alternative approach would be to consider the Gini coefficient as half of the relative mean difference, which is a mathematical equivalence. The mean difference is the average absolute difference between two items selected randomly from a population, and the relative mean difference is the mean difference divided by the average, to normalize for scale.

Gini Coefficient of Income Distributions

Gini coefficients of income are calculated on market income as well as disposable income basis. The Gini coefficient on market income - sometimes referred to as pre-tax Gini index - is calculated on income before taxes and transfers, and it measures inequality in income without considering the effect of taxes and social spending already in place in a country. The Gini coefficient on disposable income - sometimes referred to as after-tax Gini index - is calculated on income after taxes and transfers, and it measures inequality in income after considering the effect of taxes and social spending already in place in a country. The difference in Gini indices between OECD countries, on after-taxes and transfers basis, is significantly narrower. For OECD countries, over 2008-2009 period, Gini coefficient on pre-taxes and transfers basis for total population ranged between 0.34 to 0.53, with South Korea the lowest and Italy the highest. Gini coefficient on after-taxes and transfers basis for total population ranged between 0.25 to 0.48, with Denmark the lowest and Mexico the highest. For United States, the country with the largest population in OECD countries, the pre-tax Gini index was 0.49, and after-tax Gini index was 0.38, in 2008-2009. The OECD averages for total population in OECD countries was 0.46 for pre-tax income Gini index and 0.31 for after-tax income Gini Index. Taxes and social spending that were in place in 2008-2009 period in OECD countries significantly lowered effective income inequality.

Using the Gini can help quantify differences in welfare and compensation policies and philosophies. However it should be borne in mind that the Gini coefficient can be misleading when used to make political comparisons between large and small countries or those with different immigration policies. The Gini index for the entire world has been estimated by various parties to be between 0.61 and 0.68. The graph shows the values expressed as a percentage, in their historical development for a number of countries.

Regional Income Gini Indices

According to UNICEF, Latin America and the Caribbean region had the highest net income Gini index in the world at 48.3, on unweighted average basis in 2008. The remaining regional averages were: sub-Saharan Africa (44.2), Asia (40.4), Middle East and North Africa (39.2), Eastern Europe and Central Asia (35.4), and High-income Countries (30.9). Using the same method, the United States is claimed to have a Gini index of 36, while South Africa the highest income Gini index score of 67.8.

Gini Coefficients of Social Development

Gini coefficient is widely used in fields as diverse as sociology, economics, health science, ecology, engineering and agriculture. For example, in social sciences and economics, in addition to income Gini coefficients, scholars have published education Gini coefficients and opportunity Gini coefficients.

Gini Coefficient of Education

Education Gini index estimates the inequality in education for a given population. It is used to discern trends in social development through educational attainment over time. From a study of 85 countries, Thomas et al. estimate Mali had the highest education Gini index of 0.92 in 1990 (implying very high inequality in education attainment across the population), while the United States had the lowest education inequality Gini index of 0.14. Between 1960 and 1990, South Korea, China and India had the fastest drop in education inequality Gini Index. They also claim education Gini index for the United States slightly increased over the 1980 - 1990 period.

Gini Coefficient of Opportunity

Similar in concept to income Gini coefficient, opportunity Gini coefficient measures inequality of opportunity. The concept builds on Amartya Sen's suggestion that inequality coefficients of social development should be premised on the process of enlarging people's choices and enhancing their capabilities, rather than process of reducing income inequality. Kovacevic in a review of opportunity Gini coefficient explains that the coefficient estimates how well a society enables its citizens to achieve success in life where the success is based on a person's choices, efforts and talents, not his background defined by a set of predetermined circumstances at birth, such as, gender, race, place of birth, parent's income and circumstances beyond the control of that individual.

In 2003, Roemer reported Italy and Spain exhibited the largest opportunity inequality Gini index amongst advanced economies.

Gini Coefficients and Income Mobility

In 1978, A. Shorrocks introduced a measure based on income Gini coefficients to estimate income mobility. This measure, generalized by Maasoumi and Zandvakili, is now generally referred to as Shorrocks index, sometimes as Shorrocks mobility index or Shorrocks rigidity index. It attempts to estimate whether the income inequality Gini coefficient is permanent or temporary, and to what extent a country or region enables economic mobility to its people so that they can move from one (e.g. bottom 20%) income quantile to another (e.g. middle 20%) over time. In other words, Shorrocks index compares inequality of short-term earnings such as annual income of households, to inequality of long-term earnings such as 5-year or 10-year total income for same households.

Shorrocks index is calculated in number of different ways, a common approach being from the ratio of income Gini coefficients between short-term and long-term for the same region or country.

A 2010 study using social security income data for the United States since 1937 and Gini-based Shorrocks indexes concludes that its income mobility has had a complicated history, primarily due to mass influx of women into the country's labour force after World War II. Income inequality and income mobility trends have been different for men and women workers between 1937 and the 2000s.

When men and women are considered together, the Gini coefficient-based Shorrocks Index trends imply long-term income inequality has been substantially reduced among all workers, in recent decades for the United States. Other scholars, using just 1990s data or other short periods have come to different conclusions.

For example, Sastre and Ayala, conclude from their study of income Gini coefficient data between 1993 and 1998 for six developed economies, that France had the least income mobility, Italy the highest, and the United States and Germany intermediate levels of income mobility over those 5 years.

Features of Gini Coefficient

Gini coefficient has features that make it useful as a measure of dispersion in a population, and inequalities in particular. It is a ratio analysis method making it easier to interpret. It also avoids references to a statistical average or position unrepresentative of most of the population, such as per capita income or gross domestic product.

For a given time interval, Gini coefficient can therefore be used to compare diverse countries and different regions or groups within a country; for example states, counties, urban versus rural areas, gender and ethnic groups. Gini coefficients can be used to compare income distribution over time, thus it is possible to see if inequality is increasing or decreasing independent of absolute incomes.

Other useful features of Gini coefficient include:

- *Anonymity*: it does not matter who the high and low earners are.
- *Scale independence*: the Gini coefficient does not consider the size of the economy, the way it is measured, or whether it is a rich or poor country on average.
- *Population independence*: it does not matter how large the population of the country is.
- *Transfer principle*: if income (less than the difference), is transferred from a rich person to a poor person the resulting distribution is more equal.

Limitations of Gini Coefficient

Gini coefficient is inherently limited because of its relative nature. Its proper use and interpretation of income Gini coefficient is controversial. As example, Mellor explains, income Gini index of developing countries can rise, that is the income distribution get more unequal at the same time that the number of people in absolute poverty are reduced substantially.

Kwok claims income inequality implied by Gini coefficients over time is misleading because Gini ignores structural changes in a society, changes such as growing population (baby boom, elderly population households, increased divorces, extended family households splitting into nuclear families), population changes from emigration, immigration and income mobility. Gini coefficient is simple, and this simplicity encourages misunderstandings.

The simplicity can confuse comparison of two different populations; for example, while both Bangladesh with per capita income of $1,693 and Netherlands with per capita income of $42,183 had an income Gini index of 0.31 in 2010, it does not mean the quality of life, economic opportunities and income equality are same for Bangladesh and Netherlands.

Countries may have identical Gini coefficients, but differ greatly in wealth. Basic necessities may be equal and available to all in a developed economy population, while in an undeveloped economy with same Gini coefficient, even basic necessities are unequally available.

Table: *Different income distributionswith the same Gini Index*

Householdnumber	***Country AAnnualIncome ($)***	***Country BAnnualIncome($)***
1	20,000	9,000
2	30,000	40,000
3	40,000	48,000
4	50,000	48,000
5	60,000	55,000
Total Income	$200,000	$200,000
Country's Gini	0.2	0.2

Different income inequality, yet same Gini

Even when the total income of a population is the same, in certain situations two countries with very different income distributions can have the same Gini index (e.g. cases when income Lorenz Curves cross). Table A in this section illustrates one such situation. Both countries have a Gini index of 0.2, but the income distributions are very different. As another example, a less equal society *EE* where bottom 50% of individuals had no income and the other 50% shared all the income equally has a Gini coefficient of 0.5; a more equal society *FF* where bottom 75% of people equally shared 25% of income while the top 25% equally shared 75% also has a Gini index of 0.5. Economies with similar incomes and Gini coefficients can still have very different income distributions. Bellù and Liberati claim ranking income inequality between two different populations with same or different Gini indices is sometimes not possible, or misleading.

Extreme wealth inequality, yet low income Gini coefficient. Gini index loses information about absolute national and personal incomes. Populations can have very low income inequality Gini indices yet simultaneously very high wealth Gini index. By measuring inequality in income, the Gini ignores the differential efficiency of use of household income. By ignoring wealth (except as it contributes to income) the Gini can create the appearance of inequality when the people compared are at different stages in their life.

Wealthy countries such as Sweden can show a low Gini coefficient for disposal income of 0.31 thereby appearing equal, yet have very high Gini coefficient for wealth of 0.79 to 0.86 thereby suggesting an extremely unequal wealth distribution in its society. These factors are not assessed in income-based Gini.

Table: *Same income distributionsbut different Gini Index*

Household number	Country A Annual Income ($)	Household combined number	Country A combined Annual Income ($)
1	20,000	1 & 2	50,000
2	30,000		
3	40,000	3 & 4	90,000
4	50,000		
5	60,000	5 & 6	130,000
6	70,000		
7	80,000	7 & 8	170000
8	90,000		
9	120,000	9 & 10	270000
10	150,000		
Total Income	$710,000		$710,000
Country's Gini	**0.303**		**0.293**

Small sample bias - sparsely populated regions more likely to have low Gini coefficient

Gini index has a downward-bias for small populations. Counties or states or countries with small populations and less diverse economies will tend to report small Gini coefficients. For economically diverse large population groups, a much higher coefficient is expected than for each of its regions. Taking world economy as one, and income distribution for all human beings, for example, different scholars estimate global Gini index to range between 0.61 and 0.68.

Same population with same income distribution, analyzed differently, yields different Gini coefficients. As with other inequality coefficients, the Gini coefficient is influenced by the granularity of the measurements. For example, five 20% quantiles (low granularity) will usually yield a lower Gini coefficient than twenty 5% quantiles (high granularity) for the same distribution. Philippe Monfort has shown inconsistent or unspecified granularity limits usefulness of Gini coefficient measurements.

The Gini coefficient measure gives different results when applied to individuals instead of households, for the same economy and same income distributions. If household data is used, the measured value of income Gini depends on how the household is defined. When different populations are not measured with consistent definitions, comparison is not meaningful.

Deininger and Squire show that income Gini coefficient based on individual income, rather than household income, are different. For United States, for example, they find that individual income-based Gini index was 0.35, while for France they report individual income-based Gini index to be 0.43.

According to their individual focussed method, in the 108 countries they studied, South Africa had the world's highest Gini index at 0.62, Malaysia had Asia's highest Gini index at 0.5, Brazil the highest at 0.57 in Latin America and Caribbean region, and Turkey the highest at 0.5 in OECD countries.

Table: *Household money incomedistributions and Gini Index, USA*

Income bracket (in 2010 adjusted dollars)	% of Population 1979	% of Population 2010
Under $15,000	14.6%	13.7%
$15,000 – $24,999	11.9%	12.0%
$25,000 – $34,999	12.1%	10.9%
$35,000 – $49,999	15.4%	13.9%
$50,000 – $74,999	22.1%	17.7%
$75,000 – $99,999	12.4%	11.4%
$100,000 – $149,999	8.3%	12.1%
$150,000 – $199,999	2.0%	4.5%
$200,000 and over	1.2%	3.9%
Total Households	80,776,000	118,682,000
United State's Gini on pre-tax basis	**0.404**	**0.469**

Gini coefficient is unable to discern the effects of structural changes in populations

Expanding on the importance of life-span measures, the Gini coefficient as a point-estimate of equality at a certain time, ignores life-span changes in income. Typically, increases in the proportion of young or old members of a society will drive apparent changes in equality, simply because people generally have lower incomes and wealth when they are young than when they are old. Because of this, factors such as age distribution within a population and mobility within income classes can create the appearance of inequality when none exist taking into account demographic effects.

Thus a given economy may have a higher Gini coefficient at any one point in time compared to another, while the Gini coefficient calculated over individuals' lifetime income is actually lower than the apparently more equal (at a given point in time) economy's. Essentially, what matters is not just inequality in any particular year, but the composition of the distribution over time.

Kwok claims income Gini index for Hong Kong has been high (0.434 in 2010), in part because of structural changes in its population. Over recent decades, Hong Kong has witnessed increasing numbers of small households, elderly households and elderly living alone.

The combined income is now split into more households. Many old people are living separately from their children in Hong Kong. These social changes have caused substantial changes in household income distribution. Income Gini coefficient, claims Kwok, does not discern these structural changes in its society.

Household money income distribution for the United States, summarized in Table C of this section, confirms that this issue is not limited to just Hong Kong. According to the US Census Bureau, between 1979 and 2010, the population of United States experienced structural changes in overall households, the income for all income brackets increased in inflation-adjusted terms, household income distributions shifted into higher income brackets over time, while the income Gini coefficient increased.

Another limitation of Gini coefficient is that it is not a proper measure of egalitarianism, as it is only measures income dispersion. For example, if two equally egalitarian countries pursue different immigration policies, the country accepting a higher proportion of low-income or impoverished migrants will report a higher Gini coefficient and therefore may appear to exhibit more income inequality.

Gini coefficient falls yet the poor gets poorer, Gini coefficient rises yet everyone getting richer.

Table: *Effect of incomechanges on Gini Index*

Income bracket	**Year 1 Annual Income ($)**	**Year 2 Annual Income ($)**	**Year 3 Annual Income ($)**
Bottom 20%	0	500	0
20% – 40%	1,000	1,200	500
40% – 60%	2,000	2,200	1,000
60% – 80%	5,000	5,500	2,000
Top 20%	7,000	12,000	2,500
Country's Gini	0.48	0.51	0.43
		Everyone better off	Everyone poorer

Arnold describes one limitation of Gini coefficient to be income distribution situations where it misleads. The income of poorest fifth of households can be lower when Gini coefficient is lower, than when the poorest income bracket is earning a larger percentage of all income.

Table D illustrates this case, where the lowest income bracket has an average household market income of $500 per year at Gini index of 0.51, and zero income at Gini index of 0.48. This is counter-intuitive and Gini coefficient cannot tell what is happening to each income bracket or the absolute income, cautions Arnold.

Feldstein similarly explains one limitation of Gini coefficient as its focus on relative income distribution, rather than real levels of poverty and prosperity in society. He claims Gini coefficient analysis is limited because in many situations it intuitively implies inequality that violate the so-called Pareto improvement principle.

The Pareto improvement principle, named after the Italian economist Vilfredo Pareto, states that a social, economic or income change is good if it makes one or more people better off without making anyone else worse off. Gini coefficient can rise if some or all income brackets experience a rising income. Feldstein's explanation is summarized in Table D.

The table shows that in a growing economy, consistent with Pareto improvement principle, where income of every segment of the population has increased, from one year to next, the income inequality Gini coefficient can rise too. In contrast, in another economy, if everyone gets poorer and is worse off, income inequality is less and Gini coefficient lower. Inability to value benefits and income from informal economy affects Gini coefficient accuracy

Some countries distribute benefits that are difficult to value. Countries that provide subsidized housing, medical care, education or other such services are difficult to value objectively, as it depends on quality and extent of the benefit. In absence of free markets, valuing these income transfers as household income is subjective. The theoretical model of Gini coefficient is limited to accepting correct or incorrect subjective assumptions.

In subsistence-driven and informal economies, people may have significant income in other forms than money, for example through subsistence farming or bartering. These income tend to accrue to the segment of population that is below-poverty line or very poor, in emerging and transitional economy countries such as those in sub-

Saharan Africa, Latin America, Asia and Eastern Europe. Informal economy accounts for over half of global employment and as much as 90 per cent of employment in some of the poorer sub-Saharan countries with high official Gini inequality coefficients. Schneider et al., in their 2010 study of 162 countries, report about 31.2%, or about $20 trillion, of world's GDP is informal.

In developing countries, the informal economy predominates for all income brackets except for the richer, urban upper income bracket populations. Even in developed economies, between 8% (United States) to 27% (Italy) of each nation's GDP is informal, and resulting informal income predominates as a livelihood activity for those in the lowest income brackets.

The value and distribution of the incomes from informal or underground economy is difficult to quantify, making true income Gini coefficients estimates difficult. Different assumptions and quantifications of these incomes will yield different Gini coefficients.

Gini has some mathematical limitations as well. It is not additive and different sets of people cannot be averaged to obtain the Gini coefficient of all the people in the sets.

Alternatives to Gini Coefficient

Given the limitations of Gini coefficient, other statistical methods are used in combination or as an alternative measure of population dispersity. For example, *entropy measures* are frequently used (e.g. the Theil Index and the Atkinson index). These measures attempt to compare the distribution of resources by intelligent agents in the market with a maximum entropy random distribution, which would occur if these agents acted like non-intelligent particles in a closed system following the laws of statistical physics.

Relation to Other Statistical Measures

Gini coefficient closely related to the AUC (Area Under receiver operating characteristic Curve) measure of performance. The relation follows the formula $AUC = (G+1)/2$ Gini coefficient is also closely related to Mann–Whitney *U*.

Gini index is also related to Pietra index - both of which are a measure of statistical heterogeneity and are derived from Lorenz curve and the diagonal line.

In certain fields such as ecology, Simpson's index is used, which is related to Gini. Simpson index scales as mirror opposite to Gini;

that is, with increasing diversity Simpson index takes a smaller value (0 means maximum, 1 means minimum heterogeneity per classic Simpson index). Simpson index is sometimes transformed by subtracting the observed value from the maximum possible value of 1, and then it is known as Gini-Simpson Index.

Other Uses

Although the Gini coefficient is most popular in economics, it can in theory be applied in any field of science that studies a distribution. For example, in ecology the Gini coefficient has been used as a measure of biodiversity, where the cumulative proportion of species is plotted against cumulative proportion of individuals. In health, it has been used as a measure of the inequality of health related quality of life in a population.

In education, it has been used as a measure of the inequality of universities. In chemistry it has been used to express the selectivity of protein kinase inhibitors against a panel of kinases. In engineering, it has been used to evaluate the fairness achieved by Internet routers in scheduling packet transmissions from different flows of traffic. In statistics, building decision trees, it is used to measure the purity of possible child nodes, with the aim of maximising the average purity of two child nodes when splitting, and it has been compared with other equality measures.

The Gini coefficient is sometimes used for the measurement of the discriminatory power of rating systems in credit risk management.The discriminatory power refers to a credit risk model's ability to differentiate between defaulting and non-defaulting clients. The formula G_1, in calculation section above, may be used for the final model and also at individual model factor level, to quantify the discriminatory power of individual factors. It is related to accuracy ratio in population assessment models.

Variance

In probability theory and statistics, the variance is a measure of how far a set of numbers is spread out. It is one of several descriptors of a probability distribution, describing how far the numbers lie from the mean (expected value). In particular, the variance is one of the moments of a distribution. In that context, it forms part of a systematic approach to distinguishing between probability distributions. While other such approaches have been developed, those based on moments are advantageous in terms of mathematical and computational simplicity.

The variance is a parameter describing in part either the actual probability distribution of an observed population of numbers, or the theoretical probability distribution of a sample (a not-fully-observed population) of numbers. In the latter case a sample of data from such a distribution can be used to construct an estimate of its variance: in the simplest cases this estimate can be the sample variance, defined below.

Basic Discussion

Examples

The variance of a random variable or distribution is the expectation, or mean, of the squared deviation of that variable from its expected value or mean. Thus the variance is a measure of the amount of variation of the values of that variable, taking account of all possible values and their probabilities or weightings (not just the extremes which give the range).

For example, a perfect six-sided die, when thrown, has expected value of

$$\frac{1}{6}(1+2+3+4+5+6) = 3.5.$$

Its expected absolute deviation—the mean of the equally likely absolute deviations from the mean—is

$$\frac{1}{6}(|1-3.5|+|2-3.5|+|3-3.5|+|4-3.5|+|5-3.5|+|6-3.5|) =$$

$$\frac{1}{6}(2.5+1.5+0.5+0.5+1.5+2.5) = 1.5.$$

But its expected *squared* deviation—its variance (the mean of the equally likely squared deviations)—is

$$\frac{1}{6}(2.5^2+1.5^2+0.5^2+0.5^2+1.5^2+2.5^2) = 17.5/6 \approx 2.9.$$

As another example, if a coin is tossed twice, the number of heads is: 0 with probability 0.25, 1 with probability 0.5 and 2 with probability 0.25. Thus the expected value of the number of heads is:

$$0.25\times 0+0.5\times 1+0.25\times 2 = 1,$$

and the variance is:

$$0.25\times(0-1)^2+0.5\times(1-1)^2+0.25\times(2-1)^2$$
$$= 0.25+0+0.25 = 0.5.$$

Units of Measurement

Unlike expected absolute deviation, the variance of a variable has units that are the square of the units of the variable itself. For example, a variable measured in inches will have a variance measured in square inches. For this reason, describing data sets via their standard deviation or root mean square deviation is often preferred over using the variance. In the dice example the standard deviation is $-2.9 \approx 1.7$, slightly larger than the expected absolute deviation of 1.5.

The standard deviation and the expected absolute deviation can both be used as an indicator of the "spread" of a distribution. The standard deviation is more amenable to algebraic manipulation than the expected absolute deviation, and, together with variance and its generalization covariance, is used frequently in theoretical statistics; however the expected absolute deviation tends to be more robust as it is less sensitive to outliers arising from measurement anomalies or an unduly heavy-tailed distribution.

Estimating the Variance

Real-world distributions such as the distribution of yesterday's rain throughout the day are typically not fully known, unlike the behaviour of perfect dice or an ideal distribution such as the normal distribution, because it is impractical to account for every raindrop. Instead one estimates the mean and variance of the whole distribution as the computed mean and variance of a sample of n observations drawn suitably randomly from the whole sample space, in this example the set of all measurements of yesterday's rainfall in all available rain gauges.

This method of estimation is close to optimal, with the caveat that it underestimates the variance by a factor of $(n - 1) / n$. (For example, when $n = 1$ the variance of a single observation is obviously zero regardless of the true variance). This gives a bias which should be corrected for when n is small by multiplying by $n / (n - 1)$. If the mean is determined in some other way than from the same samples used to estimate the variance then this bias does not arise and the variance can safely be estimated as that of the samples.

To illustrate the relation between the population variance and the sample variance, suppose that in the (not entirely observed) population of numerical values, the value 1 occurs 1/3 of the time, the value 2 occurs 1/3 of the time, and the value 4 occurs 1/3 of the time. The population mean is $(1/3)[1 + 2 + 4] = 7/3$. The equally likely deviations from the population mean are $1 - 7/3$, $2 - 7/3$, and $4 - 7/$

3. The population variance — the expected squared deviation from the mean 7/3 — is $(1/3)[(-4/3)^2 + (-1/3)^2 + (5/3)^2] = 14/9$. Now suppose for the sake of a simple example that we take a very small sample of $n = 2$ observations, and consider the nine equally likely possibilities for the set of numbers within that sample: (1, 1), (1, 2), (1,4), (2, 1), (2,2), (2, 4), (4,1), (4, 2), and (4, 4).

For these nine possible samples, the sample variance of the two numbers is respectively 0, 1/4, 9/4, 1/4, 0, 4/4, 9/4, 4/4, and 0. With our plan to observe two values, we could end up computing any of these sample variances (and indeed if we hypothetically could observe a pair of numbers many times, we would compute each of these sample variances 1/9 of the time). So the expected value, over all possible samples that might be drawn from the population, of the computed sample variance is $(1/9)[0 + 1/4 + 9/4 + 1/4 + 0 + 4/4 + 9/4 + 4/4 + 0] = 7/9$.

This value of 7/9 for the expected value of our sample variance computation is a substantial underestimate of the true population variance, which we computed as 14/9, because our sample size of just two observations was so small. But if we adjust for this downward bias by multiplying our computed sample variance, whichever it may be, by $n/(n - 1) = 2/(2 - 1) = 2$, then our estimate of the population variance would be any one of 0, 1/2, 9/2, 1/2, 0, 4/2, 9/2, 4/2, and 0. The average of these is indeed the correct population variance of 14/9, so on average over all possible samples we would have the correct estimate of the population variance.

The variance of a real-valued random variable is its second central moment, and it also happens to be its second cumulant. Just as some distributions do not have a mean, some do not have a variance. The mean exists whenever the variance exists, but the converse is not necessarily true.

Index of Dispersion

In probability theory and statistics, the index of dispersion, dispersion index, coefficient of dispersion, or variance-to-mean ratio (VMR), like the coefficient of variation, is a normalized measure of the dispersion of a probability distribution: it is a measure used to quantify whether a set of observed occurrences are clustered or dispersed compared to a standard statistical model.

It is defined as the ratio of the variance σ^2 to the mean μ,

$$D = \frac{\sigma^2}{\mu}.$$

It is also known as the Fano factor, though this term is sometimes reserved for *windowed* data (the mean and variance are computed over a subpopulation), where the index of dispersion is the special case where the window is infinite. Windowing data is frequently done: the VMR is frequently computed over various intervals in time or small regions in space, which may be called "windows", and the resulting statistic called the Fano factor.

It is only defined when the mean μ is non-zero, and is generally only used for positive statistics, such as count data or time between events, or where the underlying distribution is assumed to be the exponential distribution or Poisson distribution.

Terminology

In this context, the observed dataset may consist of the times of occurrence of predefined events, such as earthquakes in a given region over a given magnitude, or of the locations in geographical space of plants of a given species. Details of such occurrences are first converted into counts of the numbers of events or occurrences in each of a set of equal-sized time- or space-regions.

The above defines a *dispersion index for counts.* A different definition applies for a *dispersion index for intervals*, where the quantities treated are the lengths of the time-intervals between the events, and where the index is equivalent to the square of the coefficient of variation of the interval lengths. Common usage is that "index of dispersion" means the dispersion index for counts.

Interpretation

Some distributions, most notably the Poisson distribution, have equal variance and mean, giving them a VMR = 1. The geometric distribution and the negative binomial distribution have VMR > 1, while the binomial distribution has VMR < 1, and the constant random variable has VMR = 0. This yields the following table:

Distribution	***VMR***	
constant random variable	VMR = 0	not dispersed
binomial distribution	0 < VMR < 1	under-dispersed
Poisson distribution	VMR = 1	
negative binomial distribution	VMR > 1	over-dispersed

This can be considered analogous to the classification of conic sections by eccentricity.

When the coefficient of dispersion is less than 1, a dataset is said to be "under-dispersed": this condition can relate to patterns of occurrence that are more regular than the randomness associated with a Poisson process. For instance, points spread uniformly in space or regular, periodic events will be under-dispersed.

If the index of dispersion is larger than 1, a dataset is said to be over-dispersed: this can correspond to the existence of clusters of occurrences. Clumped, concentrated data is over-dispersed.

In terms of the interval-counts, over-dispersion corresponds to there being more intervals with low counts and more intervals with high counts, compared to a Poisson distribution: in contrast, under-dispersion is characterised by there being more intervals having counts close to the mean count, compared to a Poisson distribution.

The relevance of the index of dispersion is that it has a value of one when the probability distribution of the number of occurrences in an interval is a Poisson distribution. Thus the measure can be used to assess whether observed data can be meddled using a Poisson process.

A sample-based estimate of the dispersion index can be used to construct a formal statistical hypothesis test for the adequacy of the model that a series of counts follow a Poisson distribution.

The VMR is a good measure of the degree of randomness of a given phenomenon. This technique is also commonly used in currency management.

Example

For randomly diffusing particles (Brownian motion), the distribution of the number of particle inside a given volume is poissonian, i.e. VMR=1. Therefore, to assess if a given spatial pattern (assuming you have a way to measure it) is due purely to diffusion or if some particle-particle interaction is involved : divide the space into patches, Quadrats or Sample Units (SU), count the number of individuals in each patch or SU, and compute the VMR. VMRs significantly higher than 1 denote a clustered distribution, where random walk is not enough to smother the attractive inter-particle potential.

A Partial Ordering of Dispersion

A mean-preserving spread (MPS) is a change from one probability distribution A to another probability distribution B, where B is formed by spreading out one or more portions of A's probability density function while leaving the mean (the expected value) unchanged. The concept of a mean-preserving spread provides a partial ordering of probability distributions according to their dispersions: of two probability distributions, one may be ranked as having more dispersion than the other, or alternatively neither may be ranked as having more dispersion.

Outlier

In statistics, an outlier is an observation that is numerically distant from the rest of the data. Grubbs defined an outlier as: An outlying observation, or outlier, is one that appears to deviate markedly from other members of the sample in which it occurs.

Outliers can occur by chance in any distribution, but they are often indicative *either* of measurement error or that the population has a heavy-tailed distribution. In the former case one wishes to discard them or use statistics that are robust to outliers, while in the latter case they indicate that the distribution has high kurtosis and that one should be very cautious in using tools or intuitions that assume a normal distribution. A frequent cause of outliers is a mixture of two distributions, which may be two distinct sub-populations, or may indicate 'correct trial' versus 'measurement error'; this is meddled by a mixture model.

In most larger samplings of data, some data points will be further away from the sample mean than what is deemed reasonable. This can be due to incidental systematic error or flaws in the theory that generated an assumed family of probability distributions, or it may be that some observations are far from the center of the data. Outlier points can therefore indicate faulty data, erroneous procedures, or areas where a certain theory might not be valid. However, in large samples, a small number of outliers is to be expected (and not due to any anomalous condition).

Outliers, being the most extreme observations, may include the sample maximum or sample minimum, or both, depending on whether they are extremely high or low. However, the sample maximum and minimum are not always outliers because they may not be unusually far from other observations.

Naive interpretation of statistics derived from data sets that include outliers may be misleading. For example, if one is calculating the average temperature of 10 objects in a room, and nine of them are between 20 and 25 degrees Celsius, but an oven is at 175 °C, the median of the data could be between 20 and 25 °C but the mean temperature will be between 35.5 and 40 °C. In this case, the median better reflects the temperature of a randomly sampled object than the mean; however, naively interpreting the mean as "a typical sample", equivalent to the median, is incorrect. As illustrated in this case, outliers may be indicative of data points that belong to a different population than the rest of the sample set.

Estimators capable of coping with outliers are said to be robust: the median is a robust statistic, while the mean is not.

Occurrence and Causes

In the case of normally distributed data, roughly 1 in 22 observations will differ by twice the standard deviation or more from the mean, and 1 in 370 will deviate by three times the standard deviation; see three sigma rule for details. In a sample of 1000 observations, the presence of up to five observations deviating from the mean by more than three times the standard deviation is within the range of what can be expected, being less than twice the expected number and hence within 1 standard deviation of the expected number – and not indicative of an anomaly.

If the sample size is only 100, however, just three such outliers are already reason for concern, being more than 11 times the expected number.

In general, if the nature of the population distribution is known a priori, it is possible to test if the number of outliers deviate significantly from what can be expected: for a given cutoff (so samples fall beyond the cutoff with probability p) of a given distribution, the number of outliers will follow a binomial distribution with parameter p, which can generally be well-approximated by the Poisson distribution with $\lambda = pn$.

Thus if one takes a normal distribution with cutoff 3 standard deviations from the mean, p is approximately .3%, and thus for 1,000 trials one can approximate the number of samples whose deviation exceeds 3 sigmas by a Poisson distribution with $\lambda = 3$.

Causes

Outliers can have many anomalous causes. A physical apparatus for taking measurements may have suffered a transient malfunction. There may have been an error in data transmission or transcription. Outliers arise due to changes in system behaviour, fraudulent behaviour, human error, instrument error or simply through natural deviations in populations.

A sample may have been contaminated with elements from outside the population being examined. Alternatively, an outlier could be the result of a flaw in the assumed theory, calling for further investigation by the researcher. Additionally, the pathological appearance of outliers of a certain form appears in a variety of datasets, indicating that the causative mechanism for the data might differ at the extreme end (King effect).

Caution

Unless it can be ascertained that the deviation is not significant, it is ill-advised to ignore the presence of outliers. Outliers that cannot be readily explained demand special attention.

Identifying Outliers

There is no rigid mathematical definition of what constitutes an outlier; determining whether or not an observation is an outlier is ultimately a subjective exercise.

Outlier detection has been used for centuries to detect and, where appropriate, remove anomalous observations from data. Outlier detection can identify system faults and fraud before they escalate with potentially catastrophic consequences. The original outlier detection methods were arbitrary but now, principled and systematic techniques are used, drawn from the full gamut of computer science and statistics.

There are three fundamental approaches to the problem of outlier detection:

- Type 1 - Determine the outliers with no prior knowledge of the data. This is essentially a learning approach analogous to unsupervised clustering. The approach processes the data as a static distribution, pinpoints the most remote points, and flags them as potential outliers.
- Type 2 - Model both normality and abnormality. This approach is analogous to supervised classification and requires pre-labeled data, tagged as normal or abnormal.
- Type 3 - Model only normality (or in a few cases model abnormality). This is analogous to a semi-supervised recognition or detection task. It may be considered semi-supervised as the normal class is taught but the algorithm learns to recognize abnormality.

Model-based methods which are commonly used for identification assume that the data are from a normal distribution, and identify observations which are deemed "unlikely" based on mean and standard deviation:

- Chauvenet's criterion
- Grubbs' test for outliers
- Peirce's criterion

It is proposed to determine in a series of *m*observations the limit of error, beyond which all observations involving so great an error may be rejected, provided there are as many as *n*such observations. The principle upon which it is proposed to solve this problem is, that the proposed observations should be rejected when the probability of the system of errors obtained by retaining them is less than that of the system of errors obtained by their rejection multiplied by the probability of making so many, and no more, abnormal observations. (Quoted in the editorial note on page 516 to Peirce (1982 edition) from *A Manual of Astronomy* 2:558 by Chauvenet.)

- Dixon's Q test
- ASTM E178 Standard Practice for Dealing With Outlying Observations

Other methods flag observations based on measures such as the interquartile range. For example, if Q_1 and Q_3 are the lower and upper quartiles respectively, then one could define an outlier to be any observation outside the range:

$$\left[Q_1 - k(Q_3 - Q_1), Q_3 + k(Q_3 - Q_1)\right]$$

for some constant k.

Other approaches are distance-based and density-based , and all of them frequently use the distance to the k-nearest neighbours to label observations as outliers or non-outliers.

Working with Outliers

The choice of how to deal with an outlier should depend on the cause.

Retention

Even when a normal distribution model is appropriate to the data being analyzed, outliers are expected for large sample sizes and should not automatically be discarded if that is the case. The application should use a classification algorithm that is robust to outliers to model data with naturally occurring outlier points.

Exclusion

Deletion of outlier data is a controversial practice frowned on by many scientists and science instructors; while mathematical criteria provide an objective and quantitative method for data rejection, they do not make the practice more scientifically or methodologically sound, especially in small sets or where a normal distribution cannot be assumed. Rejection of outliers is more acceptable in areas of practice where the underlying model of the process being measured and the usual distribution of measurement error are confidently known. An outlier resulting from an instrument reading error may be excluded but it is desirable that the reading is at least verified.

In regression problems, an alternative approach may be to only exclude points which exhibit a large degree of influence on the parameters, using a measure such as Cook's distance.

If a data point (or points) is excluded from the data analysis, this should be clearly stated on any subsequent report.

Non-normal Distributions

The possibility should be considered that the underlying distribution of the data is not approximately normal, having "fat tails". For instance, when sampling from a Cauchy distribution, the sample variance increases with the sample size, the sample mean fails to converge as the sample size increases, and outliers are expected at far larger rates than for a normal distribution.

Alternative Models

In cases where the cause of the outliers is known, it may be possible to incorporate this effect into the model structure, for example by using a hierarchical Bayes model or a mixture model.

Formula and Calculation

Most F-tests arise by considering a decomposition of the variability in a collection of data in terms of sums of squares. The test statistic in an F-test is the ratio of two scaled sums of squares reflecting different sources of variability. These sums of squares are constructed so that the statistic tends to be greater when the null hypothesis is not true. In order for the statistic to follow the F-distribution under the null hypothesis, the sums of squares should be statistically independent, and each should follow a scaled chi-squared distribution. The latter condition is guaranteed if the data values are independent and normally distributed with a common variance.

Multiple-comparison ANOVA Problems

The F-test in one-way analysis of variance is used to assess whether the expected values of a quantitative variable within several pre-defined groups differ from each other. For example, suppose that a medical trial compares four treatments. The ANOVA F-test can be used to assess whether any of the treatments is on average superior, or inferior, to the others versus the null hypothesis that all four treatments yield the same mean response.

This is an example of an "omnibus" test, meaning that a single test is performed to detect any of several possible differences. Alternatively, we could carry out pairwise tests among the treatments (for instance, in the medical trial example with four treatments we could carry out six tests among pairs of treatments). The advantage of the ANOVA F-test is that we do not need to pre-specify which treatments are to be compared, and we do not need to adjust for making multiple comparisons. The disadvantage of the ANOVA F-test is that if we reject the null hypothesis, we do not know which treatments can be said to be significantly different from the others — if the F-test is performed at level α we cannot state that the treatment pair with the greatest mean difference is significantly different at level α.

The formula for the one-way ANOVA F-test statistic is

$$F = \frac{\text{explained variance}}{\text{unexplained variance}},$$

or

$$F = \frac{\text{between-group variability}}{\text{within-group variability}}.$$

The "explained variance", or "between-group variability" is

$$\sum_i n_i(\bar{Y}_{i\cdot} - \bar{Y})^2 / (K-1)$$

where $\bar{Y}_{i\cdot}$ denotes the sample mean in the ith group, ni is the number of observations in the ith group, $\bar{Y}$ denotes the overall mean of the data, and K denotes the number of groups.

The "unexplained variance", or "within-group variability" is

$$\sum_{ij}(Y_{ij} - \bar{Y}_{i\cdot})^2 / (N-K),$$

where Y_{ij} is the jth observation in the ith out of K groups and N is the overall sample size. This F-statistic follows the F-distribution with

$K - 1$, $N - K$ degrees of freedom under the null hypothesis. The statistic will be large if the between-group variability is large relative to the within-group variability, which is unlikely to happen if the population means of the groups all have the same value.

Note that when there are only two groups for the one-way ANOVA *F*-test, $F = t^2$ where *t* is the Student's *t* statistic.

Regression Problems

Consider two models, 1 and 2, where model 1 is 'nested' within model 2. Model 1 is the Restricted model, and Model 2 is the Unrestricted one. That is, model 1 has *p1* parameters, and model 2 has *p2* parameters, where $p2 > p1$, and for any choice of parameters in model 1, the same regression curve can be achieved by some choice of the parameters of model 2. (We use the convention that any constant parameter in a model is included when counting the parameters. For instance, the simple linear model $y = mx + b$ has $p = 2$ under this convention.)

The model with more parameters will always be able to fit the data at least as well as the model with fewer parameters. Thus typically model 2 will give a better (i.e. lower error) fit to the data than model 1. But one often wants to determine whether model 2 gives a significantly better fit to the data. One approach to this problem is to use an F test.

If there are n data points to estimate parameters of both models from, then one can calculate the F statistic, given by

$$F = \frac{\left(\dfrac{\text{RSS}_1 - \text{RSS}_2}{p_2 - p_1}\right)}{\left(\dfrac{\text{RSS}_2}{n - p_2}\right)},$$

where RSS*i* is the residual sum of squares of model *i*. If your regression model has been calculated with weights, then replace RSS*i* with χ^2, the weighted sum of squared residuals. Under the null hypothesis that model 2 does not provide a significantly better fit than model 1, F will have an F distribution, with $(p_2 - p_1, n - p_2)$ degrees of freedom. The null hypothesis is rejected if the F calculated from the data is greater than the critical value of the F-distribution for some desired false-rejection probability (e.g. 0.05). The F-test is a Wald test.

One-way ANOVA Example

Consider an experiment to study the effect of three different levels of a factor on a response (e.g. three levels of a fertilizer on plant growth). If we had 6 observations for each level, we could write the outcome of the experiment in a table like this, where a_1, a_2, and a_3 are the three levels of the factor being studied.

a_1	a_2	a_3
6	8	13
8	12	9
4	9	11
5	11	8
3	6	7
4	8	12

The null hypothesis, denoted H_0, for the overall F-test for this experiment would be that all three levels of the factor produce the same response, on average. To calculate the F-ratio:

Step 1: Calculate the mean within each group:

$$\bar{Y}_1 = \frac{1}{6}\sum Y_{1i} = \frac{6+8+4+5+3+4}{6} = 5$$

$$\bar{Y}_2 = \frac{1}{6}\sum Y_{2i} = \frac{8+12+9+11+6+8}{6} = 9$$

$$\bar{Y}_3 = \frac{1}{6}\sum Y_{3i} = \frac{13+9+11+8+7+12}{6} = 10$$

Step 2: Calculate the overall mean:

$$\bar{Y} = \frac{\sum_i \bar{Y}_i}{a} = \frac{\bar{Y}_1 + \bar{Y}_2 + \bar{Y}_3}{a} = \frac{5+9+10}{3} = 8$$

where a is the number of groups.

Step 3: Calculate the "between-group" sum of squares:

$$S_B = n(\bar{Y}_1 - \bar{Y})^2 + n(\bar{Y}_2 - \bar{Y})^2 + n(\bar{Y}_3 - \bar{Y})^2$$

$$[8pt] = 6(5-8)^2 + 6(9-8)^2 + 6(10-8)^2 = 84$$

where n is the number of data values per group.

The between-group degrees of freedom is one less than the number of groups

$$f_b = 3 - 1 = 2$$

so the between-group mean square value is

$$MS_B = 84/2 = 42$$

Step 4: Calculate the "within-group" sum of squares. Begin by centering the data in each group:

a_1	a_2	a_3
6 - 5 = 1	8 - 9 = -1	13 - 10 = 3
8 - 5 = 3	12 - 9 = 3	9 - 10 = -1
4 - 5 = -1	9 - 9 = 0	11 - 10 = 1
5 - 5 = 0	11 - 9 = 2	8 - 10 = -2
3 - 5 = -2	6 - 9 = -3	7 - 10 = -3
4 - 5 = -1	8 - 9 = -1	12 - 10 = 2

The within-group sum of squares is the sum of squares of all 18 values in this table

$$S_W = 1+9+1+0+4+1+1+9+0+4+9+1+9+1+1+4+9+4 = 68$$

The within-group degrees of freedom is

$$f_W = a(n-1) = 3(6-1) = 15$$

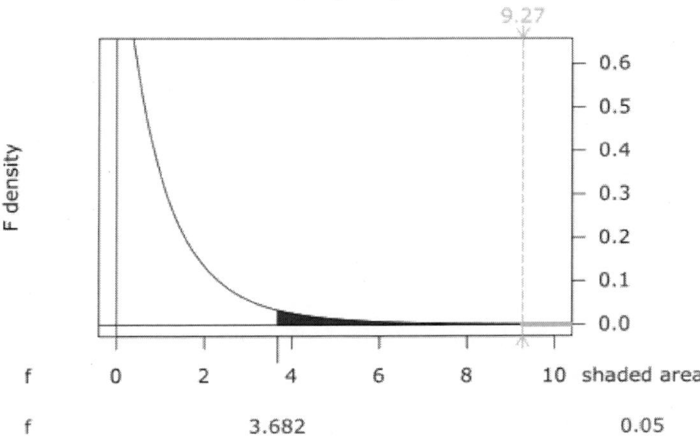

Thus the within-group mean square value is

$$MS_W = S_W / f_W = 68/15 \approx 4.5$$

Step 5: The F-ratio is

$$F = \frac{MS_B}{MS_W} \approx 42/4.5 \approx 9.3$$

The critical value is the number that the test statistic must exceed to reject the test. In this case, F*crit*(2,15) = 3.68 at $\alpha = 0.05$.

Since F = 9.3 > 3.68, the results are significant at the 5% significance level. One would reject the null hypothesis, concluding that there is strong evidence that the expected values in the three groups differ. The p-value for this test is 0.002.

After performing the F-test, it is common to carry out some "post-hoc" analysis of the group means. In this case, the first two group means differ by 4 units, the first and third group means differ by 5 units, and the second and third group means differ by only 1 unit. The standard error of each of these differences is $\sqrt{4.5/6+4.5/6}=1.2$. Thus the first group is strongly different from the other groups, as the mean difference is more times the standard error, so we can be highly confident that the population mean of the first group differs from the population means of the other groups. However there is no evidence that the second and third groups have different population means from each other, as their mean difference of one unit is comparable to the standard error.

Note $F(x, y)$ denotes an F-distribution with x degrees of freedom in the numerator and y degrees of freedom in the denominator.

ANOVA's Robustness with Respect to Type I errors for Departures from Population Normality

The oneway ANOVA can be generalized to the factorial and multivariate layouts, as well as to the analysis of covariance. None of these F-tests, however, are robust when there are severe violations of the assumption that each population follows the normal distribution, particularly for small alpha levels and unbalanced layouts. Furthermore, if the underlying assumption of homoscedasticity is violated, the Type I error properties degenerate much more severely. For nonparametric alternatives in the factorial layout.

Extended Logic

ANOVA consists of separable parts; partitioning sources of variance and hypothesis testing can be used individually. ANOVA is used to support other statistical tools. Regression is first used to fit more complex models to data, then ANOVA is used to compare models with the objective of selecting simple(r) models that adequately describe the data. "Such models could be fit without any reference to ANOVA, but ANOVA tools could then be used to make some sense of the fitted models, and to test hypotheses about batches of coefficients." "We think of the analysis of variance as a way of understanding and structuring multilevel models—not as an alternative to regression but as a tool for summarizing complex high-dimensional inferences..."

One-way Analysis of Variance

In statistics, one-way analysis of variance (abbreviated one-way ANOVA) is a technique used to compare means of two or more samples (using the F distribution). This technique can be used only for numerical data.

The ANOVA tests the null hypothesis that samples in two or more groups are drawn from populations with the same mean values. To do this, two estimates are made of the population variance. These estimates rely on various assumptions. The ANOVA produces an F-statistic, the ratio of the variance calculated among the means to the variance within the samples. If the group means are drawn from populations with the same mean values, the variance between the group means should be lower than the variance of the samples, following the central limit theorem. A higher ratio therefore implies that the samples were drawn from populations with different mean values. Typically, however, the one-way ANOVA is used to test for differences among at least three groups, since the two-group case can be covered by a t-test (Gosset, 1908). When there are only two means to compare, the t-test and the F-test are equivalent; the relation between ANOVA and t is given by $F = t^2$.

Assumptions

The results of a one-way ANOVA can be considered reliable as long as the following assumptions are met:

- Response variable are normally distributed (or approximately normally distributed).
- Samples are independent.
- Variances of populations are equal.
- Responses for a given group are independent and identically distributed normal random variables (not a simple random sample (SRS)).

ANOVA is a relatively robust procedure with respect to violations of the normality assumption. If data are ordinal, a non-parametric alternative to this test should be used such as Kruskal–Wallis one-way analysis of variance.

The Case of Fixed Effects, Fully Randomized Experiment, Unbalanced Data

The Model

The normal linear model describes treatment groups with probability distributions which are identically bell-shaped (normal) curves with different means. Thus fitting the models requires only the means of each treatment group and a variance calculation (an average variance within the treatment groups is used). Calculations of the means and the variance are performed as part of the hypothesis test.

The commonly used normal linear models for a completely randomized experiment are:

$y_{i,j} = \mu_j + \varepsilon_{i,j}$ (the means model) or

$y_{i,j} = \mu + \tau_j + \varepsilon_{i,j}$ (the effects model)

where

$i = 1, \ldots, I$ is an index over experimental units

$j = 1, \ldots, J$ is an index over treatment groups

I_j is the number of experimental units in the jth treatment group

$I = \sum_j I_j$ is the total number of experimental units

$y_{i,j}$ are observations

μ_j is the mean of the observations for the jth treatment group

μ is the grand mean of the observations

τ_j is the *j*th treatment effect, a deviation from the grand mean

$\sum \tau_j = 0$

$\mu_j = \mu + \tau_j$

$\varepsilon \sim N(0, \sigma^2), \varepsilon_{i,j}$

are normally distributed zero-mean random errors.

The index i over the experimental units can be interpreted several ways. In some experiments, the same experimental unit is subject to a range of treatments; *i* may point to a particular unit. In others, each treatment group has a distinct set of experimental units; i may simply be an index into the j_{th} list.

Analysis Summary

The core ANOVA analysis consists of a series of calculations. The data is collected in tabular form. Then

- Each treatment group is summarized by the number of experimental units, two sums, a mean and a variance. The treatment group summaries are combined to provide totals for the number of units and the sums. The grand mean and grand variance are computed from the grand sums. The treatment and grand means are used in the model.
- The three DFs and SSs are calculated from the summaries. Then the MSs are calculated and a ratio determines F.
- A computer typically determines a *p*-value from *F* which determines whether treatments produce significantly different results. If the result is significant, then the model provisionally has validity.

If the experiment is balanced, all of the I_j terms are equal so the SS equations simplify.

In a more complex experiment, where the experimental units (or environmental effects) are not homogeneous, row statistics are also used in the analysis. The model includes terms dependent on *i*. Determining the extra terms reduces the number of degrees of freedom available.

Two-way Analysis of Variance

In statistics, the two-way analysis of variance (ANOVA) test is an extension of the one-way ANOVA test that examines the influence of different categorical independent variables on one dependent variable. While the one-way ANOVA measures the significant effect of one independent variable (IV), the two-way ANOVA is used when there are more than one IV and multiple observations for each IV.

The two-way ANOVA can not only determine the main effect of contributions of each IV but also identifies if there is a significant interaction effect between the IVs.

Assumptions to Use Two-way ANOVA

As with other parametric tests, we make the following assumptions when using two-way ANOVA:

- The populations from which the samples are obtained must be normally distributed.
- Sampling is done correctly. Observations for within and between groups must be independent.

- The variances among populations must be equal (homogeneity).
- Data are interval or nominal.

Understanding the Result

There are multiple ways that one can go about obtaining statistical data from an experiment. In psychology, there is a pool of different experimental tests that can be run in order to obtain statistical data.

However, it is important to note that there are different ways to report different types of data for different types of tests. One type of test is the Two-Way BG (Between Groups) Anova Test. Anova simply is the study and/or analysis of variance, the difference between a set of scores, and is commonly used by most psychologists to help determine or measure, whether or not, there is some degree of difference between groups on some variable. In the results section of a formal lab report, is where test results done from a study should be located.

According to APA (6th ed.) when reporting your results, no do not only "mention" what happened in the experiment, but provide enough information that will help and assist the reader in fully understanding the background information of the study that was conducted. In any instance where one's experiment is multileveled or "omnibus" and has various subjects being compared in numerous ways, such as a two-way Anova, for each degree be sure to also provide a concentrated summary of the analyses conducted.

Also, be sure to refer to your hypothesis and state whether or not your hypothesis was proven or unproven and provide the necessary data that helps to support their argument of how their hypothesis was confirmed or unverified (Kahn, 2010). When reporting data you should include a number of things in your results section of your lab report. Of those things should be: the mean, standard deviation, degrees of freedom, obtained values and the *p*-value(s) (Kahn, 2010).

1. *P-value:* In reporting data, the p-value, the indicator of significant difference, is one finding that is extremely vital and is reported immensely. There are two ways in which p-values can be stated in a report. One way to report the p-value is to use the criterion or alpha level of .05 or to exactly state what the p-value is, for example $p = 0.04$ (Kahn, 2010). However, according to APA standards, the p-value should always be stated exactly, unless it is "less than .001" (Little, 2010). In the first case, when one chooses to report the p-value using the criterion you should use the more than or less than signs

(<, >) and state the criterion, for example: $p < .05$. When reporting the exact p-value, like in example two, make sure to use the equal sign (=), for example: $p = .04$. *f* & (Note that the "*P*" is lowercased and italicized and there is a period that follows after.)

2. *ANOVA:* When reporting statistical data for two-way ANOVA tests, there are three things needed in order to report the statistical data correctly. First, the degrees of freedom are needed for both the between and within group subjects (BG and WG). Followed by the *F*-value or statistic and then, lastly the significant value or p-value (Little, 2010).
   (*a*) *Degrees of Freedom (df):* When reporting this value you should first report the degrees of freedom for between groups and then the within Groups value. Each value should both be between parentheses and separated only by a comma.
   (*b*) *F Statistic (F):* This value should be reported next and rounded to the hundredths place (2 decimal spaces).
   (*c*) *P-value (p):* The significance level should follow the *F*-value, separated by only a comma. So that the end product should look like this: $F(2, 100) = 3.33$, ($p =.01$). f& (Note that the "*F*" is capitalized and italicized and the degrees of freedom follow promptly in parenthesis.)
3. *Report in APA format:* There is an assumption that for the baseball World Series of the United States there is a home-field advantage when winning. Due to the differences in various baseball parks across the nation, some players become familiarized and customary to playing in one park versus another, and as a result, different players have leads and gains across different fields in the U.S. Thus, my goal of this study is to test, whether those assumptions can be proven true or false.

This example comes from a study comparing the scores of two teams, the American League (AL) and the National League (NL), that have played and competed in the World Series in the past year and have collected data to help determine whether the myth of home-field advantage really exist. The data collected is based on whether the team (AL or NL) won the game, and on where they won the game, whether it was at home or away. A 2x2 (location x league) between groups two-way ANOVA was used to showed that for our first independent variable, "location" that there was statistical significant difference, F(1, 284) = 126.36, p = .000. For the second variable, "league" there was also statistically significant difference, F(1, 284) = 5.81, p = .017. However, no significance was indicated when analysing the interaction between both variables, F(1, 284) = 3.80, p = .080. In all, for the two independent variables, the null is rejected and the alternative hypothesis is accepted in that there is a significant difference between home-field advantages versus away, p < .05.

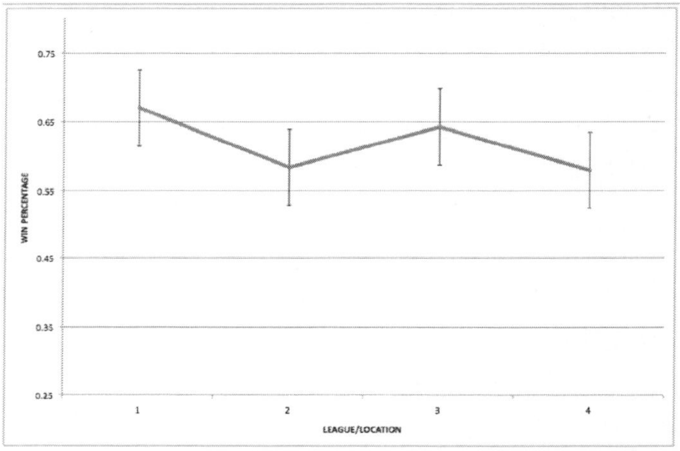

Figure: *The Myth of Home Field Advantage, True or False?*

Figure displays the average winning percentages of each team, and the significance between the League and Home/Away factors. Both teams tended to do better (1- American Home, 3- National Home) when playing on their home field as oppose to playing away (2- American Away, 4- National Away). Significant at the *p < 0.05 level.

Related Literature Review

In the study from Personality and Individual Differences (Ekermans et al. 2010), the researchers sought to examine two measures of score on Bar-On EQ-i: S, an emotional quotient inventory, over workplace and student data. Workplace data was from Australia and South Africa, and student data was from Canada and Scotland. One of the methods of measurement, differential item functioning (DIF) was measured across these four groups using a 2-way ANOVA.

DIF is one independent variable, and it has six possible scores which are its six levels. The country the subject was from was the other independent variable, and had four different levels. The researchers rejected the null hypothesis of normality in all of the samples. After finding significance in the omnibus test, the researchers used the Robust Maximum Likelihood Estimation as a post hoc test to determine significance at each level.

In this example, a two-way ANOVA was the appropriate tool to analyse the data. The data for the 2-way ANOVA came from a part of the study with two independent variables, each with multiple levels. It's assumed that by running the tests the researchers violated none of the assumptions of a parametric test, and there's no evidence in the study to contradict that.

In the conclusions the researchers mention that a two-way ANOVA may not have been the best choice of test because it may be a less sensitive test to recognize any bias in the data as opposed to other SEM techniques, but it was still a statistically appropriate test to use. In the study from Journal of Neurological Sciences (Diserens et al. 2007), Repetitive arm cycling and spasticity were measured before, during, and after athletic training by a set of subjects.

The same set of subjects were tested in four separate trials, and they were measured on the Ashworth Scale of elbow flexors and extenders, the maximum active extension of the biceps, and the minimum torque during arm cycling.

One of the independent variables was the time of trial, which had four levels (before, at the beginning of, at the end of, and two weeks after training). The other was arm cycling and spasticity, which was measured at four different levels. The null hypothesis that training doesn't affect the force and range of movement significantly was rejected. The spasticity data was standardized and pooled, and a significant decrease in spasticity was determined with a p-value of 0.076.

A two-way ANOVA was an appropriate statistical test to use in this example. There were two independent variables, and each had multiple levels. There's no information to suggest that the assumptions for a parametric test weren't met, and in the confidence intervals for spasticity, the error bars didn't overlap, further verifying a significant difference across the levels.

Worked Numeric Examples

Several fully worked numerical examples are available. A simple case uses one-way (a single factor) analysis. A more complex case uses two-way (two-factor) analysis.

Associated Analysis

Some analysis is required in support of the design of the experiment while other analysis is performed after changes in the factors are formally found to produce statistically significant changes in the responses. Because experimentation is iterative, the results of one experiment alter plans for following experiments.

Preparatory Analysis

The Number of Experimental Units

In the design of an experiment, the number of experimental units is planned to satisfy the goals of the experiment. Experimentation is often sequential. Early experiments are often designed to provide mean-unbiased estimates of treatment effects and of experimental error. Later experiments are often designed to test a hypothesis that a treatment effect has an important magnitude; in this case, the number of experimental units is chosen so that the experiment is within budget and has adequate power, among other goals.

Reporting sample size analysis is generally required in psychology. "Provide information on sample size and the process that led to sample size decisions." The analysis, which is written in the experimental protocol before the experiment is conducted, is examined in grant applications and administrative review boards. Besides the power analysis, there are less formal methods for selecting the number of experimental units. These include graphical methods based on limiting the probability of false negative errors, graphical methods based on an expected variation increase (above the residuals) and methods based on achieving a desired confident interval.

Power Analysis

Power analysis is often applied in the context of ANOVA in order to assess the probability of successfully rejecting the null hypothesis if we assume a certain ANOVA design, effect size in the population, sample size and significance level. Power analysis can assist in study design by determining what sample size would be required in order to have a reasonable chance of rejecting the null hypothesis when the alternative hypothesis is true.

Effect Size

In statistics, an effect size is a measure of the strength of a phenomenon (for example, the relationship between two variables in a statistical population) or a sample-based estimate of that quantity.

An effect size calculated from data is a descriptive statistic that conveys the estimated magnitude of a relationship without making any statement about whether the apparent relationship in the data reflects a true relationship in the population. In that way, effect sizes complement inferential statistics such as p-values. Among other uses, effect size measures play an important role in meta-analysis studies that summarize findings from a specific area of research, and in statistical power analyses.

The concept of effect size appears already in everyday language. For example, a weight loss programme may boast that it leads to an average weight loss of 30 pounds. In this case, 30 pounds is an indicator of the claimed effect size. Another example is that a tutoring programme may claim that it raises school performance by one letter grade. This grade increase is the claimed effect size of the programme. These are both examples of "absolute effect sizes", meaning that they convey the average difference between two groups without any discussion of the variability within the groups. For example, if the weight loss programme results in an average loss of 30 pounds, it is possible that every participant loses exactly 30 pounds, or half the participants lose 60 pounds and half lose no weight at all.

Reporting effect sizes is considered good practice when presenting empirical research findings in many fields. The reporting of effect sizes facilitates the interpretation of the substantive, as opposed to the statistical, significance of a research result. Effect sizes are particularly prominent in social and medical research. Relative and absolute measures of effect size convey different information, and can be used complementarily. A prominent task force in the psychology research community expressed the following recommendation:

> Always present effect sizes for primary outcomes...If the units of measurement are meaningful on a practical level (e.g., number of cigarettes smoked per day), then we usually prefer an unstandardized measure (regression coefficient or mean difference) to a standardized measure (r or d).
>
> — *L. Wilkinson and APA Task Force on Statistical Inference (1999, p. 599)*

Overview

Population and Sample Effect Sizes

The term effect size can refer to a statistic calculated from a sample of data, or to a parameter of a hypothetical statistical population.

Conventions for distinguishing sample from population effect sizes follow standard statistical practices — one common approach is to use Greek letters like ρ to denote population parameters and Latin letters like r to denote the corresponding statistic; alternatively, a "hat" can be placed over the population parameter to denote the statistic, e.g. with $\hat{\rho}$ being the estimate of the parameter ρ.

As in any statistical setting, effect sizes are estimated with error, and may be biased unless the effect size estimator that is used is appropriate for the manner in which the data were sampled and the manner in which the measurements were made. An example of this is publication bias, which occurs when scientists only report results when the estimated effect sizes are large or are statistically significant. As a result, if many researchers are carrying out studies under low statistical power, the reported results are biased to be stronger than true effects, if any. Another example where effect sizes may be distorted is in a multiple trial experiment, where the effect size calculation is based on the averaged or aggregated response across the trials.

Relationship to Test Statistics

Sample-based effect sizes are distinguished from test statistics used in hypothesis testing, in that they estimate the strength of an apparent relationship, rather than assigning a significance level reflecting whether the relationship could be due to chance. The effect size does not determine the significance level, or vice-versa. Given a sufficiently large sample size, a statistical comparison will always show a significant difference unless the population effect size is exactly zero. For example, a sample Pearson correlation coefficient of 0.1 is strongly statistically significant if the sample size is 1000. Reporting only the significant *p*-value from this analysis could be misleading if a correlation of 0.1 is too small to be of interest in a particular application.

Standardized and Unstandardized Effect Sizes

The term effect size can refer to a standardized measures of effect (such as r, Cohen's d, and odds ratio), or to an unstandardized measure (e.g., the raw difference between group means and unstandardized regression coefficients). Standardized effect size measures are typically used when the metrics of variables being studied do not have intrinsic meaning (e.g., a score on a personality test on an arbitrary scale), when results from multiple studies are being combined, when some or all of the studies use different scales, or when it is desired to convey the size of an effect relative to the variability in the population. In meta-analysis, standardized effect sizes are used as a common measure that can be calculated for different studies and then combined into an overall summary.

Types

Effect Sizes Based on "Variance Explained"

These effect sizes estimate the amount of the variance within an experiment that is "explained" or "accounted for" by the experiment's model.

Pearson r (correlation)

Pearson's correlation, often denoted r and introduced by Karl Pearson, is widely used as an effect size when paired quantitative data are available; for instance if one were studying the relationship between birth weight and longevity. The correlation coefficient can also be used when the data are binary. Pearson's r can vary in magnitude from −1 to 1, with −1 indicating a perfect negative linear relation, 1 indicating a perfect positive linear relation, and 0 indicating no linear relation between two variables. Cohen gives the following guidelines for the social sciences:

Effect size	r
Small	0.10
Medium	0.30
Large	0.50

Coefficient of Determination

A related effect size is r^2, the coefficient of determination (also referred to as "r-squared"), calculated as the square of the Pearson correlation r. In the case of paired data, this is a measure of the proportion of variance shared by the two variables, and varies from 0 to 1. For example, with an r of 0.21 the coefficient of determination is 0.0441, meaning that 4.4% of the variance of either variable is shared with the other variable. The r^2 is always positive, so does not convey the direction of the correlation between the two variables.

Cohen's f^2

Cohen's f^2 is one of several effect size measures to use in the context of an F-test for ANOVA or multiple regression. Note that it estimates for the sample rather than the population and is biased (overestimates effect size for the ANOVA).

The f^2 effect size measure for multiple regression is defined as:

$$f^2 = \frac{R^2}{1-R^2}$$

where R^2 is the squared multiple correlation.

The f^2 effect size measure for hierarchical multiple regression is defined as:

$$f^2 = \frac{R^2_{AB} - R^2_A}{1 - R^2_{AB}}$$

where R^2A is the variance accounted for by a set of one or more independent variables A, and R^2AB is the combined variance accounted for by A and another set of one or more independent variables B.

By convention, f^2A effect sizes of 0.02, 0.15, and 0.35 are termed small, medium, and large, respectively.

Cohen's $\hat{f}$ can also be found for factorial analysis of variance (ANOVA, aka the F-test) working backwards using :

$$\hat{f}_{\text{effect}} = \sqrt{(df_{\text{effect}} / N)(F_{\text{effect}} - 1)}.$$

In a balanced design (equivalent sample sizes across groups) of ANOVA, the corresponding population parameter of f^2 is

$$\frac{f^2 SS(\mu_1, \mu_2, \ldots, \mu_K)}{K \times \sigma^2},$$

wherein μj denotes the population mean within the jth group of the total K groups, and σ the equivalent population standard deviations within each groups. SS is the sum of squares manipulation in ANOVA. An unbiased estimator for ANOVA would be based on Omega squared, which estimates for the population.

ω^2

A more unbiased estimator of the variance explained in the population is omega-squared

$$\hat{\omega}^2 = \frac{SS_{\text{treatment}} - df_{\text{treatment}} * MS_{\text{error}}}{SS_{\text{total}} + MS_{\text{error}}}.$$

This form of the formula is limited to between-subjects analysis with equal sample sizes in all cells,. Since it less biased (although still biased), ω^2 is preferable to Cohen's f^2; however, it can be more inconvenient to calculate for complex analyses. A generalized form of the estimator has been published for between-subjects and within-subjects analysis, repeated measure, mixed design, and randomized block design experiments. In addition, methods to calculate partial Omega^2 for individual factors and combined factors in designs with up to three independent variables have been published.

Effect Sizes Based on Means or Distances Between/among Means

A (population) effect size θ based on means usually considers the standardized mean difference between two populations

$$\theta = \frac{\mu_1 - \mu_2}{\sigma},$$

where μ1 is the mean for one population, μ*2* is the mean for the other population, and σ is a standard deviation based on either or both populations.

In the practical setting the population values are typically not known and must be estimated from sample statistics. The several versions of effect sizes based on means differ with respect to which statistics are used.

This form for the effect size resembles the computation for a t-test statistic, with the critical difference that the t-test statistic includes a factor of $\sqrt{n}$. This means that for a given effect size, the significance level increases with the sample size. Unlike the t-test statistic, the effect size aims to estimate a population parameter, so is not affected by the sample size.

Cohen's d

Cohen's d is defined as the difference between two means divided by a standard deviation for the data

$$d = \frac{\bar{x}_1 - \bar{x}_2}{s},$$

Cohen's d is frequently used in estimating sample sizes. A lower Cohen's d indicates a necessity of larger sample sizes, and vice versa, as can subsequently be determined together with the additional parameters of desired significance level and statistical power.

What precisely the standard deviation s is was not originally made explicit by Jacob Cohen because he defined it (using the symbol "σ") as "the standard deviation of either population (since they are assumed equal)". Other authors make the computation of the standard deviation more explicit with the following definition for a pooled standard deviation with two independent samples.

$$s = \sqrt{\frac{(n_1 - 1)s_1^2 + (n_2 - 1)s_2^2}{n_1 + n_2}},$$

$$s_1^2 = \frac{1}{n_1 - 1}\sum_{i=1}^{n_1}(x_{1,i} - \overline{x}_1)^2$$

This definition of "Cohen's ≤ is termed the maximum likelihood estimator by Hedges and Olkin, and it is related to Hedges' g by a scaling

$$g = \sqrt{\frac{n_1 + n_2 - 2}{n_1 + n_2}}d$$

Glass's Δ

In 1976 Gene V. Glass proposed an estimator of the effect size that uses only the standard deviation of the second group

$$\Delta = \frac{\overline{x}_1 - \overline{x}_2}{s_2}$$

The second group may be regarded as a control group, and Glass argued that if several treatments were compared to the control group it would be better to use just the standard deviation computed from the control group, so that effect sizes would not differ under equal means and different variances. Under an assumption of equal population variances a pooled estimate for σ is more precise.

Hedges' g

Hedges' g, suggested by Larry Hedges in 1981, is like the other measures based on a standardized difference

$$g = \frac{\overline{x}_1 - \overline{x}_2}{s^*}$$

but its pooled standard deviation s^* is computed slightly differently from Cohen's *d*

$$s^* = \sqrt{\frac{(n_1 - 1)s_1^2 + (n_2 - 1)s_2^2}{n_1 + n_2 - 2}}.$$

As an estimator for the population effect size θ it is biased. However, this bias can be corrected for by multiplication with a factor

$$g^* = J(n_1 + n_2 - 2)g \approx \left(1 - \frac{3}{4(n_1 + n_2) - 9}\right)g$$

Hedges and Olkin refer to this unbiased estimator g^* as d, but it is not the same as Cohen's d. The exact form for the correction factor $J()$ involves the gamma function

$$J(a) = \frac{\Gamma(a/2)}{\sqrt{a/2}\Gamma((a-1)/2)}.$$

Distribution of Effect Sizes Based on Means

Provided that the data is Gaussian distributed a scaled Hedges' g, $\sqrt{(n_1 n_2 / (n_1 + n_2)} g$, follows a noncentral t-distribution with the noncentrality parameter $\sqrt{(n_1 n_2 / (n_1 + n_2)} \theta$ and $n_1 + n_2 - 2$ degrees of freedom. Likewise, the scaled Glass' Δ is distributed with $n_2 - 1$ degrees of freedom.

From the distribution it is possible to compute the expectation and variance of the effect sizes.

In some cases large sample approximations for the variance are used. One suggestion for the variance of Hedges' unbiased estimator is

$$\hat{\sigma}^2(g^*) = \frac{n_1 + n_2}{n_1 n_2} + \frac{(g^*)^2}{2(n_1 + n_2)}.$$

Odds Ratio

The odds ratio (OR) is another useful effect size. It is appropriate when both variables are binary. For example, consider a study on spelling. In a control group, two students pass the class for every one who fails, so the odds of passing are two to one (or more briefly 2/1 = 2). In the treatment group, six students pass for every one who fails, so the odds of passing are six to one (or 6/1 = 6). The effect size can be computed by noting that the odds of passing in the treatment group are three times higher than in the control group (because 6 divided by 2 is 3). Therefore, the odds ratio is 3. However, odds ratio statistics are on a different scale to Cohen's d. So, this '3' is not comparable to a Cohen's d of 3.

Relative Risk

The relative risk (RR), also called risk ratio, is simply the risk (probability) of an event relative to some independent variable. This measure of effect size differs from the odds ratio in that it compares probabilities instead of odds, but asymptotically approaches the latter for small probabilities. Using the example above, the probabilities for those in the control group and treatment group passing is 2/3 (or 0.67) and 6/7 (or 0.86), respectively. The effect size can be computed the same as above, but using the probabilities instead. Therefore, the relative risk is 1.28. Since rather large probabilities of passing were used, there is a large difference between relative risk and odds ratio. Had failure (a smaller probability) been used as the event (rather than passing), the difference between the two measures of effect size would not be so great.

While both measures are useful, they have different statistical uses. In medical research, the odds ratio is commonly used for case-control studies, as odds, but not probabilities, are usually estimated. Relative risk is commonly used in randomized controlled trials and cohort studies. When the incidence of outcomes are rare in the study population (generally interpreted to mean less than 10%), the odds ratio is considered a good estimate of the risk ratio. However, as outcomes become more common, the odds ratio and risk ratio diverge, with the odds ratio overestimating or underestimating the risk ratio when the estimates are greater than or less than 1, respectively. When estimates of the incidence of outcomes are available, methods exist to convert odds ratios to risk ratios.

Confidence Intervals by Means of Noncentrality Parameters

Confidence intervals of standardized effect sizes, especially Cohen's *d* and f^2, rely on the calculation of confidence intervals of noncentrality parameters (ncp). A common approach to construct the confidence interval of ncp is to find the critical ncp values to fit the observed statistic to tail quantiles $\alpha/2$ and $(1 - \alpha/2)$. The SAS and R-package MBESS provides functions to find critical values of ncp.

T Test for Mean Difference of Single Group or Two Related Groups

In case of single group, M (μ) denotes the sample (population) mean of single group, and SD (σ) denotes the sample (population) standard deviation. N is the sample size of the group. T test is used for the hypothesis on the difference between mean and a baseline μ*baseline*. Usually, μ*baseline* is zero, while not necessary. In case of two related groups, the single group is constructed by difference in each pair of samples, while SD (σ) denotes the sample (population) standard deviation of differences rather than within original two groups.

$$t := \frac{M}{SD/\sqrt{N}} = \frac{\sqrt{N}\,\frac{M-\mu}{\sigma} + \sqrt{N}\,\frac{\mu-\mu_{\text{baseline}}}{\sigma}}{\frac{SD}{\sigma}}$$

$$ncp = \sqrt{N}\,\frac{\mu - \mu_{\text{baseline}}}{\sigma}$$

and Cohen's

$$d := \frac{M - \mu_{\text{baseline}}}{SD}$$

is the point estimate of

$$\frac{\mu - \mu_{\text{baseline}}}{\sigma}. \text{ So, } \tilde{d} = \frac{ncp}{\sqrt{N}}.$$

T Test for Mean Difference Between two Independent Groups

n_1 or n_2 is sample size within the respective group.

$$t := \frac{M_1 - M_2}{SD_{\text{within}} \Big/ \sqrt{\dfrac{n_1 n_2}{n_1 + n_2}}},$$

wherein

$$SD_{\text{within}} := \sqrt{\frac{SS_{\text{within}}}{df_{\text{within}}}} = \sqrt{\frac{(n_1 - 1)SD_1^2 + (n_2 - 1)SD_2^2}{n_1 + n_2 - 2}}.$$

$$ncp = \sqrt{\frac{n_1 n_2}{n_1 + n_2}}\,\frac{\mu_1 - \mu_2}{\sigma}$$

and Cohen's

$$d := \frac{M_1 - M_2}{SD_{\text{within}}} \text{ is the point estimate of } \frac{\mu_1 - \mu_2}{\sigma}.$$

So, $$\tilde{d} = \frac{ncp}{\sqrt{\dfrac{n_1 n_2}{n_1 + n_2}}}.$$

One-way ANOVA Test for Mean Difference Across Multiple Independent Groups

One-way ANOVA test applies noncentral F distribution. While with a given population standard deviation σ, the same test question applies noncentral chi-squared distribution.

$$F := \frac{\dfrac{SS_{\text{between}}}{\sigma^2} \Big/ df_{\text{between}}}{\dfrac{SS_{\text{within}}}{\sigma^2} \Big/ df_{\text{within}}}$$

For each j-th sample within i-th group $X_{i,j}$, denote

$$M_i\left(X_{i,j}\right) := \frac{\sum_{w=1}^{n_i} X_{i,w}}{n_i};\ \mu_i\left(X_{i,j}\right) := \mu_i.$$

While,

$$\begin{aligned}
& SS_{\text{between}} / \sigma^2 \\
= & \frac{SS\left(M_i\left(X_{i,j}\right); i = 1,2,\ldots,K,\ j = 1,2,\ldots,n_i\right)}{\sigma^2} \\
= & SS\left(\frac{M_i\left(X_{i,j} - \mu_i\right)}{\sigma} + \frac{\mu_i}{\sigma}; i = 1,2,\ldots,K,\ j = 1,2,\ldots,n_i\right) \\
\sim & \chi^2\left(df = K-1,\ ncp = SS\left(\frac{\mu_i\left(X_{i,j}\right)}{\sigma}; i = 1,2,\ldots,K,\ j = 1,2,\ldots,n_i\right)\right)
\end{aligned}$$

So, both ncp(s) of F and χ^2 equate

$$SS\left(\mu_i(X_{i,j})/\sigma; i = 1,2,\ldots,K,\ j = 1,2,\ldots,n_i\right)$$

In case of $n := n_1 = n_2 = \cdots = n_K$ for K independent groups of same size, the total sample size is N := n ·K.

$$\begin{aligned}
\text{Cohens } \tilde{f}^2 &:= \frac{SS(\mu_1, \mu_2, \ldots, \mu_K)}{K \cdot \sigma^2}. \\
&= \frac{SS\left(\mu_i\left(X_{i,j}\right)/\sigma; i = 1,2,\ldots,K,\ j = 1,2,\ldots,n_i\right)}{n \cdot K} \\
&= \frac{ncp}{n \cdot K} = \frac{ncp}{N}.
\end{aligned}$$

T-test of pair of independent groups is a special case of one-way ANOVA. Note that noncentrality parameter ncp_F of F is not comparable to the noncentrality parameter ncp_t of the corresponding t. Actually, $ncp_F = ncp_t^2$, and $\tilde{f} = \left|\frac{\tilde{d}}{2}\right|$ in the case.

"Small", "medium", "large"

Some fields using effect sizes apply words such as "small", "medium" and "large" to the size of the effect. Whether an effect size should be interpreted small, medium, or large depends on its substantial context and its operational definition. Cohen's conventional criteria small, medium, or big are near ubiquitous across many fields. Power analysis or sample size planning requires an assumed population parameter of effect sizes. Many researchers adopt Cohen's standards as default alternative hypotheses. Russell Lenth criticized them as T-shirt effect sizes.

This is an elaborate way to arrive at the same sample size that has been used in past social science studies of large, medium, and small size (respectively). The method uses a standardized effect size as the goal. Think about it: for a "medium" effect size, you'll choose the same *n* regardless of the accuracy or reliability of your instrument, or the narrowness or diversity of your subjects. Clearly, important considerations are being ignored here. "Medium" is definitely not the message!

For Cohen's d an effect size of 0.2 to 0.3 might be a "small" effect, around 0.5 a "medium" effect and 0.8 to infinity, a "large" effect. (But note that the d might be larger than one)

Cohen's text anticipates Lenth's concerns:

"The terms 'small,' 'medium,' and 'large' are relative, not only to each other, but to the area of behavioural science or even more particularly to the specific content and research method being employed in any given investigation....In the face of this relativity, there is a certain risk inherent in offering conventional operational definitions for these terms for use in power analysis in as diverse a field of enquiry as behavioural science.

This risk is nevertheless accepted in the belief that more is to be gained than lost by supplying a common conventional frame of reference which is recommended for use only when no better basis for estimating the ES index is available." (p. 25)

In an ideal world, researchers would interpret the substantive significance of their results by grounding them in a meaningful context or by quantifying their contribution to knowledge. Where this is problematic, Cohen's effect size criteria may serve as a last resort.

Followup Analysis

It is always appropriate to carefully consider outliers. They have a disproportionate impact on statistical conclusions and are often the result of errors.

Model Confirmation

It is prudent to verify that the assumptions of ANOVA have been met. Residuals are examined or analyzed to confirm homoscedasticity and gross normality. Residuals should have the appearance of (zero mean normal distribution) noise when plotted as a function of anything including time and meddled data values. Trends hint at interactions among factors or among observations. One rule of thumb: "If the largest standard deviation is less than twice the smallest standard deviation, we can use methods based on the assumption of equal standard deviations and our results will still be approximately correct."

Follow-up Tests

A statistically significant effect in ANOVA is often followed up with one or more different follow-up tests. This can be done in order to assess which groups are different from which other groups or to test various other focused hypotheses. Follow-up tests are often distinguished in terms of whether they are planned (a priori) or post hoc. Planned tests are determined before looking at the data and post hoc tests are performed after looking at the data.

Often one of the "treatments" is none, so the treatment group can act as a control. Dunnett's test (a modification of the t-test) tests whether each of the other treatment groups has the same mean as the control.

Post hoc tests such as Tukey's range test most commonly compare every group mean with every other group mean and typically incorporate some method of controlling for Type I errors. Comparisons, which are most commonly planned, can be either simple or compound. Simple comparisons compare one group mean with one other group mean. Compound comparisons typically compare two sets of groups means where one set has two or more groups (e.g., compare average group means of group A, B and C with group D). Comparisons can also look at tests of trend, such as linear and quadratic relationships, when the independent variable involves ordered levels. Following ANOVA with pair-wise multiple-comparison tests has been criticized on several grounds. There are many such tests (10 in one table) and recommendations regarding their use are vague or conflicting.

Study Designs and ANOVAs

There are several types of ANOVA. Many statisticians base ANOVA on the design of the experiment, especially on the protocol that specifies the random assignment of treatments to subjects; the protocol's description of the assignment mechanism should include a specification of the structure of the treatments and of any blocking. It is also common to apply ANOVA to observational data using an appropriate statistical model.

Some popular designs use the following types of ANOVA:

- One-way ANOVA is used to test for differences among two or more independent groups (means),e.g. different levels of urea application in a crop. Typically, however, the one-way ANOVA is used to test for differences among at least three groups, since the two-group case can be covered by a t-test. When there are only two means to compare, the t-test and the ANOVA *F*-test are equivalent; the relation between ANOVA and t is given by $F = t^2$.
- Factorial ANOVA is used when the experimenter wants to study the interaction effects among the treatments.
- Repeated measures ANOVA is used when the same subjects are used for each treatment (e.g., in a longitudinal study).
- Multivariate analysis of variance (MANOVA) is used when there is more than one response variable.

ANOVA Cautions

Balanced experiments (those with an equal sample size for each treatment) are relatively easy to interpret; Unbalanced experiments offer more complexity. For single factor (one way) ANOVA, the adjustment for unbalanced data is easy, but the unbalanced analysis lacks both robustness and power. For more complex designs the lack of balance leads to further complications. "The orthogonality property of main effects and interactions present in balanced data does not carry over to the unbalanced case. This means that the usual analysis of variance techniques do not apply.

Consequently, the analysis of unbalanced factorials is much more difficult than that for balanced designs." In the general case, "The analysis of variance can also be applied to unbalanced data, but then the sums of squares, mean squares, and *F*-ratios will depend on the order in which the sources of variation are considered."

The simplest techniques for handling unbalanced data restore balance by either throwing out data or by synthesizing missing data. More complex techniques use regression. ANOVA is (in part) a significance test. The American Psychological Association holds the view that simply reporting significance is insufficient and that reporting confidence bounds is preferred. While ANOVA is conservative (in maintaining a significance level) against multiple comparisons in one dimension, it is not conservative against comparisons in multiple dimensions.

Generalizations

ANOVA is considered to be a special case of linear regression which in turn is a special case of the general linear model. All consider the observations to be the sum of a model (fit) and a residual (error) to be minimized. The Kruskal–Wallis test and the Friedman test are nonparametric tests, which do not rely on an assumption of normality.

History

While the analysis of variance reached fruition in the 20th century, antecedents extend centuries into the past according to Stigler. These include hypothesis testing, the partitioning of sums of squares, experimental techniques and the additive model. Laplace was performing hypothesis testing in the 1770s.

The development of least-squares methods by Laplace and Gauss circa 1800 provided an improved method of combining observations (over the existing practices of astronomy and geodesy). It also initiated much study of the contributions to sums of squares.

Laplace soon knew how to estimate a variance from a residual (rather than a total) sum of squares. By 1827 Laplace was using least squares methods to address ANOVA problems regarding measurements of atmospheric tides. Before 1800 astronomers had isolated observational errors resulting from reaction times (the "personal equation") and had developed methods of reducing the errors.

The experimental methods used in the study of the personal equation were later accepted by the emerging field of psychology which developed strong (full factorial) experimental methods to which randomization and blinding were soon added. An eloquent non-mathematical explanation of the additive effects model was available in 1885.

Sir Ronald Fisher introduced the term "variance" and proposed a formal analysis of variance in a 1918 article The Correlation Between Relatives on the Supposition of Mendelian Inheritance. His first application of the analysis of variance was published in 1921. Analysis of variance became widely known after being included in Fisher's 1925 book Statistical Methods for Research Workers. Randomization models were developed by several. The first was published in Polish by Neyman in 1923.

One of the attributes of ANOVA which ensured its early popularity was computational elegance. The structure of the additive model allows solution for the additive coefficients by simple algebra rather than by matrix calculations. In the era of mechanical calculators this simplicity was critical.

The determination of statistical significance also required access to tables of the F function which were supplied by early statistics texts.

Mixed Model

A mixed model is a statistical model containing both fixed effects and random effects, that is mixed effects. These models are useful in a wide variety of disciplines in the physical, biological and social sciences.

They are particularly useful in settings where repeated measurements are made on the same statistical units, or where measurements are made on clusters of related statistical units.

History and Current Status

Ronald Fisher introduced random effects models to study the correlations of trait values between relatives. In the 1950s, Charles Roy Henderson provided best linear unbiased estimates (BLUE) of fixed effects and best linear unbiased predictions (BLUP) of random effects. Subsequently, mixed modelling has become a major area of statistical research, including work on computation of maximum likelihood estimates, non-linear mixed effect models, missing data in mixed effects models, and Bayesian estimation of mixed effects models. Mixed models are applied in many disciplines where multiple correlated measurements are made on each unit of interest.

They are prominently used in research involving human and animal subjects in fields ranging from genetics to marketing, and have also been used in industrial statistics.

Definition

In matrix notation a mixed model can be represented as

$$y = X\beta + Zu + \epsilon$$

where

- y is a vector of observations, with mean $E(y) = X\beta$

- β is a vector of fixed effects
- u is a vector of random effects with mean $E(u) = 0$ and variance-covariance matrix $\text{var}(u) = G$
- ∈ is a vector of IID random error terms with mean E(∈) and variance var(∈) = R
- X and Z are matrices of regressors relating the observations to and

Estimation

Henderson's "mixed model equations" (MME) are:

$$\begin{pmatrix} X'R^{-1}X & X'R^{-1}Z \\ Z'R^{-1}X & Z'R^{-1}Z + G^{-1} \end{pmatrix} \begin{pmatrix} \tilde{\beta} \\ \tilde{u} \end{pmatrix} = \begin{pmatrix} X'R^{-1}y \\ Z'R^{-1}y \end{pmatrix}$$

The solutions to the MME, $\tilde{\beta}$ and $\tilde{u}$ are best linear unbiased estimates (BLUE) and predictors for β and u, respectively. This is a consequence of the Gauss-Markov theorem when the conditional variance of the outcome is not scalable to the identity matrix. When the conditional variance is known, then the inverse variance weighted least squares estimate is BLUE.

However, the conditional variance is rarely, if ever, known. So it is desirable to jointly estimate the variance and weighted parameter estimates when solving MMEs.

One method used to fit such mixed models is that of the EM algorithm where the variance components are treated as unobserved nuisance parameters in the joint likelihood. Currently, this is the implemented method for the major statistical software packages R (lme in the nlme library) and SAS (proc mixed). The solution to the mixed model equations is a maximum likelihood estimate when the distribution of the errors is normal.

Chi-squared Test

A chi-squared test, also referred to as chi-square test or x^2 test, is any statistical hypothesis test in which the sampling distribution of the test statistic is a chi-squared distribution when the null hypothesis is true, or any in which this is asymptotically true, meaning that the sampling distribution (if the null hypothesis is true) can be made to approximate a chi-squared distribution as closely as desired by making the sample size large enough.

Some examples of chi-squared tests where the chi-squared distribution is only approximately valid:

- Pearson's chi-squared test, also known as the chi-squared goodness-of-fit test or chi-squared test for independence. When mentioned without any modifiers or without other precluding context, this test is usually understood.
- Yates's correction for continuity, also known as Yates' chi-squared test.
- Cochran–Mantel–Haenszel chi-squared test.
- McNemar's test, used in certain 2×2 tables with pairing
- Linear-by-linear association chi-squared test
- The portmanteau test in time-series analysis, testing for the presence of autocorrelation
- Likelihood-ratio tests in general statistical modelling, for testing whether there is evidence of the need to move from a simple model to a more complicated one (where the simple model is nested within the complicated one).

One case where the distribution of the test statistic is an exact chi-squared distribution is the test that the variance of a normally distributed population has a given value based on a sample variance. Such a test is uncommon in practice because values of variances to test against are seldom known exactly.

Chi-squared Test for Variance in a Normal Population

If a sample of size n is taken from a population having a normal distribution, then there is a well-known result which allows a test to be made of whether the variance of the population has a pre-determined value.

For example, a manufacturing process might have been in stable condition for a long period, allowing a value for the variance to be determined essentially without error.

Suppose that a variant of the process is being tested, giving rise to a small sample of product items whose variation is to be tested. The test statistic T in this instance could be set to be the sum of squares about the sample mean, divided by the nominal value for the variance (i.e. the value to be tested as holding).

Then T has a chi-squared distribution with $n - 1$ degrees of freedom. For example if the sample size is 21, the acceptance region for T for a significance level of 5% is the interval 9.59 to 34.17.

Correlation and Dependence

In statistics, dependence refers to any statistical relationship between two random variables or two sets of data. Correlation refers to any of a broad class of statistical relationships involving dependence. Familiar examples of dependent phenomena include the correlation between the physical statures of parents and their offspring, and the correlation between the demand for a product and its price. Correlations are useful because they can indicate a predictive relationship that can be exploited in practice.

For example, an electrical utility may produce less power on a mild day based on the correlation between electricity demand and weather. In this example there is a causal relationship, because extreme weather causes people to use more electricity for heating or cooling; however, statistical dependence is not sufficient to demonstrate the presence of such a causal relationship (i.e., Correlation does not imply causation).

Formally, dependence refers to any situation in which random variables do not satisfy a mathematical condition of probabilistic independence. In loose usage, correlation can refer to any departure of two or more random variables from independence, but technically it refers to any of several more specialized types of relationship between mean values. There are several correlation coefficients, often denoted ρ or r, measuring the degree of correlation. The most common of these is the Pearson correlation coefficient, which is sensitive only to a linear relationship between two variables (which may exist even if one is a nonlinear function of the other). Other correlation coefficients have been developed to be more robust than the Pearson correlation – that is, more sensitive to nonlinear relationships.

8

Bivariate Normal Distribution

If a pair (X, Y) of random variables follows a bivariate normal distribution, the conditional mean $E(X|Y)$ is a linear function of Y, and the conditional mean $E(Y|X)$ is a linear function of X. The correlation coefficient r between X and Y, along with the marginal means and variances of X and Y, determines this linear relationship:

$$E(Y \mid X) = E(Y) + r\sigma_y \frac{X - E(X)}{\sigma_x},$$

where $E(X)$ and $E(Y)$ are the expected values of X and Y, respectively, and σ_x and σ_y are the standard deviations of X and Y, respectively.

Partial Correlation

In probability theory and statistics, partial correlation measures the degree of association between two random variables, with the effect of a set of controlling random variables removed.

Formal Definition

Formally, the partial correlation between X and Y given a set of n controlling variables $Z = \{Z_1, Z_2, \ldots, Z_n\}$, written $\rho XY{\cdot}Z$, is the correlation between the residuals RX and RY resulting from the linear regression of X with Z and of Y with Z, respectively. In fact, the first-order partial correlation (i.e. when $n = 1$) is nothing else than a difference between a correlation and the product of the removable correlations divided by the product of the coefficients of alienation of the removable correlations. The coefficient of alienation, and its relation with joint variance through correlation are available in Guilford (1973, pp. 344–345).

Computation

Using Linear Regression

A simple way to compute the partial correlation for some data is to solve the two associated linear regression problems, get the residuals, and calculate the correlation between the residuals. If we write x_i, y_i and z_i to denote i.i.d. samples of some joint probability distribution over X, Y and Z, solving the linear regression problem amounts to finding n-dimension vectors

$$\mathrm{w}_X^* = \arg\min_{\mathrm{w}} \left\{ \sum_{i=1}^{N} (x_i - \langle \mathrm{w}, \mathrm{z}_i \rangle)^2 \right\}$$

$$\mathrm{w}_Y^* = \arg\min_{\mathrm{w}} \left\{ \sum_{i=1}^{N} (y_i - \langle \mathrm{w}, \mathrm{z}_i \rangle)^2 \right\}$$

with N being the number of samples and $\langle \mathrm{v}, \mathrm{w} \rangle$ the scalar product between the vectors v and w. Note that in some implementations the regression includes a constant term, so the matrix **Z** would have an additional column of ones. The residuals are then:

$$r_{X,i} = x_i - \langle \mathrm{w}_X^*, \mathrm{z}_i \rangle$$

$$r_{Y,i} = y_i - \langle \mathrm{w}_Y^*, \mathrm{z}_i \rangle$$

and the sample partial correlation is

$$\hat{\rho}_{XY \cdot Z} = \frac{N \sum_{i=1}^{N} r_{X,i} r_{Y,i} - \sum_{i=1}^{N} r_{X,i} \sum_{i=1}^{N} r_{Y,i}}{\sqrt{N \sum_{i=1}^{N} r_{X,i}^2 - \left(\sum_{i=1}^{N} r_{X,i} \right)^2} \sqrt{N \sum_{i=1}^{N} r_{Y,i}^2 - \left(\sum_{i=1}^{N} r_{Y,i} \right)^2}}.$$

Using Recursive Formula

It can be computationally expensive to solve the linear regression problems. Actually, the nth-order partial correlation (i.e., with $|Z| = n$) can be easily computed from three $(n - 1)$th-order partial correlations. The zeroth-order partial correlation $\rho XY \cdot \emptyset$ is defined to be the regular correlation coefficient ρXY.

It holds, for any $Z_0 \in Z$:

$$\rho_{XY \cdot Z} = \frac{\rho_{XY \cdot Z \setminus \{Z_0\}} - \rho_{XZ_0 \cdot Z \setminus \{Z_0\}} \rho_{Z_0 Y \cdot Z \setminus \{Z_0\}}}{\sqrt{1 - \rho_{XZ_0 \cdot Z \setminus \{Z_0\}}^2} \sqrt{1 - \rho_{Z_0 Y \cdot Z \setminus \{Z_0\}}^2}}.$$

Naïvely implementing this computation as a recursive algorithm yields an exponential time complexity. However, this computation has the overlapping subproblems property, such that using dynamic programming or simply caching the results of the recursive calls yields a complexity of $\mathcal{O}(n^3)$.

Note in the case where Z is a single variable, this reduces to:

$$\rho_{XY\cdot Z} = \frac{\rho_{XY} - \rho_{XZ}\rho_{ZY}}{\sqrt{1-\rho_{XZ}^2}\sqrt{1-\rho_{ZY}^2}}.$$

Using Matrix Inversion

In $\mathcal{O}(n^3)$ time, another approach allows all partial correlations to be computed between any two variables X_i and X_j of a set V of cardinality n, given all others, i.e., $V \setminus \{X_i, X_j\}$ if the correlation matrix (or alternatively covariance matrix) $\Omega = (\omega_{ij})$, where $\omega_{ij} = \rho XiXj$, is invertible. If we define $P = \Omega^{-1}$, we have:

$$\rho_{X_iX_j\cdot V\setminus\{X_i,X_j\}} = -\frac{p_{ij}}{\sqrt{p_{ii}p_{jj}}}.$$

Interpretation

Geometrical

Let three variables X, Y, Z [where x is the Independent Variable (IV), y is the Dependent Variable (DV), and Z is the "control" or "extra variable"] be chosen from a joint probability distribution over n variables V.

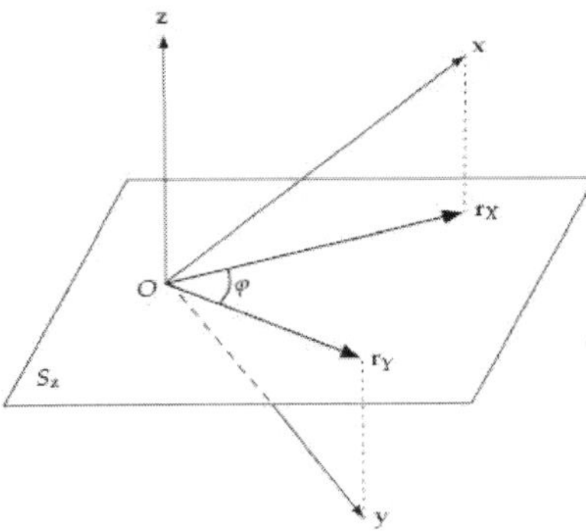

Figure: *Geometrical interpretation of partial correlation*

Further let v*i*, $1 \le i \le N$, be N n-dimensional i.i.d. samples taken from the joint probability distribution over V. We then consider the N-dimensional vectors x (formed by the successive values of X over the samples), y (formed by the values of Y) and z (formed by the values of Z).

It can be shown that the residuals RX coming from the linear regression of X using Z, if also considered as an N-dimensional vector rX, have a zero scalar product with the vector z generated by Z. This means that the residuals vector lives on a hyperplane Sz that is perpendicular to z. The same also applies to the residuals RY generating a vector rY. The desired partial correlation is then the cosine of the angle φ between the projections rX and rY of x and y, respectively, onto the hyperplane perpendicular to z.

As Conditional Independence Test

With the assumption that all involved variables are multivariate Gaussian, the partial correlation $\rho XY{\cdot}Z$ is zero if and only if X is conditionally independent from Y given Z. This property does not hold in the general case. To test if a sample partial correlation $\hat{\rho}_{XY\cdot Z}$ vanishes, Fisher's z-transform of the partial correlation can be used:

$$z(\hat{\rho}_{XY\cdot Z}) = \frac{1}{2}\ln\left(\frac{1+\hat{\rho}_{XY\cdot Z}}{1-\hat{\rho}_{XY\cdot Z}}\right).$$

The null hypothesis is $H_0 : \hat{\rho}_{XY\cdot Z} = 0$, to be tested against the two-tail alternative $H_A : \hat{\rho}_{XY\cdot Z} \neq 0$ We reject H0 with significance level α if:

$$\sqrt{N-|Z|-3}\cdot|z(\hat{\rho}_{XY\cdot Z})| > \Phi^{-1}(1-\alpha/2),$$

where $\Phi(\cdot)$ is the cumulative distribution function of a Gaussian distribution with zero mean and unit standard deviation, and N is the sample size. Note that this z-transform is approximate and that the actual distribution of the sample (partial) correlation coefficient is not straightforward. However, an exact t-test based on a combination of the partial regression coefficient, the partial correlation coefficient and the partial variances is available.

The distribution of the sample partial correlation was described by Fisher.

Semipartial Correlation (part correlation)

The semipartial (or part) correlation statistic is similar to the partial correlation statistic. Both measure variance after certain factors are controlled for, but to calculate the semipartial correlation one holds the third variable constant for either X or Y, whereas for partial correlations one holds the third variable constant for both. The semipartial correlation measures unique and joint variance while the partial correlation measures unique variance.

The semipartial (or part) correlation can be viewed as more practically relevant "because it is scaled to (i.e., relative to) the total variability in the dependent (response) variable." Conversely, it is less theoretically useful because it is less precise about the unique contribution of the independent variable. Although it may seem paradoxical, the semipartial correlation of X with Y is always less than the partial correlation of X with Y.

Use in Time Series Analysis

In time series analysis, the partial autocorrelation function (sometimes "partial correlation function") of a time series is defined, for lag h, as

$$\phi(h) = \rho_{X_0 X_h \cdot \{X_1,\dots,X_{h-1}\}}.$$

Interpretation

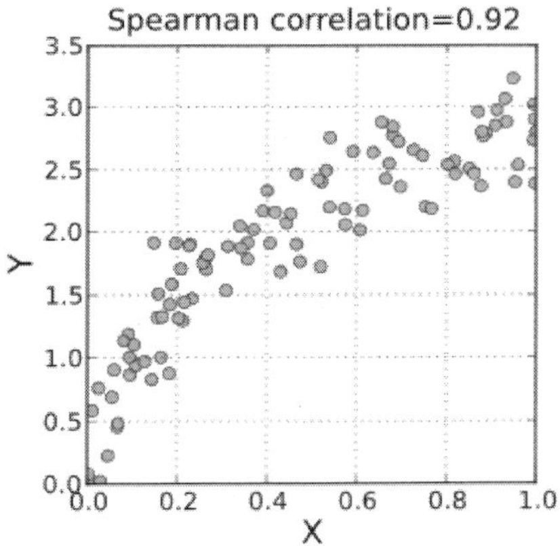

A positive Spearman correlation coefficient corresponds to an increasing monotonic trend between X and Y.

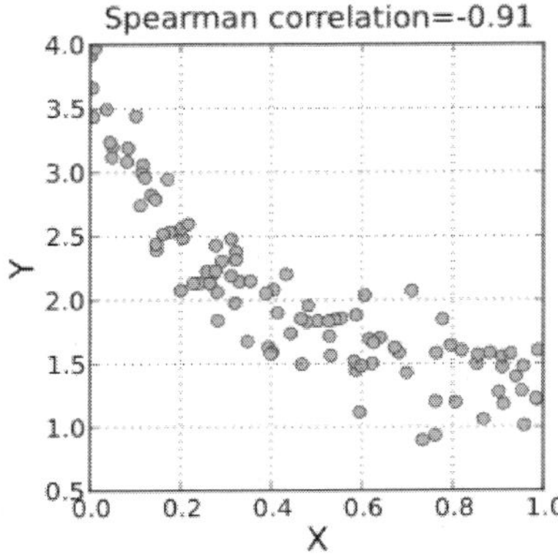

A negative Spearman correlation coefficient corresponds to a decreasing monotonic trend between X and Y.

The sign of the Spearman correlation indicates the direction of association between X (the independent variable) and Y (the dependent variable). If Y tends to increase when X increases, the Spearman correlation coefficient is positive. If Y tends to decrease when X increases, the Spearman correlation coefficient is negative. A Spearman correlation of zero indicates that there is no tendency for Y to either increase or decrease when X increases. The Spearman correlation increases in magnitude as X and Y become closer to being perfect monotone functions of each other. When X and Y are perfectly monotonically related, the Spearman correlation coefficient becomes 1. A perfect monotone increasing relationship implies that for any two pairs of data values X_i, Y_i and X_j, Y_j, that $X_i - X_j$ and $Y_i - Y_j$ always have the same sign. A perfect monotone decreasing relationship implies that these differences always have opposite signs.

The Spearman correlation coefficient is often described as being "nonparametric." This can have two meanings. First, the fact that a perfect Spearman correlation results when X and Y are related by any monotonic function can be contrasted with the Pearson correlation, which only gives a perfect value when X and Y are related by a linear function. The other sense in which the Spearman correlation is non-parametric in that its exact sampling distribution can be obtained without requiring knowledge (i.e., knowing the parameters) of the joint probability distribution of X and Y.

Determining Significance

One approach to testing whether an observed value of ρ is significantly different from zero (r will always maintain $-1 \le r \le 1$) is to calculate the probability that it would be greater than or equal to the observed r, given the null hypothesis, by using a permutation test. An advantage of this approach is that it automatically takes into account the number of tied data values there are in the sample, and the way they are treated in computing the rank correlation.

Another approach parallels the use of the Fisher transfor-mation in the case of the Pearson product-moment correlation coefficient. That is, confidence intervals and hypothesis tests relating to the population value ρ can be carried out using the Fisher transformation:

$$F(r) = \frac{1}{2}\ln\frac{1+r}{1-r} = \operatorname{arctanh}(r).$$

If F(r) is the Fisher transformation of r, the sample Spearman rank correlation coefficient, and n is the sample size, then

$$z = \sqrt{\frac{n-3}{1.06}} F(r)$$

is a z-score for r which approximately follows a standard normal distribution under the null hypothesis of statistical independence ($\rho = 0$).

One can also test for significance using

$$t = r\sqrt{\frac{n-2}{1-r^2}}$$

which is distributed approximately as Student's t distribution with n – 2 degrees of freedom under the null hypothesis. A justification for this result relies on a permutation argument.

A generalization of the Spearman coefficient is useful in the situation where there are three or more conditions, a number of subjects are all observed in each of them, and it is predicted that the observations will have a particular order. For example, a number of subjects might each be given three trials at the same task, and it is predicted that performance will improve from trial to trial. A test of the significance of the trend between conditions in this situation was developed by E. B. Page and is usually referred to as Page's trend test for ordered alternatives.

Correspondence Analysis Based on Spearman's Rho

Classic correspondence analysis is a statistical method that gives a score to every value of two nominal variables. In this way the Pearson correlation coefficient between them is maximized. There exists an equivalent of this method, called grade correspondence analysis, which maximizes Spearman's rho or Kendall's tau.

Other Measures of Dependence Among Random Variables

The information given by a correlation coefficient is not enough to define the dependence structure between random variables. The correlation coefficient completely defines the dependence structure only in very particular cases, for example when the distribution is a multivariate normal distribution. In the case of elliptical distributions it characterizes the (hyper-)ellipses of equal density, however, it does not completely characterize the dependence structure (for example, a multivariate t-distribution's degrees of freedom determine the level of tail dependence). Distance correlation and Brownian covariance /

Brownian correlation were introduced to address the deficiency of Pearson's correlation that it can be zero for dependent random variables; zero distance correlation and zero Brownian correlation imply independence.

The correlation ratio is able to detect almost any functional dependency, and the entropy-based mutual information, total correlation and dual total correlation are capable of detecting even more general dependencies. These are sometimes referred to as multi-moment correlation measures, in comparison to those that consider only second moment (pairwise or quadratic) dependence.

The polychoric correlation is another correlation applied to ordinal data that aims to estimate the correlation between theorised latent variables.

One way to capture a more complete view of dependence structure is to consider a copula between them.

Sensitivity to the Data Distribution

The degree of dependence between variables X and Y does not depend on the scale on which the variables are expressed. That is, if we are analysing the relationship between X and Y, most correlation measures are unaffected by transforming X to $a + bX$ and Y to $c + dY$, where a, b, c, and d are constants. This is true of some correlation statistics as well as their population analogues. Some correlation statistics, such as the rank correlation coefficient, are also invariant to monotone transformations of the marginal distributions of X and/or Y.

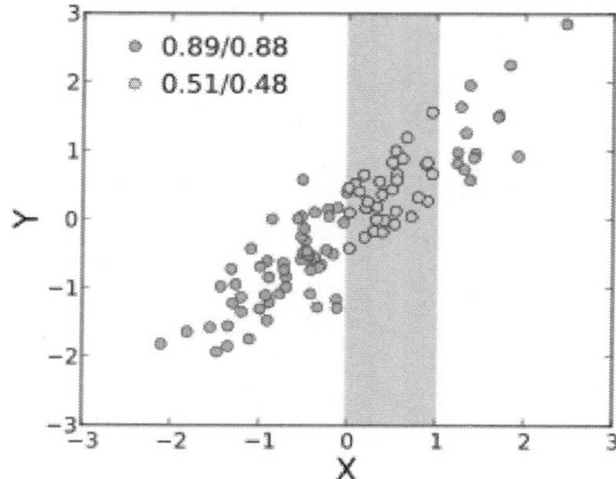

Pearson/Spearman correlation coefficients between X and Y are shown when the two variables' ranges are unrestricted, and when the

range of X is restricted to the interval (0,1). Most correlation measures are sensitive to the manner in which X and Y are sampled. Dependencies tend to be stronger if viewed over a wider range of values.

Thus, if we consider the correlation coefficient between the heights of fathers and their sons over all adult males, and compare it to the same correlation coefficient calculated when the fathers are selected to be between 165 cm and 170 cm in height, the correlation will be weaker in the latter case. Several techniques have been developed that attempt to correct for range restriction in one or both variables, and are commonly used in meta-analysis; the most common are Thorndike's case II and case III equations.

Various correlation measures in use may be undefined for certain joint distributions of X and Y. For example, the Pearson correlation coefficient is defined in terms of moments, and hence will be undefined if the moments are undefined. Measures of dependence based on quantiles are always defined. Sample-based statistics intended to estimate population measures of dependence may or may not have desirable statistical properties such as being unbiased, or asymptotically consistent, based on the spatial structure of the population from which the data were sampled.

Sensitivity to the data distribution can be used to an advantage. For example, scaled correlation is designed to use the sensitivity to the range in order to pick out correlations between fast components of time series. By reducing the range of values in a controlled manner, the correlations on long time scale are filtered out and only the correlations on short time scales are revealed.

Correlation Matrices

The correlation matrix of n random variables $X_1, \ldots, X_n$ is the $n \times n$ matrix whose i,j entry is corr(X_i, X_j). If the measures of correlation used are product-moment coefficients, the correlation matrix is the same as the covariance matrix of the standardized random variables $X_i / \sigma(X_i)$ for $i = 1, \ldots, n$. This applies to both the matrix of population correlations (in which case "σ" is the population standard deviation), and to the matrix of sample correlations (in which case "σ" denotes the sample standard deviation). Consequently, each is necessarily a positive-semidefinite matrix.

The correlation matrix is symmetric because the correlation between X_i and X_j is the same as the correlation between X_j and X_i.

Correlation Does not Imply Causation

"Correlation does not imply causation" is a phrase used in science and statistics to emphasize that a correlation between two variables does not necessarily imply that one causes the other. Many statistical tests calculate correlation between variables. A few go further and calculate the likelihood of a true causal relationship; examples are the Granger causality test and convergent cross mapping.

The opposite assumption, that correlation proves causation, is one of several questionable cause logical fallacies by which two events that occur together are taken to have a cause-and-effect relationship. The fallacy is also known as cum hoc ergo propter hoc (Latin for "with this, therefore because of this") and false cause. A similar fallacy, that an event that follows another was necessarily a consequence of the first event, is sometimes described as post hoc ergo propter hoc.

In a widely studied example, numerous epidemiological studies showed that women who were taking combined hormone replacement therapy (HRT) also had a lower-than-average incidence of coronary heart disease (CHD), leading doctors to propose that HRT was protective against CHD.

But randomized controlled trials showed that HRT caused a small but statistically significant increase in risk of CHD. Re-analysis of the data from the epidemiological studies showed that women undertaking HRT were more likely to be from higher socio-economic groups (ABC1), with better-than-average diet and exercise regimens.

The use of HRT and decreased incidence of coronary heart disease were coincident effects of a common cause (i.e. the benefits associated with a higher socioeconomic status), rather than cause and effect, as had been supposed.

As with any logical fallacy, identifying that the reasoning behind an argument is flawed does not imply that the resulting conclusion is false. In the instance above, if the trials had found that hormone replacement therapy caused an decrease in coronary heart disease, but not to the degree suggested by the epidemiological studies, the assumption of causality would have been correct, although the logic behind the assumption would still have been flawed.

Usage

In logic, the technical use of the word "implies" means "to be a sufficient circumstance." This is the meaning intended by statisticians when they say causation is not certain. Indeed, p implies q has the technical meaning of logical implication: if p then q symbolized as $p \rightarrow q$. That is "if circumstance p is true, then q necessarily follows." In this sense, it is always correct to say "Correlation does not imply causation."

However, in casual use, the word "imply" loosely means suggests rather than requires. The idea that correlation and causation are connected is certainly true; where there is causation, there is likely to be correlation. Indeed, correlation is used when inferring causation; the important point is that such inferences are not always correct because there are other possibilities, as explained later in this article.

Edward Tufte, in a criticism of the brevity of "correlation does not imply causation," deprecates the use of "is" to relate correlation and causation (as in "Correlation is not causation"), citing its inaccuracy as incomplete. While it is not the case that correlation is causation, simply stating their nonequivalence omits information about their relationship. Tufte suggests that the shortest true statement that can be made about causality and correlation is one of the following:

- "Empirically observed covariation is a necessary but not sufficient condition for causality."
- "Correlation is not causation but it sure is a hint."

General Pattern

For any two correlated events A and B, the following relationships are possible:

- A causes B;
- B causes A;
- A and B are consequences of a common cause, but do not cause each other;
- There is no connection between A and B, the correlation is coincidental.

Less clear-cut correlations are also possible. For example, causality is not necessarily one-way; in a predator-prey relationship, predator numbers affect prey, but prey numbers, i.e. food supply, also affect predators.

The cum hoc ergo propter hoc logical fallacy can be expressed as follows:

1. A occurs in correlation with B.
2. Therefore, A causes B.

In this type of logical fallacy, one makes a premature conclusion about causality after observing only a correlation between two or more factors. Generally, if one factor (A) is observed to only be correlated with another factor (B), it is sometimes taken for granted that A is causing B, even when no evidence supports it. This is a logical fallacy because there are at least five possibilities:

1. A may be the cause of B.
2. B may be the cause of A.
3. Some unknown third factor C may actually be the cause of both A and B.
4. There may be a combination of the above three relationships. For example, B may be the cause of A at the same time as A is the cause of B (contradicting that the only relationship between A and B is that A causes B). This describes a self-reinforcing system.
5. The "relationship" is a coincidence or so complex or indirect that it is more effectively called a coincidence (i.e. two events occurring at the same time that have no direct relationship to each other besides the fact that they are occurring at the same time). A larger sample size helps to reduce the chance of a coincidence, unless there is a systematic error in the experiment.

In other words, there can be no conclusion made regarding the existence or the direction of a cause and effect relationship only from the fact that A and B are correlated. Determining whether there is an actual cause and effect relationship requires further investigation, even when the relationship between A and B is statistically significant, a large effect size is observed, or a large part of the variance is explained.

Examples of Illogically Inferring Causation from Correlation

B Causes A (reverse causation)

The more firemen fighting a fire, the bigger the fire is observed to be. Therefore firemen cause an increase in the size of a fire. In this example, the correlation between the number of firemen at a scene and the size of the fire does not imply that the firemen cause the fire. Firemen are sent according to the severity of the fire and if there is a large fire, a greater number of firemen are sent; therefore, it is rather that fire causes firemen to arrive at the scene. So the above conclusion is false.

A Causes B and B Causes A (bidirectional causation)

Increased pressure is associated with increased temperature. Therefore pressure causes temperature. The ideal gas law, $PV = nRT$, describes the direct relationship between pressure and temperature (along with other factors) to show that there is a direct correlation between the two properties. For a fixed volume and mass of gas, an increase in temperature will cause an increase in pressure; likewise, increased pressure will cause an increase in temperature. This demonstrates bidirectional causation. The conclusion that pressure causes temperature is true but is not logically guaranteed by the premise.

Spurious Relationship

In statistics, a spurious relationship (or, sometimes, spurious correlation or spurious regression) is a mathematical relationship in which two events or variables have no direct causal connection, yet it may be wrongly inferred that they do, due to either coincidence or the presence of a certain third, unseen factor (referred to as a "confounding factor" or "lurking variable"). Suppose there is found to be a correlation between A and B. Aside from coincidence, there are three possible relationships:

A causes B,

B causes A,

OR

C causes both A and B.

In the last case there is a spurious correlation between A and B. In a regression model where A is regressed on B but C is actually the true causal factor for A, this misleading choice of independent variable (B instead of C) is called specification error.

Because correlation can arise from the presence of a lurking variable rather than from direct causation, it is often said that "Correlation does not imply causation".

General Example

An example of a spurious relationship can be illuminated examining a city's ice cream sales. These sales are highest when the rate of drownings in city swimming pools is highest. To allege that ice cream sales cause drowning, or vice-versa, would be to imply a spurious relationship between the two. In reality, a heat wave may have caused both. The heat wave is an example of a hidden or unseen variable, also known as a confounding variable.

Another popular example is a series of Dutch statistics showing a positive correlation between the number of storks nesting in a series of springs and the number of human babies born at that time. Of course there was no causal connection; they were correlated with each other only because they were correlated with the weather nine months before the observations. However Hoefer et al showed the correlatin to be stronger than just weather variations as he could show in post reunification Germany that the number of clinical deliveries was inversly linked with the rise in stork population whilst out of hospital deliveries correlate with the stork population.

Detecting Spurious Relationships

The term "spurious relationship" is commonly used in statistics and in particular in experimental research techniques, both of which attempt to understand and predict direct causal relationships (X → Y).A non-causal correlation can be spuriously created by an antecedent which causes both (W → X and W → Y). Intervening variables(X → W → Y), if undetected, may make indirect causation look direct. Because of this, experimentally identified correlations do not represent causal relationships unless spurious relationships can be ruled out.

Experiments

In experiments, spurious relationships can often be identified by controlling for other factors, including those that have been theoretically identified as possible confounding factors. For example, consider a researcher trying to determine whether a new drug kills bacteria; when the researcher applies the drug to a bacterial culture, the bacteria die. But to help in ruling out the presence of a confounding variable, another culture is subjected to conditions that are as nearly identical as possible to those facing the first-mentioned culture, but the second culture is not subjected to the drug. If there is an unseen confounding factor in those conditions, this control culture will die as well, so that no conclusion of efficacy of the drug can be drawn from the results of the first culture. On the other hand, if the control culture does not die, then the researcher cannot reject the hypothesis that the drug is efficacious.

Relation to the Ecological Fallacy

There is a relation between this subject-matter and the Ecological fallacy, described in a 1950 paper by William S. Robinson. Robinson shows that ecological correlations, where the statistical object is a group of persons (i.e. an ethnic group), does not show the same behaviour as individual correlations, where the objects of enquiry are individuals: "The relation between ecological and individual correlations which is discussed in this paper provides a definite answer as to whether ecological correlations can validly be used as substitutes for individual correlations. They cannot." (...) "(a)n ecological correlation is almost certainly not equal to its corresponding individual correlation."

Determining Causation

David Hume argued that causality is based on experience, and experience similarly based on the assumption that the future models the past, which in turn can only be based on experience – leading to circular logic. In conclusion, he asserted that causality is not based on actual reasoning: only correlation can actually be perceived.

In order for a correlation to be established as causal, the cause and the effect must be connected through an impact mechanism in accordance with known laws of nature.

Intuitively, causation seems to require not just a correlation, but a counterfactual dependence. Suppose that a student performed poorly on a test and guesses that the cause was his not studying. To prove this, one thinks of the counterfactual – the same student writing the same test under the same circumstances but having studied the night before. If one could rewind history, and change only one small thing (making the student study for the exam), then causation could be observed (by comparing version 1 to version 2). Because one cannot rewind history and replay events after making small controlled changes, causation can only be inferred, never exactly known. This is referred to as the Fundamental Problem of Causal Inference – it is impossible to directly observe causal effects.

A major goal of scientific experiments and statistical methods is to approximate as best as possible the counterfactual state of the world. For example, one could run an experiment on identical twins who were known to consistently get the same grades on their tests.

One twin is sent to study for six hours while the other is sent to the amusement park. If their test scores suddenly diverged by a large degree, this would be strong evidence that studying (or going to the amusement park) had a causal effect on test scores. In this case, correlation between studying and test scores would almost certainly imply causation.

Well-designed experimental studies replace equality of individuals as in the previous example by equality of groups. This is achieved by randomization of the subjects to two or more groups.

Although not a perfect system, the likeliness of being equal in all aspects rises with the number of subjects placed randomly in the treatment/placebo groups. From the significance of the difference of the effect of the treatment vs. the placebo, one can conclude the likeliness of the treatment having a causal effect on the disease. This likeliness can be quantified in statistical terms by the P-value.

When experimental studies are impossible and only pre-existing data are available, as is usually the case for example in economics, regression analysis can be used. Factors other than the potential causative variable of interest are controlled for by including them as regressors in addition to the regressor representing the variable of interest. False inferences of causation due to reverse causation (or wrong estimates of the magnitude of causation due the presence of bidirectional causation) can be avoided by using explanators (regressors) that are necessarily exogenous, such as physical explanators like rainfall amount (as a determinant of, say, futures prices), lagged variables whose values were determined before the dependent variable's value was determined, instrumental variables for the explanators (chosen based on their known exogeneity), etc.

Spurious correlation due to mutual influence from a third, common, causative variable, is harder to avoid: the model must be specified such that there is a theoretical reason to believe that no such underlying causative variable has been omitted from the model; in particular, underlying time trends of both the dependent variable and the independent (potentially causative) variable must be controlled for by including time as another independent variable.

Kendall Tau Rank Correlation Coefficient

In statistics, the Kendall rank correlation coefficient, commonly referred to as Kendall's tau (τ) coefficient, is a statistic used to measure the association between two measured quantities. A tau test is a non-parametric hypothesis test for statistical dependence based on the tau coefficient.

Specifically, it is a measure of rank correlation, i.e., the similarity of the orderings of the data when ranked by each of the quantities. It is named after Maurice Kendall, who developed it in 1938, though Gustav Fechner had proposed a similar measure in the context of time series in 1897.

Definition

Let $(x_1, y_1), (x_2, y_2), \ldots, (x_n, y_n)$ be a set of observations of the joint random variables X and Y respectively, such that all the values of (x_i) and (y_i) are unique. Any pair of observations (x_i, y_i) and (x_j, y_j) are said to be concordant if the ranks for both elements agree: that is, if both $x_i > x_j$ and $y_i > y_j$ or if both $x_i < x_j$ and $y_i < y_j$. They are said to be discordant, if $x_i > x_j$ and $y_i < y_j$ or if $x_i < x_j$ and $y_i > y_j$. If $x_i = x_j$ or $y_i = y_j$, the pair is neither concordant nor discordant.

The Kendall τ coefficient is defined as:

$$\tau = \frac{(\text{number of concordant pairs}) - (\text{number of discordant pairs})}{\frac{1}{2}n(n-1)}.$$

Properties

The denominator is the total number pair combinations, so the coefficient must be in the range $-1 \le \tau \le 1$.

- If the agreement between the two rankings is perfect (i.e., the two rankings are the same) the coefficient has value 1.
- If the disagreement between the two rankings is perfect (i.e., one ranking is the reverse of the other) the coefficient has value –1.
- If X and Y are independent, then we would expect the coefficient to be approximately zero.

Hypothesis Test

The Kendall rank coefficient is often used as a test statistic in a statistical hypothesis test to establish whether two variables may be regarded as statistically dependent.

This test is non-parametric, as it does not rely on any assumptions on the distributions of X or Y or the distribution of (X, Y).

Under the null hypothesis of independence of X and Y, the sampling distribution of τ has an expected value of zero.

The precise distribution cannot be characterized in terms of common distributions, but may be calculated exactly for small samples; for larger samples, it is common to use an approximation to the normal distribution, with mean zero and variance:

$$\frac{2(2n+5)}{9n(n-1)}.$$

Accounting for Ties

A pair $\{(x_i, y_i), (x_j, y_j)\}$ is said to be tied if $x_i = x_j$ or $y_i = y_j$; a tied pair is neither concordant nor discordant. When tied pairs arise in the data, the coefficient may be modified in a number of ways to keep it in the range [-1, 1]:

Tau-a

Tau-a statistic tests the strength of association of the cross tabulations. Both variables have to be ordinal. Tau-a will not make any adjustment for ties.

Tau-b

Tau-b statistic, unlike tau-a, makes adjustments for ties. Values of tau-b range from −1 (100% negative association, or perfect inversion) to +1 (100% positive association, or perfect agreement). A value of zero indicates the absence of association.

The Kendall tau-b coefficient is defined as:

$$\tau_B = \frac{n_c - n_d}{\sqrt{(n_0 - n_1)(n_0 - n_2)}}$$

Tau-c

Tau-c differs from tau-b as in being more suitable for rectangular tables than for square tables.

Factor Analysis

Factor analysis is a statistical method used to describe variability among observed, correlated variables in terms of a potentially lower number of unobserved variables called factors.

In other words, it is possible, for example, that variations in three or four observed variables mainly reflect the variations in fewer unobserved variables. Factor analysis searches for such joint variations in response to unobserved latent variables. The observed variables are meddled as linear combinations of the potential factors, plus "error" terms. The information gained about the interdependencies between observed variables can be used later to reduce the set of variables in a dataset. Computationally this technique is equivalent to low rank approximation of the matrix of observed variables. Factor analysis originated in psychometrics, and is used in behavioural sciences, social sciences, marketing, product management, operations research, and other applied sciences that deal with large quantities of data.

Factor analysis is related to principal component analysis (PCA), but the two are not identical. Latent variable models, including factor analysis, use regression modelling techniques to test hypotheses producing error terms, while PCA is a descriptive statistical technique. There has been significant controversy in the field over the equivalence or otherwise of the two techniques.

Statistical Model

Definition

Suppose we have a set of p observable random variables, $x_1,\ldots,x_p$ with means $\mu_1,\ldots,\mu_p$.

Suppose for some unknown constants l_{ij} and k unobserved random variables F_j, where $i \in 1,\ldots,p$ and $j \in 1,\ldots,k$ where $k < p$, we have

$$x_i - \mu_i = l_{i1}F_1 + \cdots + l_{ik}F_k + \varepsilon_i.$$

Here, the ε_i are independently distributed error terms with zero mean and finite variance, which may not be the same for all i. Let $\text{Var}(\varepsilon_i) = \psi_i$, so that we have

$$\text{Cov}(\varepsilon) = \text{Diag}(\psi_1,\ldots,\psi_p) = \Psi \text{ and } \text{E}(\varepsilon) = 0.$$

In matrix terms, we have

$$x - \mu = LF + \varepsilon.$$

If we have n observations, then we will have the dimensions $x_{p\times n}, L_{p\times k}$, and $F_{k\times n}$. Each column of x and F denote values for one particular observation, and matrix L does not vary across observations.

Also we will impose the following assumptions on F.

1. F and ε are independent.
2. $\text{E}(F) = 0$
3. $\text{Cov}(F) = I$ (to make sure that the factors are uncorrelated)

Any solution of the above set of equations following the constraints for F is defined as the factors, and L as the loading matrix. Suppose $\text{Cov}(x - \mu) = \Sigma$. Then note that from the conditions just imposed on F, we have

$$\text{Cov}(x - \mu) = \text{Cov}(LF + \varepsilon),$$

or

$$\Sigma = L\text{Cov}(F)L^T + \text{Cov}(\varepsilon),$$

or $\Sigma = LL^T + \Psi.$

Note that for any orthogonal matrix Q if we set $L = LQ$ and $F = Q^T F$, the criteria for being factors and factor loadings still hold. Hence a set of factors and factor loadings is identical only up to orthogonal transformations.

Example

The following example is for expository purposes, and should not be taken as being realistic. Suppose a psychologist proposes a theory that there are two kinds of intelligence, "verbal intelligence" and "mathematical intelligence", neither of which is directly observed. Evidence for the theory is sought in the examination scores from each of 10 different academic fields of 1000 students. If each student is chosen randomly from a large population, then each student's 10 scores are random variables. The psychologist's theory may say that for each of the 10 academic fields, the score averaged over the group of all students who share some common pair of values for verbal and mathematical "intelligences" is some constant times their level of verbal intelligence plus another constant times their level of mathematical intelligence, i.e., it is a linear combination of those two "factors". The numbers for a particular subject, by which the two kinds of intelligence are multiplied to obtain the expected score, are posited by the theory to be the same for all intelligence level pairs, and are called "factor loadings" for this subject. For example, the theory may hold that the average student's aptitude in the field of taxonomy is

{10 × the student's verbal intelligence} + {6 × the student's mathematical intelligence}.

The numbers 10 and 6 are the factor loadings associated with taxonomy. Other academic subjects may have different factor loadings.

Two students having identical degrees of verbal intelligence and identical degrees of mathematical intelligence may have different aptitudes in taxonomy because individual aptitudes differ from average aptitudes. That difference is called the "error" — a statistical term that means the amount by which an individual differs from what is average for his or her levels of intelligence.

The observable data that go into factor analysis would be 10 scores of each of the 1000 students, a total of 10,000 numbers. The factor loadings and levels of the two kinds of intelligence of each student must be inferred from the data.

Mathematical Model of the Same Example

In the example above, for $i = 1, ..., 1{,}000$ the ith student's scores are

$$\begin{array}{ccccccccc} x_{1,i} & = & \mu_1 & + & \ell_{1,1}v_i & + & \ell_{1,2}m_i & + & \varepsilon_{1,i} \\ \vdots & & \vdots & & \vdots & & \vdots & & \vdots \\ x_{10,i} & = & \mu_{10} & + & \ell_{10,1}v_i & + & \ell_{10,2}m_i & + & \varepsilon_{10,i} \end{array}$$

where

- $x_{k,i}$ is the ith student's score for the kth subject
- μ_k is the mean of the students' scores for the kth subject (assumed to be zero, for simplicity, in the example as described above, which would amount to a simple shift of the scale used)
- v_i is the ith student's "verbal intelligence",
- m_i is the ith student's "mathematical intelligence",
- $\ell_{k,j}$ are the factor loadings for the kth subject, for j = 1, 2.
- $\varepsilon_{k,i}$ is the difference between the ith student's score in the kth subject and the average score in the kth subject of all students whose levels of verbal and mathematical intelligence are the same as those of the ith student,

In matrix notation, we have

$$X = \mu \otimes 1_{1\times N} + LF + \epsilon$$

where

- N is 1000 students
- X is a 10 × 1,000 matrix of observable random variables,
- μ is a 10 × 1 column vector of unobservable constants (in this case "constants" are quantities not differing from one individual student to the next; and "random variables" are those assigned to individual students; the randomness arises from the random way in which the students are chosen),
- L is a 10 × 2 matrix of factor loadings (unobservable constants, ten academic topics, each with two intelligence parameters that determine success in that topic),
- F is a 2 × 1,000 matrix of unobservable random variables (two intelligence parameters for each of 1000 students),
- ε is a 10 × 1,000 matrix of unobservable random variables.

Observe that by doubling the scale on which "verbal intelligence"—the first component in each column of F—is measured, and simultaneously halving the factor loadings for verbal intelligence makes no difference to the model.

Thus, no generality is lost by assuming that the standard deviation of verbal intelligence is 1. Likewise for mathematical intelligence. Moreover, for similar reasons, no generality is lost by assuming the two factors are uncorrelated with each other. The "errors" ε are taken to be independent of each other. The variances of the "errors" associated with the 10 different subjects are not assumed to be equal. Note that, since any rotation of a solution is also a solution, this makes interpreting the factors difficult.

In this particular example, if we do not know beforehand that the two types of intelligence are uncorrelated, then we cannot interpret the two factors as the two different types of intelligence. Even if they are uncorrelated, we cannot tell which factor corresponds to verbal intelligence and which corresponds to mathematical intelligence without an outside argument.

The values of the loadings L, the averages μ, and the variances of the "errors" ε must be estimated given the observed data X and F (the assumption about the levels of the factors is fixed for a given F).

Bibliography

Anderson, D.R., Sweeney, D.J., Williams, T.A.: *Introduction to Statistics: Concepts and Applications*, West Group, 1994.

Bonola, R.: *History of Non-Euclidean Geometry.* Hafner Publishing Company, New York, USA, 1912.

Boothby, W. M.: *An Introduction to Differentiable Manifolds and Riemannian Geometry,* Academic Press, New York, USA, 1975.

Chance, Beth L.; Rossman, Allan J.: *Investigating Statistical Concepts, Applications, and Methods*, Duxbury Press, 2005.

Douglas C. Montgomery: *Design and Analysis of Experiments*, John Wiley and Sons, Inc. New York, 2000.

Eadie, Drijard, James, Roos, and Sadoulet: *Statistical Methods in Experimental Physics*, American Elsevier, 1971.

Ferguson, T. S.: *Mathematical Statistics: A Decision Theoretic Approach*, Academic Press, Inc., New York, 1967.

George Casella, Roger L. Berger: *Statistical Inference*, Duxbury Press, 2001.

Hays, William Lee: *Statistics for the Social Sciences*, Rinehart and Winston, Holt, 1973.

Henry Scheffé: *The Analysis of Variance*, Wiley-Interscience, 1999.

Henry Scheffé: *The Analysis of Variance*, Wiley-Interscience, 1999.

Huff, Darrell: *How to Lie With Statistics*, WW Norton & Company, Inc. New York, 1954.

Huff, Darrell; Irving Geis: *How to Lie with Statistics*, Norton, New York, 1954.

Leonard J. Savage: *The Foundations of Statistics*, Dover Publications, Inc. New York, 1972.

Louis Lyons: *Statistics for Nuclear and Particle Physics*, Cambridge University Press, Cambridge, 1986.

Moore, David: *Statistics for the Twenty-First Century*, The Mathematical Association of America, Washington, DC, 1992.

Morris H. DeGroot, Mark J.: *Schervish Probability and Statistics*, Addison Wesley, NY, 2001.

Morris H. DeGroot, Mark J.: *Schervish Probability and Statistics*, Addison Wesley, NY, 2001.

Moses, Lincoln E.: *Think and Explain with Statistics*, Addison-Wesley, NY, 1986.

Moses, Lincoln E.: *Think and Explain with Statistics*, Addison-Wesley, NY, 1986.

Peter J. Bickel, Kjell A.: *Doksum, Mathematical Statistics*, Prentice Hall, NY, 2001.

Peter McCullagh, J. A. Nelder: *Monographs on Statistics and Applied Probability,* Chapman & Hall/CRC, 1999.

Peter McCullagh, J. A. Nelder: *Monographs on Statistics and Applied Probability,* Chapman & Hall/CRC, 1999.

Postnikov, M. M.: *The Variational Theory of Geodesics,* Dover, Publications, New York, 1983.

Robert V. Hogg, Allen T. Craig, Joseph W. McKean: *An Introduction to Mathematical Statistics*, Prentice Hall, NY, 2004.

Robert V. Hogg, Allen T. Craig, Joseph W. McKean: *An Introduction to Mathematical Statistics*, Prentice Hall, NY, 2004.

Robinson, E. A.: *Least Squares Regression Analysis in Terms of Linear Algebra*, Goose Pond Press, Houston, USA, 1981.

Saville, D. J. and G. R. Wood: *Statistical Methods: The Geometric Approach*, Springer-Verlag, New York, USA, 1991.

Singh, Simon: *The Code Book : the Science of Secrecy from Ancient Egypt to Quantum Cryptography,* Anchor Books, New York, 1998.

Singh, Simon: *The Code Book : the Science of Secrecy from Ancient Egypt to Quantum Cryptography,* Anchor Books, New York, 1998.

Theodore W. Anderson: *An Introduction to Multivariate Statistical Analysis*, Wiley-Interscience, NY, 2003

Theodore W. Anderson: *An Introduction to Multivariate Statistical Analysis*, Wiley-Interscience, NY, 2003

Thompson, B.: *Foundations of Behavioral Statistics*, Guilford Press, New York, NY, 2006.

Thompson, B.: *Foundations of Behavioral Statistics*, Guilford Press, New York, NY, 2006.

Weintraub, S. H.: *Differential Forms: A Complement to Vector Calculus,* Academic Press, San Diego, CA, USA, 1997.

Index

❑❑❑